Praise for *They Poured Fire on Us From the Sky*

"[The authors'] accounts, written first in lesson books and then on computer have been skillfully put together in a narrative, each boy carrying both history and that of their joint flight and reunion forward. The result is both fascinating and immediate, not least because of the guilelessness of the language and the particularly African use of metaphor and imagery. . . . *They Poured Fire* . . . conjures up a world of marabou storks, acacia trees, termite mounds taller than men, scorpions and snakes that move in the dark, a world governed by traditions, rituals, seasons, weather, and obligations." —*New York Review of Books*

"Tender and lyrical . . . one of the most riveting stories ever told of African childhoods—and a stirring tale of courage. . . . Anyone interested in Africa, its children, or the human will to survive should read this book. This beautifully told volume . . . will remain on my desk for years to come." —*Washington Post*

"Lovely and unusual. . . . [V]ital stories . . . that can help readers understand events in Sudan on a human level. But *They Poured Fire on Us From the Sky* is no mere historical document; it is a wise and sophisticated examination of the arbitrary cruelties and joys of being alive." —*Minneapolis Star Tribune*

"Their serious tone, broken by the occasional wry smile, memorializes their parents, the land, and animals that wove the tapestry of their early childhoods. . . . One reviewer called the book 'deceptively understated,' but the soft plainness of the young writers' voices, combined with their moral insight, throws the surreal danger and strife into sharp relief." —*San Diego Union-Tribune*

"[*They Poured Fire*] is an amazing account of boys who managed to survive a terrifying ordeal. . . . [T]here's a kind of haunting beauty to their story. . . . After reading this book, readers may feel like they've been on an adventure—or in hell, depending on your point of view. Whatever the case, this book is an eye-opener." —*Rocky Mountain News*

"[The book] represent[s] genuine, heartfelt examples of what war does to young people and how they may adjust to life outside the country of their birth, especially the social and intellectual problems they experience." —*Deseret Morning News*

"In a harrowing account of the war, three young refugees in California . . . remember how they were driven from their homes in Southern Sudan in the ethnic and religious conflicts that have left two million dead. They tell their stories quietly with the help of their mentor, coauthor Judy Bernstein, in clear, interwoven, narratives that put a personal face on statistics." —*Booklist*

"The memories of the horrors they faced—from hunger, thirst, and desert conditions to the constant terror and death they witnessed—tumble forth, raw and fresh, on the pages." —MSNBC.com

"As the news of Darfur demonstrates, Sudan is still in crisis. But these authors made it to the US 14 years after their personal horror began. Their lives are still not easy, but they endure." —*Book Page*

"The trio's lyrical eloquence, combined with the gut-wrenching clarity of their recollections, powers this testament to human endurance in the face of overwhelming trauma." —*East Bay Express*

"Heartbreaking, stunning book." —*Good Times Santa Cruz*

They Poured
Fire on Us
From the Sky

They Poured Fire on Us From the Sky

The True Story of Three Lost Boys from Sudan

ALEPHONSION DENG

BENSON DENG

BENJAMIN AJAK

WITH JUDY A. BERNSTEIN

PublicAffairs
New York

Book design by Jane Raese
Text set in Mrs Eaves

Library of Congress Cataloging-in-Publication Data
Deng, Benson.
They poured fire on us from the sky: the true story
of three lost boys from Sudan /
Benson Deng, Alephonsion Deng, Benjamin Ajak; with Judy Bernstein.
p. cm.
ISBN 1-58648-269-6
1. Deng, Benson. 2. Deng, Alephonsion. 3. Ajak, Benjamin.
4. Refugees—Sudan—Bibliography. 5. Sudan—History—Civil War, 1983– .
I. Deng, Alephonsion. II. Ajak, Benjamin. III. Bernstein, Judy.
IV. Title.
DT157.63.D46 2005
962.404'3'0922—dc22
[B]
2005042566

978-1-61039-598-4 (PB)
978-1-61039-599-1 (EB)

6 2020

Dedicated to Monyde
and all of the children throughout time
who've been caught up in adult wars

When two elephants fight,
it is the grass that gets trampled.

—AFRICAN PROVERB

The name Lost Boys came to be when our village was
attacked by fierce Arab horsemen. We, little boys,
spewed out of the blazing village like a colony of ants
disturbed in their nest. We ran in different directions
not knowing where we are going. We gathered some
fruits for our breakfast and lunch. We, little boys,
were so messy, all chaos and cries filling the dark,
fiercely lightless night.

—ALEPHONSION DENG

Contents

An Introduction to
the Lost Boys

It was Joseph Jok, a caseworker in the San Diego offices of the International Rescue Committee, who introduced me to the authors of this book when he asked if I'd like to mentor some Lost Boys of Sudan. I'd read how twenty thousand or so boys, many no more than five or six years old, fled a thousand miles across Africa's largest country. I was intrigued.

"I'd love to meet them," I told Joseph, who is a Sudanese refugee himself. "But I have to be honest with you: I'm not sure about the mentoring part."

I didn't want to admit that mentoring scared me. It was such a serious commitment—and to three young men who might need a great deal of help.

"You could just show a couple of them around San Diego," Joseph suggested. "You know, the zoo or Sea World. They need acculturation."

Being a part-time tour guide sounded much less threatening. Still, I worried about what I was getting into. They wouldn't be boys now, but young men, nineteen years or older, who had grown up in refugee camps without parents. I conjured up visions from William Golding's *Lord of the Flies.*

Relax, I told myself. You're just showing them around town for a day or two, not adopting them. Acquainting these young men with our culture will be fun. They're coming from a place without cars, running water, or enough food to survive, to a land of freeways, faucets that spout water without being touched and so much food it's probably our biggest health threat. They're being dropped from the sky into an utterly alien place, like that Coca-Cola bottle that shows up in South Africa in the movie *The Gods Must Be Crazy*.

So I set off with my twelve-year-old son, Cliff, to wait, rather nervously, on a couch in the International Rescue Committee offices to meet three refugee Lost Boys from Sudan.

"Will they speak English?" Cliff asks.

"Oh yes," I answer, but becoming less sure as I look around the room at the eight or so desks that surround us, and the refugees, mostly families, huddled on chairs, muttering in strange tongues. It's a colorful scene, a full palette of skin tones and an Epcot of clothing and languages. Cliff is quiet and wide-eyed. The menagerie of people is nothing like what he's used to, where the faces are mostly white and occasional Spanish the only foreign language.

A few minutes later Joseph arrives with three Lost Boys. I don't know what I'd expected, but they are not it. Tall, around six feet, they are dressed like prep students, have short-cropped hair, and beautiful, impossibly black, flawless skin. Cliff and I stand across from the three of them. I extend my hand to one young man who is wearing a bright yellow neon shirt and introduce Cliff and myself. He shakes my hand and Cliff's and says his name is Benson. The Lost Boy beside him, who looks so much like Benson they could brothers, holds out his hand. It sounds like he says Alfonso, but I'm not sure, and it seems an unlikely name for someone from Africa, but then so does Benson. The third Lost Boy, who is the tallest by an inch or so, shakes our hands too. I understand his name clearly; it's Lino.

As planned, we head for the car and something to eat. I whisper to Joseph to give me the names again and he tells me the one who looks so much like Benson is his brother, Alephonsion, and that I can call him Alepho.

"Please put on your seat belts," I say when they climb into the back of my Explorer. As I prepare to pull out, I hear shuffling and look behind me. "Would you like help?"

Benson lifts the strap. "Please, may I just hold it?"

Cliff climbs into the backseat and helps them get snapped in. Accustomed to teenagers demanding reasons for things, I caution them about the seat belt law, police stopping us if they don't wear them and the threat of a ticket. My voice trails off when it dawns on me that I'm painting America like some sort of police state. I must sound silly to young men who've just spent fifteen years surviving in a war zone.

As we drive toward the east part of San Diego, the avenue roughens with potholes that have sprouted like garden weeds. I haven't been in this part of town for years and notice that the larger businesses, such as Sears and car dealers, have gone and the small stores have signs—some hand-painted—in more foreign languages than I can identify.

Alepho suddenly asks, "You know Payson?"

"Does he live here?"

"Yes, he live here," Alepho confirms.

"No, I'm sorry. I don't know him." I assume Payson is a Lost Boy who arrived here earlier.

"How do you know Payson?" I ask.

"He is my friend."

"Where did you *meet* Payson?"

"I met him in the airport. He gave me his phone number. He want me to call him. I cannot find the piece of paper. You do not know Payson?"

Alepho sounds a bit desperate, and I realize he hasn't quite yet fathomed the size of this city. "No, I'm so sorry," I say. "I hope you find the piece of paper again."

Our first stop is a fast food restaurant. Nothing on the menu is familiar to them except the word "chicken," so we order chicken strips. We each receive an empty cup and it is the moment Cliff has been looking forward to—teaching them the finer points of a soda machine. As he demonstrates, the young men tower over him, watching his every move with the levers and buttons. When Cliff steps aside, his protégés jostle to be next. Alepho gets in there first, jumping a bit when the ice bursts into his cup, but completing the task like a pro.

Lids and straws in place, they all join me and Joseph at the table. Cliff looks pleased by his successful soda lesson.

Alepho eagerly dives into his box of chicken, only pausing momentarily over the barbecue sauce before plunging the strip into it. His next bite is drenched in ranch dressing. I imagine these must be strange and exotic explosions to a palate that's known only cornmeal and water for ten years. Undaunted by the foreign flavors, he dares even the sweet and sour.

I haven't touched my salad and can't take my eyes off the young men across the table. They've been in America for three days only, coming from a place *60 Minutes* described as "stone age," yet their manners are impeccable. They are like finishing school graduates as they hold the food delicately and wipe their mouths with napkins after each bite.

"Do you like the chicken?" I inquire.

"It is good," Alepho declares and goes back to his dipping sauces.

I can't stop grinning. They make a routine event feel like a wonderful adventure. Although the restaurant is crowded and noisy, communications flow easily, buoying my confidence. Their English is good, their vocabulary extensive, but their accent is like nothing I've heard before. I'd anticipated a primarily British influence and there is a tinge of that; however, something totally foreign dominates.

"Were you in school in Kenya?"

"That is where we studied English," Benson says. He has delicate features and it's difficult to imagine anything other than a warm smile on his kind face. "Now we come to America to get education."

Still curious about the accent, I ask, "What language did you speak before?"

"I speak Dinka at home in our village then learn Arabic and Kswahili."

So English is their fourth language. The more I listen to them speak, the better I'm able to follow. Lino, who has only said a few words, has broad shoulders. Although none of their bodies are much more than bones and wiry muscles, Lino looks like a particularly strong fellow and is poised at the edge of his seat, constantly looking around, as though he's ready to head off for the next thing.

For all of his bravado with food, Alepho seems the most reserved of the three. His slightly distant manner could easily be mistaken for aloofness or even arrogance. His expression is serious; his eyes wide-set, especially dark and heavy lidded as though shadowed by sadness. I have the instant impression he's seen too much for his age, regardless of what that age is. He looks up at me. "Do you only have one son?"

I sense that is a surprising idea to him. "Yes, only one," I answer, but am left with the feeling that he wants more explanation. "I was working until I was thirty-six. My husband, Paul, was in medical school for many years." I'm not sure this clarifies anything for him, but I'm getting the impression he won't be too shy to ask if he wants to know more. With his question, I become braver and ask what is really on my mind. "How old were you when you left home?"

"I was seven," Benson says. "I was away at my sister's house in her village. Alepho was only five then. He was at home with our mother until he was seven."

"I was five," says Lino.

"Lino is our cousin," Benson adds.

Five and seven years old. I've been worrying, five years ahead of time, about the day Cliff will go off to college. How does a mother bear letting her child go at any age, much less seven? Benson is twenty-one now. He's been gone from his home and parents fourteen years.

"Our cousin, Benjamin, is coming next month," Benson says. "He was with us going to Ethiopia. Just a little, little boy, like five years."

Benjamin and Lino, five years old, crossing that desert. "So young," I say, and thinking of nothing to adequately express my feelings, add, "I look forward to meeting him."

"He is very, very tall now and the most black. He talk a lot too."

I sip my tea, touched and in disbelief that these heroic survivors are across the table from me. It is as though Lewis and Clark just stopped in for a bite. "Would you like to go to the store?" I ask.

We climb into the car and the seat belts snap in place. Traveling farther east we pass scattered tattoo shops, liquor stores and a tacked up cardboard sign that reads "Big Ass Yard Sale," before pulling into the Wal-Mart parking lot.

As we walk across the lot, Benson says, "Cars stand here like cattle in cattle camp."

Just ahead of us reverse lights go on. With a mother's instincts, my arms reflexively spread to protect them. "Be careful in parking lots," I caution. "Those white lights mean the car is backing up."

"Oh!" Benson exclaims. "It is like when walking among the cows. One must use caution. A cow may swing her head very, very fast to get a fly. The horns, very long, can injure a boy."

"That must be dangerous. Why don't you remove the horns of the cows?"

"Cows need horn to fight lion."

Cliff's eyes widen and he mouths, "Lions! *Real* lions?"

Inside the store, they stop and crane their necks up at the voluminous space above. Benson reaches his arms toward the ceiling and with reverential awe in his voice declares, "This is like a king's palace."

A king's palace. It's a Wal-Mart—an old, small one.

"What do you need most?" I ask.

"Pants."

They aren't interested in jeans, which surprises me. After examining all the options, each one selects a pair of Dockers. As we cruise down other aisles, Cliff has a great time showing them things, bouncing excitedly from one mysterious object to another.

"This opens cans."

"Cans?"

"Is that gun?"

"No! It dries your hair."

"Why? It dries by itself."

When Cliff explains something, they gather closely around him, listening intently, as though it is a chemistry lab demonstration and they mustn't miss a thing. Then Cliff reminds me that he needs some back-to-school supplies. The two aisles full of notebooks and folders excite them more than anything we've seen yet. They focus on the composition books and I'm amazed and impressed that of all the things we'd seen and touched in this store, these sixty-nine-cent spiral notebooks captivate them the most.

"Would you like to get one?"

Their eyes light up.

"What will you use them for?"

"Write down what we see," Alepho says.

"Do you like to write?"

"Yes. I wrote stories when I was in Africa."

"I hope you write some stories about your experience here, too."

"We will do that," Benson replies. "And about Africa too."

Once I've delivered them at their apartment with their Dockers and composition books, I return home with many more questions about the situation in Sudan. What happened to the girls? Their parents? Where did the boys walk to? And what did the refugee camp look like? The Internet provides more historical background, and I watch a *Sixty Minutes* segment tape I ordered.

Fourteen years ago the fundamentalist jihad of the northern government drove an estimated twenty thousand boys from their families and villages in southern Sudan. Walking barefoot without food or water, they crossed a thousand miles of lion and crocodile country, eating mud to stave off thirst and starvation. In an interview, one boy says that because he was older—eleven at the time—he kept the lions away from the younger ones. Wandering for years, half of them died before the others at last found sanctuary in a Kenyan refugee camp.

Ignited in 1983, Africa's longest-running war is still going on. North against south, Muslims against animists and Christians, Arabs against blacks. Huge oil reserves in southern Sudan being held by the northern Muslim government fuel the war. Race, religion and riches. The same things people always kill each other over. With no solution in sight, 2 million blacks in the south have already died. More casualties than Angola, Bosnia, Chechnya, Kosovo, Liberia, the Persian Gulf, Sierra Leone, Somalia and Rwanda combined. *Two million dead. Five million displaced and at risk.* A holocaust happening today. I recall the news stories over the years of famine related to drought and war somewhere in Africa, but somehow I thought it was mostly in Ethiopia. These boys fled *to* Ethiopia. Who flees to Ethiopia? I read two papers a day and three weekly news magazines. Why don't I know more about this war? Bosnia was in the headlines for months, but the only thing I've read recently about Sudan was that Osama bin Laden was there for five years.

Sixty Minutes reporter Bob Simon says the boys survived because most of them were outside their villages tending herds of cattle and goats when their villages were invaded. However, their parents were killed and many of their sisters sold into slavery and taken to northern Sudan. *Slavery?* In our time?

Sixty Minutes concludes, "If ever there were tired, poor, huddled masses yearning to breathe free, it is these boys, and that so far a thousand of Sudan's best and brightest were coming to the U.S."

At Joseph's suggestion, we have a couple of acculturation sessions a week—going to the zoo, beach or museums. My hesitation at accepting the mentoring responsibility dissipates immediately, and Benson, Alepho and Lino become very dear to our family. Soon we're searching for jobs and investigating educational options for them.

One day, over a month later, when I'm visiting them in their modest apartment, Benson and Alepho hand me several sheets of light green composition paper with spiral-ripped edges. "These are stories we wrote."

I want to sit down and devour them immediately, but, anticipating the emotional wallop they might pack, I am afraid to do so in their company. "May I take them home and read them when I can really concentrate?"

"They are for you."

"Thank-you. I can't wait to read them."

"Benjamin, our cousin, is coming now," Benson announces.

His flight had left Nairobi on September 10, 2001, and

his plane into New York on September 11 had been diverted to Canada. Ten days have passed since the 9/11 disaster without word from Benjamin, and where he has been is a worry and a mystery.

I wait around for a while but Benjamin doesn't arrive. "Are you sure he's coming?"

"He is coming now."

I sense we have differing concepts of "now." "Do you mean right now, at 2:00 P.M. or sometime today?"

"He is walking from IRC."

That's five miles away, assuming he doesn't mistake the route.

"I'm sorry," I say. "I sure hope he arrives safely, but I'm going to miss him. I must leave to pick up Cliff at school."

As I pull out of the parking lot, two unmistakably Sudanese young men, one very tall, are walking down the other side of the street. I'm relieved to see they've made it safely. I pull to the side of the road, roll down my window and yell, "Hello!"

They stop and eye me warily from afar.

"Is either of you Benjamin?"

The taller one cocks his head cautiously—like a forewarned child offered candy from a stranger—and says nothing. I recall what Benson had relayed to me once. They'd been warned while still in Africa that because American men marry only a single wife, there are many women here who are not married and looking for husbands. "Whatever your skin color," they were told, "it doesn't matter. You must be careful about going with American women. Stick to your education. Some American women may kidnap men by threatening them with weapons like a gun or a pistol to make them be their husband. It may be very difficult to escape because she may hide you in a most dangerous mountain or on an island."

I shout, "I know your cousins, Benson, Alepho and Lino."

The taller one raises his arms into the air, "Oh! Yes!" and takes sweeping strides across the street with the shorter man trailing behind and comes around to my passenger window. "I am Benjamin!" His face lights up with a huge smile that unveils a dazzling set of the whitest teeth.

"Hi, welcome." I extend my hand to his outstretched one. "I'm a friend, well, mentor, of your cousins."

"Ah, yes, Ju. . . dee!" He is exuberant, flashing that smile all over the place and pumping my hand.

"You went to Canada, I hear."

"Yes. We fly to New York but captain say we cannot be permitted to land. Smoke everywhere covering the city."

I shake my head wondering at his upbeat attitude, especially since the same zealotry that had driven him from his home fourteen years ago greeted him in this new one.

"You are my mentor, yes?"

He's caught me off guard. "Yes, of course," I agree and think a second later that he will be a lot of fun to mentor. "But I'm very sorry, I must leave now and pick up my son from school. I will see you soon, okay? You can tell me about your trip."

He lets go of my hand. "Okay. I see you later. Bye, bye, Ju. . . dee."

The first thing I do when I arrive home is settle onto the couch with the stories Benson and Alepho have given me. They have both written about the attack on their villages and the beginning of their journey across Sudan. Hearing the accounts from them individually, how they experienced it as such young children is nothing like seeing the newsreels of thousands of boys. Their stories take my breath away and break my heart.

Soon Benjamin is writing too, though not as fluently. He was so young when he fled, but his indomitable spirit is evident even at that age. Their telling comes to me randomly, but from the threads and pieces, an amazing story emerges. Surviving that thousand-mile trek at the age of kindergartners is beyond belief, but the tragedy didn't end there. War separated the two brothers, Benson and Alepho, for five years, neither knowing if the other was alive. When they were reunited, it was only briefly. War thrust them apart and once again they were running for their lives.

Between struggling for employment in the post 9/11 economic downturn and dealing with daily life in an alien land without family, they continue to write. In the beginning, their accounts came on pale green composition book pages produced folded or crumpled from their pockets. But crisp white computer paper and Internet files soon replaced those first precious pieces. Touched by their accounts and outraged by the situation, I want the world to hear of their tragic and remarkable experiences and to know what is happening in Sudan. I begin to dream that if we can weave their stories into a tapestry and if we're granted a great stroke of luck, the resulting book might pay for some tuition and they can fulfill their dreams of getting an education.

Judy A. Bernstein
Rancho Santa Fe, January 2005

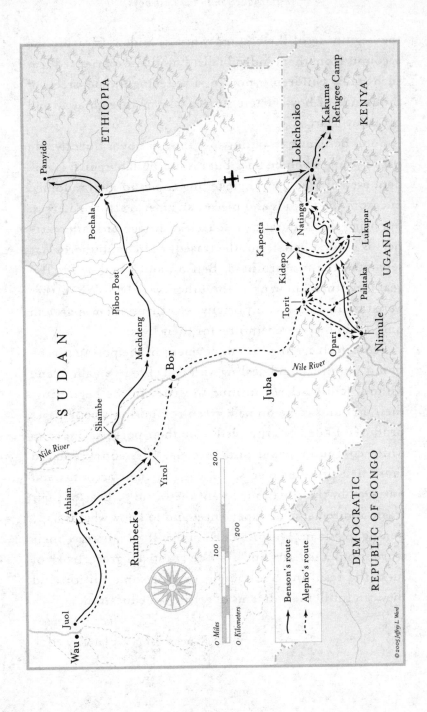

Part One

*The Village
of Juol*

The Blade Is Blunt

BENSON

Since my wandering began, there hasn't been a day or night that I do not think back to my family, our people and lovely Dinkaland. I am the fifth child from a big family with five brothers and three sisters. My parents were pastoralists and subsistence farmers of the Bahr al Ghazal region of southern Sudan. We call ourselves Dinka now, but according to our elders' stories there was no such name before the British arrived. When an explorer came to our remote area and met a group of Monyjeng men hunting, he stopped them. "Who are you young men?" he asked in a strange language.

"Ding Kak," they replied, calling themselves by the chief's name according to the tradition of our people.

The explorer wrote down "Dinka" and that is how the name came into being.

Before all the ruin and waste came, we Dinka people had cows as a source of wealth and were very proud of them. To be rich, a man needed to own more than 150 head of cattle. My father wasn't rich; he owned ninety cows. But it was enough to be happy and proud.

My mother wore the radiating five-line scarification mark on her forehead as a sign of her bravery. Any woman who had this scar could even join men in battle. Taller than my father, she was the third and most respected of his five wives. She could not be made to work for the more senior wives, as most Dinka women were, but did as she wished for the good of the family. She was very independent, and once she even fought my father for arguing with his younger wife.

We slept in small, mudded huts thatched with grasses, and when it was cold we kindled a fire inside with wood. Most of the time only my mother and us kids used the house. My father was usually away attending court because he was an important member of society who helped in difficult decisions. When he was home, he slept in our hut or in the huts of his other wives. I still hear echoes of the ground hornbill howling and weaver birds singing and building their nests in the thorny bushes. I would stand under acacia trees and watch the giraffes curl their black tongues around the leaves above. They would glance at me and then ignore me, a little boy who could do them no harm. At night, when screaming hyenas fought lions and awoke everybody, I cuddled close to my mother.

Each family member had daily chores to do as best as they could. The girls pounded the grains and only left the house to fetch water or firewood. We boys never stayed home like the girls but scattered during the day to see to our duties. My two older brothers led the cows to good pasture and water and I took the goats, sheep and calves to graze. Sometimes we hunted small animals like squirrel, rabbit or mongoose. Together we smoked them out of their holes and let the dogs do the running part. When the chores were done I played with my friends and we formed groups, walking from house to house, chewing on sorghum cane. After harvest time, we sat in the dry field and dug with our feet in the soil for peanuts to play *ketket*, my favorite game. We pretended those nuts were our cattle and the boy who had the most nuts was the most powerful that day. It was important to me to win that game, but back then small things defeated me easily. If I lost a silly game or even if food preparation took too long, I would pout in the corner, still as an empty pot.

My mother did the housework, but above all she was the best cook. From the wine to the porridge, the other wives praised her skill. She was known for making different kinds of wine on New Year's Eve and, in the morning, walking around hitting two small pieces of wood together and calling, "Come drink free wine." Those who didn't drink alcohol could have the wine made with millet flour but no yeast. This wine made you feel refreshed, as good as juice, with no intoxication at all. Even young children drank this wine. A lot of people came and finished her wine early, which made my mother happy.

She made beautiful pots from clay and huge grain storage baskets from reeds, taller than me, for my father to sell. My father exchanged the money for food and clothes in the city. As a little boy I didn't mind being naked. But by the time I was four, I wasn't happy seeing other children wearing their beautiful clothes. When my father came home with clothes for others and not for me, I wouldn't talk to him. "At your young age," he said, "it's okay to be naked for a while." But it wasn't okay; I wanted clothes too. Other children looked beautiful in their clothes compared to my shy bare body.

The life of the Dinka changed according to the seasons. We harvested in the autumn and planted at the end of summer or the middle of spring. When heavy rains came, the brooks filled with water, and the young men took the cattle to graze at the cattle camp, a huge grassy area where all of the villages collected their cows. When the sun shone again, the sky was clear except for the smoke soaring from the village cooks and an outpouring of tiny winged termites. Marabou storks, swallows, glossy starlings, shoebill herons and the egrets that walk with cows flew in to reap the termite blooming. Indolent birds perched at the tops of the heglig and acacias trees, and ground hornbills waddled lazily along the prairie, howling.

When spring planting began, my job was to sit by the nursery and protect the newly sprouted sorghum and maize. I scared the birds away with mud balls until it became too hot. Then my mother sent me to call my father to lunch. Sometimes I was sent to the neighbor's house to get the fire, and I would carry home an ember on a piece of broken calabash or dried cow dung. In the afternoons I cleaned the goat shed and arranged the goats in their pens. I worked a lot, but at night we rested and the elders told us Dinka folktales and described how life was before we were born. Our houses were surrounded by fields of grass, and so we would gather close by the fire, where we could see our surroundings while scorpions and snakes wandered about in the dark. It was on these nights with my family when I learned the most about my ancestors and the Dinka people and how we were supposed to live.

At night, the bigger termites came out from their mound, which was taller than a man. My mother harvested them by digging a hole the size of a large pumpkin in front of the mound and waiting behind it with a burning bundle of dried grasses. The termites, attracted to the light, flowed out like disturbed fire ants, and Mother swept them into the hole with her broom and singed them to death with her fire. In less than half an hour she'd have three big baskets full of them. But she had to be quick and careful because frogs and snakes appeared from all around to share in the harvest. Drying the termites took two or three days and made the heads drop off. Once the wind removed the chaff, they glowed golden with oil. I liked them best fried, but boiling them made a greasy, delicious soup that looked like gray clotted milk.

My nephew Majok was my best friend and we never quarreled or fought over playthings. Sitting in the sand, we liked to mold mud into model cows, goats, people and dogs and make houses for them. I used charcoal and ashes to make white cows, black cows and black-with-white-spots cows or white-with-black-spots cows. We could make brown cows from brown soil and gray cows from gray soil. Sometimes we picked snail shells and used them the same way, as cows. We were learning to be fond of cows, and our playing never stopped until we were called for breakfast or dinner. But Majok lived far away and we saw each other rarely.

One day my father called to me, "Majok is here to visit today. Do you want to go play with him?"

My father took me to his first wife's home, where many people had gathered. I was very excited. The women were cooking a goat and later there would be a celebration; we would sip broth and eat goat meat. My father sat under an acacia tree with many other men, among them was a man taller than my father who was wearing a blue garment. He was the center of attention, and everybody listened to him.

While the men talked, Majok and I played around the hut. Before long a girl of our age called to us. "Your father said the sun is getting hotter. He wants you to play inside the stable."

As Majok and I entered the stable, two men came from behind and blocked the door. One man grabbed for Majok. He jumped aside but the other man caught him and flung him over his shoulder and carried him out.

The door closed and I was left in the dark, listening to Majok's fading cries. "Let me go, let me go." My heart beat like bee's wings but I stood rooted to the ground. I wasn't like Majok. He was fast and alert to trouble. I was always calm and did not quickly understand danger. That was why they had grabbed him first.

After a few minutes Majok began crying even louder than before and his screams seemed to go on forever before they turned to muffled sobs. Light rays penetrated the dark stable, as my father stood at the opened door to my relief.

"Come, son, let's go."

Something in his voice told me he wasn't there to rescue me.

"Why is Majok crying?"

"He was just scared and cried pointlessly. Don't be like him. Be strong and brave like my usual son."

"I am strong and brave. I don't cry for anything."

"Good boy." He grabbed my hand, holding it tighter than I had ever felt, and led me to the acacia tree. All the men's eyes were on me like hyenas staring at a lost goat kid. I got scared and stopped walking. My father lifted me up into the air. Now I knew there was something bad. I kicked my feet and slapped my hands on his chest. Four men grabbed me and laid me on my back, holding me down and turning my face up to the sky. A pot of water boiled on a fire. The man with the blue robe was washing the blood off a razor blade. I knew that blade. My father kept it on the roof beam and had used it many times. After each use he would wash and dry it in the sun and then rub it on the grain shafts to sharpen it.

The man kneeled and leaned over me. He took hold of my penis and began cutting off the skin. I'd never felt such pain in my life. I tried to jerk away but I was held so strongly that I couldn't move a muscle. The pain felt like he was tearing my skin off with only his fingers, not cutting it with a sharp blade. I cried but it was going so slowly my voice began wearing out. My mother came and tears were flowing down her cheeks.

"The blade is blunt," said the man who was cutting off the skin.

"Ma, please help me," I cried. "They are killing me."

"Be calm, son," my father said. "It will be over soon and then you will be a strong and brave son of mine."

When the man finished they washed me with very hot water and my father carried me home on his shoulder while I dripped blood all down his shirt. After a few weeks, I was playing and wrestling with the boys again. When girls sang this song: "Uncircumcised, he is like a cow with an untrimmed tail. When he farts, it smells like broth." I was happy to have passed the uncircumcised stage, but it wasn't worth the pain I went through.

When I sometimes have nightmares about all the things that happened when our peaceful village life turned to chaos, that feeling of not being able to move during my initiation still overcomes me.

Dinkaland

ALEPHO

I was fast: that was my gift. If I did something bad, I would run. If something bad happened to me, I would run too. The night all the turmoil broke out, I ran, like my mother had told me.

When I was young and still in the village, I fought and did foolish things that people didn't like. If a person came to our house I'd say, "What do you want in our house? You come to steal some goats or something?" When people were eating, I'd hold sand in my hand and pretend-sneeze, "Achoo," and blow sand over everybody's food. Then I'd say, "You stopped eating. Why you stopped eating?"

My mother despaired of me.

Benson, my full brother and the third son, is two years older than me. He was quiet, always the good boy. He didn't do silly things. Sometimes I'd pinch him and run, but he'd just shrug and forget it.

Benson never complained. When mother gave us food I'd say, "Benson already ate." Benson would be quiet but Mother knew that Benson hadn't eaten and she would give him milk or something. Once my sister gave Benson his meal, but she forgot to give him his soup. He didn't want to eat the grains plain like that, but he didn't say, "Where is my soup?" and just sat there for hours not eating. I told him, "You are dumb. I would never do that." Sometimes even if I'd eaten my soup, I'd complain, "Where is my soup? You didn't give me my soup." I'd drink my milk and complain to our mother, "Where is my milk? My sister took my milk." My sister would say, "I gave him his milk." "No you didn't," I'd say. I tried to prove everybody wrong.

Benson liked to stay home and help our mother or go to our sister's house. I never wanted to work. I didn't know how to cook and I learned to persuade people to cook for me by saying, "I like your cooking." My mother told me I was lazy. I'd work for a little while and then complain, "I'm so tired. I need food, I need milk, I need water." I complained a lot. My mother always asked, "If I was not here, who you going to be complaining to?" I'd say, "Well I'm going to be complaining to the air you know."

My big half brother, Yier, second son of the first wife, was much older than me and he wasn't lazy. He was at the University in Wau, a five-day walk from Juol, our village. Yier wanted to be a lawyer but didn't qualify—because when the trouble started and the government starting killing all the smart students he had to flee, so he joined the freedom fighters. I hardly remember Yier except wearing the clothes of a soldier.

My full brother, Allok, the third son, had a disease and my father had to take care of him. That disease would catch him and he'd suddenly fall to the ground and retch and cry and spit saliva. But when he was well, he was the fastest runner and could catch rabbits, squirrels and even young digdigs.

Benson's and my mother was the third wife. Each wife had her own family area and the houses were built apart from each other with crops in between. Deng, my father, was a hardworking man. He ploughed many hectares of land, growing fruit, vegetables, and grains and, with my elder brothers, looked after our cows. My father, in the Dinka tradition, counted his wealth through cattle. Because he had almost a hundred cows he was quite rich. We had a lovely family despite the fact that he was famous and had to travel a lot.

Our Dinkaland had vast green grasses with trees dotted everywhere. Villages were hidden in the dense forests so that you could not recognize that anyone was there unless you heard the moo of a cow or saw the small paths. Since before our elders' time, each year when the waters of the Nile went back, and the mud became dry cracked pieces of earth, the Murahiliin came from the north on their swift Arab horses to steal our cattle. When a trail of dust rose in the sky, our young men went with their spears to defend our cows. But the Murahiliin's horses were very fast and quickly surrounded the entire area and in a few minutes were gone with some cows making that trail of dust again. When I was small, I didn't worry too much about those Murahiliin because they only wanted the cows, not women, girls or little boys, and our young men could still protect the village with their spears.

In the mornings I was always awake first and my mother opened the barricaded door for me because I made so much noise inside. A huge group of ostriches came early every day to eat the tendril plants that climb the trees and make beautiful flowers. The ostriches loved those leaves and stayed until nearly noon. I liked to go out and watch them.

The female ostrich was very smart. She laid some eggs, hid them with sand, then laid another stack and another stack. If you find the first one on top, there are more underground. I'd sit and wait for one to lay her eggs then I'd chase her away with a stone. But I had to watch out. Mothers with chicks were very dangerous. They'd open their wings and chase me.

When I did get an egg it was so heavy, I almost couldn't carry it home. My mother cooked it. It tasted so good and fed all the kids.

All sorts of animals came by our village in the wet season when holes were full of water. Antelope, giraffe, gazelle, digdig. Hunting was a huge sport. All the young men with their spears went out with their African hunting dogs in a big group. I loved to follow the hunters but they would send me home, telling me not to follow them. They knew after walking one hour I'd be tired and cry and want to return. If they killed enough, they'd bring it home and everyone shared the food. If they didn't, they'd say, "Well, we were not lucky today," but we knew it had probably been only a small digdig or gazelle and they'd roasted the meat and eaten it right there.

The hunters usually didn't kill the big animals, but once they killed an elephant that was causing trouble and the meat was brought to our house and cooked. Everybody sat looking at the food. Nobody wanted to be first to take a bite because it's a Dinka tradition that when you eat the meat of the elephant, everyone must put that first piece in their mouth together at once. People believed that if you started eating without the others when you got married your kids would have the split lip like the mouth of the elephant. My father lifted his bite first and everyone followed, putting it in their mouth at exactly the same time.

In summer, when the water holes dried up, the animals moved on to the River Nile and we survived on milk and the grain my mother kept stored in buried baskets.

My father often traveled, but when he was home, no matter which wife he was with, I stayed at that house too. He was funny and people hired him as the best talker to tell the judge things like, "He was promised eighty cows for his daughter, but he has only received fifty from the husband." The people paid my father to explain things like that on their behalf and he'd earn a cow for being the mediator between the plaintiff and defendant. He was half bald, muscular and athletic, not skinny like me.

Kids got malaria a lot and sometimes meningitis or other diseases. Once I was sick because I ran in the sun too much and got malaria. My father ground plants and soaked them in water. He poured the water into a gourd. "Now drink this." I drank and threw up, it was so bitter. "Okay now, there you go," he said. Two hours later I felt good.

Achol was my favorite friend because we had the best time together and we didn't fight. Most mornings I ran to her house and I'd wait for her if she wasn't yet awake. There was no school for us to go to in Juol, so we played under the palm tree in the courtyard collecting big snail shells, the size of coconuts, some pointy, some round. We built temporary structures to protect ourselves from the sun and play house in. "I am the husband and you are the wife. I tend the cows and you cook the food." She pretended to cook food from sand and we acted as if we were eating at a table. Although I liked to tease other kids, Achol felt safe around me because I protected her. She was an angel.

Every day I went to where the cows were because I liked to touch them. One spring a puppy of a feral dog came to stay with the cows. At first it was small but it got bigger and would jump and push me down and bite me. My father didn't know why I was coughing every day and I couldn't sleep. I told him the dog was biting me.

He took me to a witch doctor because the dog's poison had traveled into my veins. The witch doctor did witchcraft things by putting his mouth on my stomach and pulling out the hair of the dog. After some time, the coughing stopped.

When I was five, a man in our village brought home a small black monkey that had lost its mother. That baby monkey cried a lot; I think he missed his mom. The man gave milk to the little monkey but his cow was not producing enough for both of them. Late each afternoon the monkey would sit outside the man's house and cry, disturbing everybody.

"Come, come," I called to the monkey one day. I lifted my cup of milk to show him. He looked at me and I saw his eyes move to my cup. "Come." He moved a little bit toward me and then jumped around like monkeys do. I held the cup out low and tipped it so he could see the milk. "Come, little monkey. Aren't you hungry?" He looked all around, like he was going to get in trouble or something, and then put his fists on the ground and took a few hop steps closer. "Don't be afraid." I set the cup on the ground and moved away. He did his funny hand-foot hop walk over, grabbed up the cup and drank the milk just like a person.

The next day he took the cup from my hand and every day after that I shared my milk with him. He started liking me, like I was his mother, and became my monkey. Even though he grew long baboon teeth he knew people, so he didn't bite. At first he was small enough to sit on my shoulder and separate my hair, picking some stuff out of there and putting it in his mouth. People thought he was picking out lice. Even when my father hadn't cut my hair with a razor and it was long, he'd check my hair like that and pick something out. Sometimes he jumped to Achol's shoulder and tried to pick her hair. She liked my monkey, but she giggled when he did that and wouldn't hold still. He was a great monkey and I was so proud of him.

That spring, when my monkey was still small, baby goats kept disappearing. People thought a giant African eagle was taking them. We were playing under a tree one day and I sensed something moving and looked up. A huge snake had wrapped its body around the tree and the head was sticking out like it was a branch. "Snake!" I screamed and we all scattered back. "It's a python," the other kids said. I didn't know what a python was and went home and told my mother. She said, "No, I don't believe there is a python; let's go see where is it." It was gone when we got there and my mother ripped a branch from the tree. "You are a liar!" she said swatting my backside. "Mothers don't like kids to lie."

The next day behind our hut she saw that python eating a baby goat. She took her hoe and hit the back of the python. She saved the goat because the python has no teeth just very slippery saliva.

"I saw that python," I told her. "What did you hit me for?"

She apologized for beating me and I cried to make her feel worse. She rubbed my back and talked and laughed. I remember how she comforted me and can still feel her words now.

By the end of the summer my monkey had grown big and strong. One day we were under a tamarind tree and he jumped up and wanted to play and wrestle. He knocked me down. I got up and shoved him away as hard as I could. He fell against the tree, hit his head, collapsed, and lay still. I don't know why I did that, pushed him so hard. I felt so sorry. One moment we were playing, the next he was lying on the ground. I missed that monkey for a long time and learned that life can end in a careless moment.

Age-Mates

BENJAMIN

The summer before I started school, I was responsible to take our goats to graze. On the second day I already seemed to have lost one.

"Where is the other goat?" my father asked. His forehead was crunched together between his brows.

My voice wanted to tremble but I made it strong. "He disappeared in the bush. I cried out but nobody came."

The missing goat did not return that night. The next day my friends and I played in the shade of the trees behind the huts while our goats went together to eat the grasses. When the sun was at its hottest, we closed our eyes for a few minutes to rest. When I looked up again I couldn't see our brown goat, the one with a torn ear that hung down and flapped when he ran.

"Go look for your goat," my friend Duor said. "He must have gone to the bush." Duor was five and I was four. He was teaching me about the animals and how to hunt. I did as he said, trying to be brave, and walked through the long grass past the other grazing goats toward the thickets beyond our huts. I looked back hoping my friends had decided to follow but they were still resting in the shade, not even looking at me. I got close to the bush, but it was dense and I couldn't see my goat. I didn't want to enter, I couldn't see the ground and feared stepping on a sleeping snake. I picked up a stick and rattled the leaves, hoping my goat would be frightened and run back to his friends. My heart beat like the celebration drums. I hit the bush again with all my strength and bent my knees ready to run. There was a soft rustle, but I couldn't see anything, and then a loud crashing. I wondered if an elephant was about to run me over. I saw a flash of yellow brown. I meant to spring away like a gazelle, but my feet were stuck to the ground. Another crash. Not as loud but closer. An awful squeal sent my stomach through my chest and I knew it was my goat. I wished my father was behind me with his spear raised in the air. My stubborn feet finally moved and I ran back to my friends. Panicked, we rounded up the rest of the goats and herded them back to the village.

My father's hands went to his hips at the commotion of boys and goats running back into the village.

"Something took the goat in the bush," I panted.

"What did you see?"

"I just saw brown and the goat disappeared."

"That is hyena."

Everyone in the village tried to find the hyena.

"I will teach you to scare the hyena," said my father.

"Can a hyena be afraid of a little boy?" I couldn't imagine scaring the huge creature that caused my mother so much concern when she accompanied me to the latrine after dark.

That night I dreamed that a hyena was lurking outside our house and when my friends and I chased him like my father showed me, he disappeared. The next day we each found a sturdy branch the length of our arms and decided to graze the goats on a smaller patch of grass closer to the village. We were on alert but we heard nothing and saw nothing for several hours. Even some of the goats had begun to take their rest in the hot sun. I leaned against a tree and struggled to keep my sleepy eyes open. My eyes were half closed and I had that fuzzy floating feeling coming over me when I heard the snap of a small branch, no louder than the rustle of a rabbit in the loose twigs. Before I could even wonder what caused the noise, the goats were on their feet with their eyes and ears pointing, like hunters with their spears, toward the source of the disturbance. My friends and I took up our branches and jumped to our feet. We looked at each other with eyes like full moons on a dark night.

"What is it?" whispered Duor.

There was another sound, a rustling so faint we could barely hear it. But the goats heard it and one bolted; then the others followed, running in a tight pack like a bunch of blind men going one direction and then another.

I recalled my father's instructions and with both hands held one end of the thick branch at the top of my head, sticking it straight up. My friends did the same. Looking tall, we moved a few steps forward. "Hey," I shouted. "Hey," shouted Duor in his deeper voice. The others joined in, each in a different tone, hoping the hyena would believe that we were big like our fathers and had spears we were determined to kill with.

I didn't hear anything over our shouting but suddenly the little bunch of goats went into a frenzy. We raised our voices to our loudest shouts and jumped up and down like the dancing young men at initiation time.

Such a thrashing came from the bush that I could hear it over our shouts and the goats bolted from their group like pieces of clay when a pot is dropped. A streak of golden brown emerged into the sunlight and long grass. I wanted to charge forward to scare it away but it was gone again so quickly with a squealing kid goat that I couldn't even make out its shape—except to notice how large it was.

Later my father asked, "What color was that hyena?"

"It wasn't really yellow and it wasn't really red."

"What did his neck look like?"

"Big neck with lots of hair and on the head."

"You got a lion this time so we have to go and take care of it."

All of the men in the village gathered to go to the jungle to take care of this lion. I wanted to go too. It was my lion and I wanted to be the one who killed it, but they said that four was too young to hunt the lion. The men were gone all day and returned in the evening with just the big hair and the tail. They said, "This is the lion. Next time don't mess around with the lion. It is a very dangerous animal."

I learned many things from Duor. In Dinka tradition, it is important for children to be together. When it was time to eat, the children would go in a group from house to house eating together. When a boy ate alone, they said he was cruel and not following the traditional ways. His age-mates would throw bad words at him when they saw him walking on the street or in the jungle taking care of his cattle. The advantage of this tradition is that you got to know all the other boys in a wide area. It encouraged friendliness, building unity between the children's parents. Parents always knew that if a boy wasn't home, someone would bring him home. These were among the good things that I think of when I think about my home. Few of the boys who were with me at that time are still surviving.

Twist the Tongue

BENSON

Some nights the people of our village clustered around the fire to hear the elders speak of the days when we were not yet born. I began to understand many things about my area and my people and how our life became what it was. I learned that long ago the Arabs from northern Sudan came south as traders of salts and clothes. They traded with the Nubian, the Baggarra, the Fuong, the Fur, the Kabbabish, the Beja and many other plains and hills tribes. They gave clothing and salt to the chiefs so that they would be allowed to live there and trade. They told the chiefs about their God, Allah. Many chiefs converted and many tribes converted too.

Our elders told us that Islam kept spreading southward until it met the largest tribes, the Dinka and the Nuer, the tallest and the blackest people in Africa. They resisted this new religion because Islam was complicated and as cattle keepers we didn't have time to be meditating with the Qu'ran five times a day.

Later the discussions among the adults grew angry, especially when they talked of the government. They said the northern government wanted Islam to spread throughout Sudan because the northern land was all desert sand and they were jealous of the Dinka and Nuer territory, between the Blue and White Nile Rivers, which was the most fertile in all of Sudan. Our elders were upset that the government was telling the Islamic northern tribes that they should own cattle like the Dinka and Nuer, encouraging the converted tribesmen, called Murahiliin, to attack the villages and steal cattle from the Dinka tribes closest to the north. They called these attacks the Harpoon Wars because the Murahiliin came on horseback carrying one big spear that looked like the harpoon used for killing a hippopotamus.

My tribe, the Dinka Rek, and other more central tribes did not encounter a lot of hostility from the Murahiliin, just some cattle stealing, until the government declared Sharia law for all of Sudan in 1983. I was only a little boy and did not understand this Sharia law, but I heard the adults talking at our house, talking in the village, talking while they worked and talking at meetings. "They cannot make us pray to their God," they said. "We have too much to do with our cattle, our plantations and hunting. There is no time to pray five times a day." The men were angry. They also said, "They cannot force us to do this thing to our women. We love our women. We will not cut them like the castrated calf."

I was puzzled by this. Women did not have the parts like us boys or the bull calves. I asked Nieu-nieu, my oldest brother. "It is circumcision," he explained. I remembered my own circumcision and still did not understand.

———

Sometimes my mother liked to visit her sister on the other side of the River Nile. That summer, when there was too little food, she left me with my older sister, Angong, to take care of me and said that she was going to come back with some grain. But a long time passed and she did not return. I cried, disturbing my sister. "Angong, where is Mum?"

"She went to bring you food."

"Where?"

She pointed her finger in the direction my mother had gone.

"Ma eeee! Ma, come back." But there was no sign of her.

"Take me to her."

"I can't. There was an overflowing of River Nile and she is cut off from returning home."

Every day, I waited on the path, hoping to see my mother coming, but she never came because of the flood. Angong sometimes joined me to call her. She did it to encourage me and to stop me from crying. Still I wanted to see my mother because I felt more comfortable around her than my sister. People passing by would ask Angong, "Why is he crying?"

"He needs his mother."

"Take it easy, boy," they said. "Quiet is better."

It seemed to me like a year had passed, but Angong said it had only been a few months, when she called one afternoon. "Benson, come out. Mum is coming."

And there she was, walking with a baby basket on her head. Angong took the basket with my new brother, and my mother pulled me into her with strong arms. "How are you doing, my darling?"

I buried my face in her dress.

When my father was home, I stayed close to him. He talked slowly and softly and I liked that because I could understand everything he told me. He never punished me when I did wrong, but encouraged and teased me by talking about how my age-mates from the neighborhood did things better than me. He'd sing, "You are lazy like a pumpkin. You wait for your mother to cook you the food, then eat and fart loudly while you sleep."

His big *adeed*, which my mother had woven from a plant that grew in the Nile waters and covered with gazelle skin, was long and narrow. He stored his money and carried everything in it, even used it as a pillow when he was sleeping. He liked to go into the big cities, but he never bought for himself the city shoe. He wore sandals made from car tires. Every scrap of cloth he found on his journeys, even the smallest, would go into his *adeed*. While sitting and talking with people, he would sew pieces of cloth together into shirts and underwear, nodding his head, going "umh, umh," so that they knew he was listening.

On one trip to town, he returned with a shiny, soft pair of red shorts for me. I'd never seen anything so beautiful in all my life. He said they were underwear and made of nylon. I didn't care about that: I especially liked the dark blue stripes that went up each side. I wore them everywhere. The only time I took them off was when I was taking a bath.

———

My family had a traditional belief. Once, during the night, hyenas were hunting when they encountered an ailing male lion wandering about near my great-grandfather's village. The hyenas circled the lion. They howled threateningly, and the lion knew he could not win this fight. So he ran into my great-grandfather's house to save his life. Great-grandfather chased away the hyenas and protected the sick lion. Early the next morning he offered a lamb to this wounded lion and opened the door for him to leave the house.

Later, when famine came, the lion killed an antelope and dragged it to my great-grandfather's house in gratitude. My great-grandfather became friends with the lion. Our family lineage honored this partnership. The lion would not harm any of our herds; instead, he protected them and the family members gave the lion an animal to eat as a reward.

My father had grown rich with cattle, goats and sheep when a ferocious lion began massacring our animals. This lion had broken the old covenant of friendship. My father said that a lion who attacked any of our family's animals must be stopped. He and my Uncle Diing took a very fat and clean black castrated he-goat into the jungle and tied it to a tree. If the lion ate the offered goat, then he would not savage all our family's animals.

Day and night, everybody in the village heard the goat crying. But the lion would not take the offering. Other predators—like hyenas, leopards, pythons and cheetahs—knew that according to the rituals the goat was a gift for the lion and that the lion was around protecting the goat from being eaten.

After three days, Uncle Diing told my father to bring the goat home. It was wintertime; the grasses were as high as the adults' necks, the crops were ripening, and the pumpkin strands had spread their smiling yellow flowers in all directions. That morning, when my father returned with the goat through the tall grass, he didn't see the lion shadowing him. After putting the goat back in the pen with the others, he went off to the domino tree where the men of the village played.

"Help!" A neighbor screamed at the top of her voice.

"Mee aa! Ah aa!" the animals cried as the lion jumped from one goat to another like a kitten playing with its toys.

The men rushed to the cries. When my father finally arrived, he saw many of his animals lying dead and the others so scared they'd thrown away their dung.

My father was as angry as a snorting bull ready to fight over a mating cow. "Help me kill this lion, who has refused our offer of friendship," he demanded.

The other men refused. "It is a sacrilege to harm a lion according to our family rules."

They left my father standing beside the dead animals with chyme brackish on the grass.

The next time the lion attacked, Nieu-nieu, my oldest full brother, was watching the cows. "Damn, it is here!" he shouted when he saw the lion trying to scatter the cattle.

"Where is it?" My father yelled back. The lion, hearing a grown man's voice, disappeared into the tall thick grass. My father tracked its paw marks and saw that the lion wasn't going anywhere, just circling around our village from one bush to another and disappearing into our plantations.

My mother locked us in the hut while my father threw stones, trying to rouse the lion. He could hear it rustling through the sorghum stalks. Only adults were outside and the women's worried voices rose and fell with the lion's movements.

"What is he doing?" I asked.

My sister put her index finger to her lip and said, "Sss! Don't talk or make noise. Dad is going to fight the ferocious monster."

"Fetch my spears," my father said.

"Dad," said Dingmakuan, his eldest son by his first wife, "I don't think only two of us can fight a lion."

"Son, the covenant has been broken. I have to kill this lion."

Seeing my father's bravery and resolve to battle the beast, my Uncle Diing and two neighbors, Tourmakuei and his friend, offered their help. Dingmakuan came into the house to get ten small spears and the harpoon used to hunt large animals like elephants, buffaloes and lions. The hunters split into three groups: Uncle Diing, a very strong man, alone; the two neighbors together; and my father and Dingmakuan, each of the three groups tracking in a different direction.

My father and Dingmakuan followed the paw prints through tall bush to a ditch. When they looked over the lip of the trench, they came face-to-face with a big male lion. The lion was making his stand.

My father motioned to Dingmakuan. "Step backward, Son. Killing a lion needs fortitude and confidence to fight to the end."

He went down on one knee and crawled forward along the rim. When he was directly above the lion, he flung a light spear at him with all his strength. The spear split the lion's left ear, stuck into his hip and broke. The lion roared. Dingmakuan stood back, shaking with fear.

"I must harm the lion," my father said, "or he will harm me."

The lion crept partway up the embankment, his yellow eyes on my father, who went into a crouching position—the only suitable way to battle the lion. That way he cannot knock your face into the dust or bite the back of your neck.

The lion's tail swung left and right, brushing the ground and raising a cloud of dust. My father took a second spear from his left hand and shook it menacingly with his right. The lion roared and stayed in the posture of a hunting cat ready to jump on a mouse. The whole village heard it. Dingmakuan tried to shout out for help but he was made voiceless by fear. The two neighbors who were helping climbed a big baobab tree.

My father threw the second spear, aiming for the midpoint of the head. The lion dodged and charged. But my father quickly separated the harpoon from his left hand and held it with his right. The lion leaped up and onto him, scattering every spear out of his left hand over the grass. My father lay flat on the ground with the lion's fore claws dug deep into his chest. The lion paused. My father still held the harpoon in his right hand. He and the lion stared into each other's eyes. Then the lion opened his mouth wide to bite his throat and my father plunged his left hand into the lion's mouth and grabbed the tongue. The mouth was dripping slippery saliva but with all his strength he twisted and folded the tongue so that the lion could not bite down. With his right hand, my father pressed the harpoon into the lion's belly until it gored him through the navel. Then he jerked his left hand from the mouth and pushed the lion off him. It rolled down into the trench with a stream of blood oozing and the spear sticking out of its stomach. It moaned and could not move.

Dingmakuan's voice worked at last. "Oh oo, oh oo, he killed it. Dad killed the lion!" He went down into the trench. "Everybody come and see!"

All the villagers heard him and all those men who weren't

brave enough to approach a live lion showed up and stabbed the dead one saying, "You deserve it, monkey ass. Deng-mayomdit sent you to your lion graveyard for messing with his animals."

"You are a resolute man," the elders told my father. They splashed some water on him to clear the blood away, but he was bleeding badly where the lion's claws had torn his chest. That night the men voluntarily carried him on their shoulders to a clinic in a town two hours away. From there they transferred him to the big hospital in Wau.

But that was not the last of the lion war.

Deng the Slave

ALEPHO

One day in summer it rained heavily when no rain was expected. Deng, my cousin, who had left our village before I was born, returned that wet day with a young woman. Years earlier, during one of the attacks by the Murahiliin, people were killed and cattle stolen; Deng was taken away. Our people didn't know if he was alive or dead. When he came back to the village, old men and old women turned out to shower him with blessings. Everybody began crying and their mouths were full of laughter. Some were so excited they even forgot to say hello to his wife.

It is traditional in my culture for parents and elders to tell stories around the evening fire. Even though I have spent more than a decade without hearing these stories, I shall never forget the story Deng told the night he returned.

The Murahiliin had thrown him on the back of a horse and took him to a faraway place where he was sold as a slave. His new master made Deng herd his cattle and do his housework with a stern warning: "Any person caught escaping is killed in the presence of all eyes as an example."

Deng grew weak and thin, and his dark, smooth skin became pale pink and cracked like sun-baked clay. But Deng was a lighthearted person and persevered even under that harsh treatment.

In time his master bought other slaves, and Deng was sold to a man named Mohammed Zubber, who was harsher still. Every slave who came into Zubber's hands endured hardship. Deng was made to bathe everybody in the family, wash their clothes, cook their meals, and clean their house as well as herd cattle. There was enough to eat for the family of Zubber, but there wasn't any food for Deng or time to eat it. The slightest mistake provoked a severe whipping.

But Zubber's daughter, Asunta, talked to Deng as he worked, and they grew close. The master's daughter saw that Deng was a strong, hardworking man. Her family knew nothing of this. Everyone else hated Deng. One skinny sister of Asunta's despised Deng like poison. When Asunta called Deng by his name, her sister interrupted, asking, "Why do you call him by his name? He is *kadam asuwat*, 'black slave.'"

One day Deng escaped. But he was betrayed, tracked down and dragged back behind a horse, bruised and cut. The whole family, except Asunta, whipped him brutally, to the point of death. Asunta's eyes welled up with tears as she saw the man she had come to love being beaten to death. She couldn't help because her assistance would have revealed their relationship, which was forbidden according to Muslim law.

At the end of the beating, Zubber lifted Deng's head and looked into his eyes. "Will you ever escape again?"

Deng was too weak to answer.

"I will finish you tomorrow if you are still alive," Zubber said and left Deng outside half dead lying in a pool of blood.

Asunta, although she had heard her father's evil words, slipped out of the house that night. She cleaned Deng's wounds and served him a cup of hot tea. He sipped slowly with relief. He opened his eyes a little and asked, "Who is this?"

"I'm Asunta."

"Why are you doing this for me? You're a Muslim girl. I'm a slave."

"First, because I love you," she replied, her eyes downcast to the floor. "Second, because Allah said, *Challa ikun neep mabath*, 'love one another.'"

The following morning Mohammed Zubber woke up with the intention of killing Deng and was surprised to see his daughter nursing him.

"Asunta," he yelled. "What are you doing?" He thundered with anger like a regiment of drummers.

"Da, cool down! Da, do not you know he's also God's creature? He shouldn't be treated harshly like this. Otherwise Allah will punish us."

Zubber slapped his daughter. "Stupid child! What do know you about this black man?"

He angrily grabbed his sword and brandished it in the air like branch in a storm.

"Dad, if you do this," she said as tears rolled down her smooth cheeks, "I will run away and never be your daughter."

Zubber's mouth fell open in astonishment and he dropped the sword as if her words had stung him. He was quiet for a moment, glancing at the floor, before he mumbled, "Daughter, I changed my mind. I won't kill him, but he has to go a couple of days without food for his punishment."

Asunta ran to her father's arms and hugged him, tears of gratitude rolling down her smooth cheeks.

Deng had to resume his usual hard work, thoughts of escape mingling with fear, panic, and longing inside him until, one bright day, Asunta asked him, "Do you love me?"

He answered, "Yes!" But there was a faint stammer in his voice. She jumped to her feet and paused to examine the uncertain expression on his face. Deng sighed deeply and collected his courage. He had made a decision but fear kept him from expressing it.

Asunta had an understanding of people, but doubts crowded her mind. She wondered whether this black man really loved her. "Deng, if you love me, then I have decided to escape, abandoning my parents and my entire family." Tears welled up in her sparkling eyes.

"Why should you leave your family?" he asked.

"Because I love you, I don't want to be apart from you."

And so Asunta chose Deng to marry her, even though her father wanted her to marry a rich Muslim man. Deng promised to be her fiancé until death parted them. To seal their promise, he cut his skin and they licked blood as a sign that only in death would they break the relationship.

Soon the idea of escape filled their minds. They tiptoed out arm in arm to brave the wolf whistles and jeers of Sudan's dangerous roads. After a long and wearying trip, they arrived home safely in Deng's village to open arms and tears of joy.

Although I was too young to understand all of it, this much of their story still sticks in the back of my mind. I remember the big celebration. Old men who knew the background of our tradition talked and shouted at the top of their voices. I guess they were calling God, thanking him with strong words. Everyone welcomed Deng and Asunta into the village. A fat bull was slaughtered and we celebrated until the rains came again.

Lioness Revenge

BENSON

While tending the cows and goats, Nieu-nieu saw a lion in broad daylight. He brought the animals back to the village and put them in their stable. My mother locked us in the hut.

The men usually take care of their families, but my father had been in hospital for three weeks. Nieu-nieu was still a teenage boy so our mother became the man and the woman in our home.

The lioness came back that night. She battered her claws on the latch of the door to our house. My mother braced herself inside by the door and took up our father's harpoon, the same one he'd killed the lion with. She shouted, pretending to be a man, but the lioness seemed to know that she was just a woman and would not go away until the sun was above the trees and the men from the cattle camp came to see us.

The next night and every night after that the lioness returned and patrolled the compound. She clawed at the door and all night we heard her roaring. My mother couldn't sleep. Every day the men had to escort her to fetch water from the river or collect firewood to cook our dinner. Everyone in the village knew that the lioness was looking for revenge for the death of her mate. The village chief warned his men that they must not let harm come to us while our father was away.

The day my father came home, supporting himself with a big long stick, the lioness left the village and went back to the darkness of the jungle. But we could still hear her roaring at night.

The scars of that battle were printed on my father's chest and I was very proud every time I heard the villagers talking of how bravely he had fought and killed the lion. But through all these battles and all the sounds at night when they fought near our home, I had never seen a live lion and had no real idea what it, or many other animals people talked about, looked like.

One night I saw lights in the bush. "Look," I said to my father. "There is a hand torch."

"It's not a torch, son. It's the eyes of the lion glowing in the dark. That is why I always want you beside me. Creatures crawl at night searching for their dinner. Children make good meals for hyenas and lions. No child is safe wandering between the villages when darkness covers the land. But don't worry. No harm will ever come your way. You are my own warm blood and every creature knows that. I will always be here to protect you from anything. Even the small crawling ant will not dare to offend you while I'm around."

My father tried to make me feel safe, but his talk frightened me and I had nightmares. I kept seeing those lights glowing in the bush. The villagers believe it is a healthy omen to have a lion in your nightmares, but I knew the lioness was waiting for her revenge.

———

Every Dinka boy and girl looked forward to becoming a teenager and going to live in the cattle camp. It was like going to college: if parents didn't take their children, people mocked them saying that they would not be fit for marriage. According to Dinka life, young men in the village did not stand with a girl in conversation. If a young man wanted to speak to a girl, he had to give his message to her little brother, who brought the girl's response back to him. But they could mix freely in the cattle camp. Many young men and girls stayed in cattle camp until they married.

Our villages gathered their cattle at a place called Toch. It was wet and swampy with many rivers and plenty of grasses. There was a building for shelter from the rains and storms, but only girls used it. No matter how hard it rained, boys had to sleep outside. Not because of the girls inside, but because the rule was that boys should stay in the rain the way cows do.

A boy was voted to be *majok-wut,* or head of the camp. Whoever was *majok-wut* decided when to move to another place because the grass was finished or because some cattle were showing signs of sickness.

Everyone at camp had a part to play. The big boys traveled with the cattle to distant pastures. They measured their herding by cutting notches on their sticks to mark how many days they'd spent taking the cows to the grass. Anyone found cheating had to repeat his fifteen-day duty over again. Younger boys and girls walked with the calves near the camp. Girls usually milked the cows, but both boys and girls did it together if it was raining.

All the kids back in the village liked to pretend we were at the cattle camp. We would move our little clay models around in the grass, mingling them together to make a larger herd and pretending to drive them with small sticks.

My favorite time came during the competition called *luony kou*. The young men with the most cows showed off their riches by becoming the fattest to try to win the prettiest and cleverest girls. They drank only milk from their own cows: no other source of food was allowed. At first, when their stomachs were running, they could visit the toilet only once a day. By the end of summer, when the cattle camp dispersed, they returned to the villages and everyone, young and old, gathered to see who was the fattest. The champion was honored by the killing of many bulls, and the prettiest girls danced with him, even if he couldn't dance well because he was so heavy.

When small children played *luony kou*, we filled big gourds with water, laid in the bush and pretended the water was milk. We had fun beating our play drums, sticking our stomachs out and dancing like the fattest winners. But I regret that I never got to go to real cattle camp.

Since the cockcrow of Dinka culture, any girl who still had her lower six front teeth was not allowed to marry a man who owned a lot of cattle. "She is not from a rich family," people would say. "Or maybe she is from the city and that is why she has not removed her teeth." City girls are not respectful of their husband's family.

Young men were allowed to keep their lower teeth, but

they struggled to attract the pretty girl that breaks every man's heart. Girls told those with teeth, "You aren't a man. You haven't endured the pain of manhood."

Dinka remove the teeth to distinguish themselves from other tribes who bear different marks on their bodies such as scars on their head or bodies. It has been our practice since before our grandfather's grandfather's time. The initiations occur between the ages of six and twelve, because it is more difficult and more painful to remove the teeth when a person is more mature.

I didn't want to have my teeth removed, but I was young and couldn't question the tradition. I knew I must obey my parents.

When I was six, my permanent teeth emerged. My mother told me one morning, "Go to your uncle's house. It will be less painful when your teeth are weak early in the day before eating anything."

Three boys and one girl waited at my uncle's house. He called the girl first because he thought that if she was left until last, she might be scared.

"Come sit and look upward." He took out a fish spear that looked like a long nail. "Open your mouth." He pushed the fish spear between the two bottom front teeth and pressed the gum down with it. Blood filled her mouth. He pushed harder and the teeth bent as the spear penetrated the gum. When he swung the spear left and right; her teeth dropped to the ground. The girl was as silent as a grave and done in a few minutes.

I was next. I was nervous but thought it would go okay, as it had seemed to with the girl. I sat down on my knees and looked upward, as my uncle suggested. He held my head firmly in his big hand. "Don't move." He pushed the spear between my teeth as he had done with the girl and pressed down. My gum felt like it was being torn by a sharp razor blade. My mouth filled with blood. Then the fish spear penetrated through my teeth, splitting one in two and leaving half of it in the gum. I began to sob from the pain and my body convulsed. He gave me a slap on my cheek for moving before he inserted the spear again and pushed my chin upward so that I accidentally swallowed some of the blood. I began choking and couldn't cry more. He dug in my gum so hard that he tore it apart. When he finally got out the other half of the broken tooth, he scolded me for crying because I had made it so hard for him.

When he was done, my mother boiled a pot of water to wash the blood out of my mouth and gave me a small tin with sand to spit the blood into. The other two boys followed in my steps and they cried out too. We were all shamed that day for being bettered by the girl.

---

*N*ot long after my teeth were removed, my sister, Angong, became first wife to a man from a village two hours north of ours. When Angong's baby was born, my mother sent me to stay at her house to care for her goats and watch my new nephew. I liked being with my big sister, but I missed my mother and father, Akoon, Alepho and my friends.

The year I was at my sister's house, people began coming through her village from the north asking for food. They were Dinka but many spoke a different dialect. Angong told me that the Murahiliin had attacked their villages with

43

shooting helicopters and that the people were heading south to Bor and on to Ethiopia because war was coming to southern Sudan.

When Angong wasn't around, her husband's second wife gave me work and made me do things for her family. "I am not her son," I told Angong. But Angong couldn't help me; she was sick with conjunctivitis.

So one day I walked home by myself. I thought I knew the way, but it was longer and more confusing than I had remembered. When I reached Juol, it was nearly dark. My mother was angry that I had come by myself.

I told her about the other wife and how I missed my home. She said I could stay but would have to go back to Angong's house in a few months.

"People from the north come in a line every day through the village," I told her. "They are begging for something to eat and we are running out of food."

"They have been coming here too," she said.

One night when my father returned from a trip, he thought I was sleeping. He told my mother about an attack at a village called Akuac-kok. The Murahiliin had quickly surrounded the village on horseback and captured many civilians and shot dead those who tried to run away. The captives were separated into two groups. The women and children were locked inside the huts and burned to death. The men were tied up, led to the riverside, killed with a machete and dropped into the river. My father told my mother that he got away by jumping into the river.

I didn't sleep that night thinking about those women and children burning inside their homes. The next day my father gathered all of us together. "Listen carefully," he said.

"You must be prepared. The government troops are Arabs and call themselves Muslims. The Arabs wear a long white dress with a large handkerchief tied on their heads and pray by kneeling and smelling the ground everyday. They speak a strange language that we cannot understand but some speak Dinka. They call us slaves or infidels and want to kill us for not circumcising our girls and becoming Muslims like them."

Hearing my father talking about these bad things scared me more than the story the night before. Usually adults didn't mention war in front of the children. Alepho was only four years, but even he looked worried. Akoon was older and I could tell he understood all this better than me.

"If our village is attacked, don't panic or make any noise. Just leave the house and hide somewhere safe. Those men's guns shoot fire embers that search far and kill even into hiding places. If there is shooting or unusual roaring noises, remain in hiding and stay quiet there as long you can hear that sound. Stay away from the house.

"And you must beware. Some of the Muslims are traitors from Dinka tribes; they speak the way we do. They may call to you, 'Come back, we are Dinka. Don't run away. We are not your enemy, we will not harm you.' But when people come out of their hiding places, the traitors laugh and say, 'You are called by your death!' and those people are killed."

This was very confusing. I had never seen a Muslim. How would I know what to look for?

"Why do those Dinka men do that terrible thing?" asked Akoon. "Why are they killing us?"

"They are city criminals," my mother said. "They want money and they want our cattle."

My father's warnings echoed in my head. Everything was confusing. I didn't know who was evil and who was good. Sometimes rebel soldiers fighting the government came into the village and demanded food. The villagers called them *koryom*—locusts. This confused me too; how could people be locusts? The villagers seemed scared.

Once three rebel soldiers came to our home in the night and roused us from our sleep when my father wasn't home. They ordered Mother to send Akoon, my eldest brother, to open the goat shed. She begged them to take milk instead of a goat but they threatened that if they had to open it by themselves they'd take much more. Finally she gave up and sent Akoon to open the door. The greedy soldiers, who had been expected to take a lamb or kid, took our three best goats. When Akoon tried to stop them they beat him, breaking one of his teeth.

"Why didn't the men of the village stop those evil soldiers?" I asked my mother.

"These aren't evil," she said. "They are fighting for our freedom."

Although I hoped the soldiers would never come to our home again, I liked to look at their pale orange uniforms, big hats and the guns they slung on their shoulders. I sometimes pretended to be like a soldier by putting a stick on my shoulder. "I'm fighting for our freedom," I told my friends. "Give me food, give me milk, or I will take all your cows and goats."

"Don't do that," mother scolded when she heard me one day.

I looked down at the ground and said nothing.

"It's not safe playing like a soldier. The government

troops are killing everyone who has seen or talked to these rebels."

She called me inside and spoke to me in a way she had never done before.

"My son, times are dangerous. The Murahiliin gunmen are killing a lot of us. They are burning food and homes and seizing children and livestock. My son, the world is ending."

Her voice was terrible; it scared me. But I knew she spoke the truth. I'd heard a roar from the big town a two-day walk away the week before while I was out tending the cattle. "It's the roaring of the artilleries," Akoon had said. "There is fighting between the rebel forces and the government troops."

"Benson," mother said. "You don't understand what is bad and what is good. I am worried about you. You don't know how much I need you. I want you to be safe, my son, for the rest of my life. You must stay alert from now on. If you hear guns shooting louder or nearer than before, I want you to flee from the house, run fast and hide in the bush. Don't be captured and taken away or hurt." She spoke with grief in her voice that day.

"And stop your playing with guns. You must play like a Dinka child. Model cows or some other kind of animals. Dinka don't own guns. They are the most evil thing I have ever seen in my life. It's bad luck pretending to be a rebel soldier."

To my mother, many things indicated bad luck, most of all the day the sun became covered in red, leaving the world almost in darkness during daytime.

"It's happening once more," she had said. "The sun is

dying. This is bad luck. The sun is one of God's driving forces that shines on the world to see what good or bad people are doing. Its light alerts God that mankind has failed to attend to evils. If the sun sees many evils, it stops looking and takes the message and reports to God.

"You see," she said, looking at me seriously. "Long ago the sun and moon fought over that duty. The sun defeated the moon in wrestling and the moon was thrown on the hot ashes. His face was burned and that's why you see some dark scars on it. The moon is blind now and cannot see the many evils that happen at night. Only the sun does this and that is why it has disappeared and now we are left in darkness during the day."

"This hasn't happened since I was a little girl," she said. "It was a bad sign then. The first Arab horsemen began raiding our villages. But then they were only using long spears. There were no guns."

I was scared that day seeing the sun dying, hearing the hyenas crying and knowing that man's too many evils had darkened the earth.

Shortly after we were given those warnings, Aguok, a nearby village, was attacked. The men tried to fight the invaders with spears, but they were all killed in a few minutes. "There was a plane standing above trees pouring fire on them," my mother lamented.

The adults no longer hid the subject of war from us. We heard it everywhere day and night in our huts with our parents. A few days later horsemen attacked and killed countless villagers at Warawar, just north of our village. They burned the crops and nailed a baby on a fig tree like Jesus on the cross. People who knew how to read said the dot marks on the paper said, *Jesus, your God was here.*

"Tomorrow you must return to Angong's house," my mother told me. "She needs help with your nephews. No one is safe here. They want to pour fire on us from the sky."

School Bombing

BENJAMIN

My school uniform was white shorts and a white shirt, and I liked it a lot. I was five, living at my aunt's house in a town called Luonykear. My teacher's name was Apo Majen Majok and she spoke Arabic and taught high school, but used Dinka when she taught us. We learned songs and the school was fun because I met new boys.

After school and on the weekends my friends and I liked to go outside and eat the forest food. My favorite was coconut. I love coconut.

I had only been at the school a few months when my aunt came for me. She told me, "There is deployment. We must pick up the children because the rebels are coming to Luonykear to defend the town against the government troops. I must take you home. You will be back in school in a couple of months."

She took me back to my village, where I was so happy to see my mother and father and to be a family again.

My father explained to me that the northern government suspected that rebels called SPLA, Sudanese People's Liberation Army, were living among us. So the government troops were attacking our villages because we looked the same as the SPLA and spoke the same language. They were in the same skin as us. Some nights we saw fires on the horizon. In the mornings I smelled smoke.

"If our village is attacked," he said, "you must be quiet and quickly run into the bush and hide."

"I can run into the bush," I said bravely. It did not sound difficult. I had run from lion and hyena.

The next week he told me, "The government planes dropped bombs from the sky and the schoolhouses are all burned down. The SPLA was there to protect them but there was nothing they could do. You will not be going back to school."

Achol

ALEPHO

I was sleeping sweetly when my mother woke us abruptly. "Wake up! Wake up!" There was terror in her voice.

"Ma, what is wrong?"

"Shhh, don't talk. Please do me a favor. Go with your big brother and don't ask questions."

She got Akoon and me up in silence as my father stood by the door. Benson was away at Angong's house. Outside she instructed us, "I want you to walk into the bush with Nieunieu." She pulled us close and hugged us. "If something ever happens to your dad or me, please don't cry."

We shuffled into the long African elephant grass without asking questions. Nieu-nieu led us so slowly and cautiously that I knew in my heart something was very wrong. I wiped tears from my eyes and glanced back. My parents stood in front of our house looking at us as we walked away. I decided to not look back again. We walked far in the dark but no snake or nocturnal creeping creature bit us. When our fear had nearly settled, we saw a bright light from a village not far north of ours.

"The houses are on fire," Nieu-nieu whispered.

We knelt in the grass. Akoon's and Nieu-nieu's eyes were

big and round and watching like owls. There came a loud popping sound, like corn on the fire.

"Gunshots," said Nieu-nieu.

I'd never seen or heard a gun before. Cries, a child for her mother and father, and then a mother and father crying for their child, echoed out of the darkness. Suddenly a loud explosion sounded to the south. Juol was on fire. Grass roofs lit up like a cluster of torches. Guns started popping again. Cries. More explosions. The popping louder and faster. I couldn't stop worrying about my mother and father. I sobbed as we spent most of the night watching the explosions, until the cries and the fires died away.

"We must sleep here in the bushes," Nieu-nieu told us.

I couldn't sleep. The fear grew inside me. I wanted for dawn to break so that I could run back to our house and see my mother and father and infant brother.

Just before first light we started to walk back, one after the other. Our house was still standing, and my sadness, fear and worries were reduced when I saw my father and mother were alive. But they were sad, sitting apart from each other and muttering dolefully.

"I want to go see my friends," I said.

"Don't go," Mother said quietly. "They are not there."

"Where did they go? Why would Achol leave without saying good-bye to me? I am her best friend."

My mother reached for me but she had my brother at her breast. I ran down the path through the sorghum. When I reached the clearing, I gazed in shock at the roofless mud walls. *What happened to Achol's house?* I went closer, hoping Achol would come out to greet me like she did every morning. But when I looked through the doorway I saw the worst thing I had ever seen. Bodies lay on the floor, shrouded in ashes. Burned alive in their house. These were my lovely friends. Achol was my best friend ever. I loved her so much. My eyes were fixed on the sight of death in front of me. I smelled it, tasted it and felt it. I hurt so much I could not live with it.

I couldn't understand why people were killing us. Did Achol deserve to die? What wrong had we done to these people? *Oh, Ma, why the killing?*

The next day my mother was still mumbling her woeful song when Angong rushed into our courtyard.

"Ma! Da!"

We ran out and Angong fell to her knees under the palm tree, exhausted from running two hours with her newborn baby in her arms. My mother took her baby and my father helped her to her feet.

"There was noise and smoke." We could barely hear Angong's weak voice. "We thought it was a wildfire. Then there was shooting by guns and explosions." She began sobbing. "We didn't know what to do. The explosions shook the house. It was dark. We all scattered into the bush. It went on for hours." She fell against my father. "Oh, Da! We can't find Benson."

Part Two

Like Ants Spewing from the Nest

Too Many Evils
Darkened the Day

BENSON

The tuk! tuk! of nearby shots made me jump from my bed. After herding goats all day, I ate supper early and went to sleep alone in the little house next to my sister's. I ran outside to find Angong but a bright glare blinded me. "Angong!" I yelled. Dogs were barking, people screaming. Everything lit up for a moment and then went dark again. The sound thundered through my ears. The ground shook beneath my feet and it felt like I was floating on it. Then another flash like lightning and that ground-shaking, deafening noise again. Scores of houses began burning at once. There was so much smoke and dust and noise I could see and hear nothing. My body shook. Where was everyone?

A bright red fireball fell from the sky. Its thunder echoed to the edge of the forest. Troops were attacking with heavy weapons. I remembered my father's instructions. "Get away from the village. Hide where the gun's fire embers can't reach you. Hide so that they don't scoop you up onto a horse and take you as a slave to the north." But even though I remembered what he told me, I had never ever expected to have to follow his instructions. *Where was Angong?* Another flash. Once more I couldn't see anything for the smoke.

So I ran like my father told me to. I ran from the fireballs, bullets and screams into the dark where the hyena and lion and scorpion slithered and prowled. There was no moon in the sky—just a few winking stars. Only during the awful flashes could I see where my feet touched the ground, the night was so dark. I pushed through tall grass and bush. My feet felt like I was running far above the ground and my body was light, but my knees felt like they were breaking. The bright fire blinked, never growing more distant. I couldn't seem to escape it.

I ran for so long my legs became wobbly. When I felt like I had been running all night, I scrambled under a dark bush, hoping I'd be safe. Still as a rabbit, I tried to think where I should go. I was wearing only my underwear—the red shorts my father had brought from town. As I lay down to rest, I stared at the fireflies glimmering at the edge of the forest that swallowed the echoing gunfire. It was the coldest, gloomiest night. Many dogs barked but the birds were silent.

While it was still dark, a soft rustling in the grass near the bush startled me. I made a slight move and unintentionally crunched dry leaves.

"Who is there?" A voice broke through.

I hated hearing that voice. I wanted to stay calm like tortoises do.

"Don't be afraid," the voice said. "We are Dinka!"

I understood the language he was speaking but I didn't know who the man was or if he had been one of the ones shooting.

"Anybody there?" the voice interrupted again.

"Me!" I said without really meaning to.

"If you are Dinka, come out." His voice was low but clear. "It is not safe to stay here. Stop creeping in the bush like an ant. That bush belongs to cobras, scorpions and leopards at night."

I crawled out shaking with fear and cold. A man stood there with a little boy just like me beside him.

"Whose son are you?" the man asked.

"Deng Akuectoch son."

"I know your father, Dengmayomdit!" He used my father's nickname. "I met your family when we went through your village, but I don't know you. What are you doing up here?"

"I was staying at my sister's house."

"Don't be afraid. Come with me. I will take care of you for your father. I'm Kuany. This is my brother's son, Anei. You should call me uncle too."

I was just quiet because my head was feeling hollow and heavy, as if I'd placed a pumpkin on it.

"Come," Kuany said again. "We must move far away. They're killing everybody. They are killing our people."

I began to cry for my mother. My body trembled from my cries and the pounding of my heart.

"I will look after you until we meet your parents," Kuany said. "Come with me." He headed in a direction away from Juol.

"I must find my mum," I mumbled through my sobs and pointed toward my village.

He took my hand. "You can't travel alone. You may get lost on the way or even run into the enemy by mistake."

His warning scared me. I got to my feet and followed him and the boy through dewy wet grass that was over my head. I couldn't believe I was walking away from home without my family. The shooting became more distant, making a peculiar sound, *tit-tit-tit, dui! dui giim,* like a noisy water-digging machine I saw once. A fiery glow hovered above the village sky. Although I wanted to cry I remembered to be quiet. My breathing was sharp, louder than I could control, as warm tears rolled down my face.

We walked on through the tall grass and dark woodland without stopping. My bare feet grew numb in the cold. I stepped on sharp things that made them sting and ache. My body was bare and my underwear dripped wet from the dew. I put both hands across my chest, held my elbows tight and walked with my nose dripping. I hated the day I fooled around by putting the stick on my shoulder. My mother was right when she told me it was bad luck pretending to be a soldier.

Everything changed on that most terrifying night of my life. The sky was going to fall and swallow me. I believed what my mother had told me: the sun was dying. Men had done too many evil deeds and they had darkened the day.

We stopped walking when we heard the sound of people approaching. "Sit down," Kuany whispered. "Don't move till I tell you to." He moved toward them. "Who are you?" he asked.

"We are Dinka, going to Biong."

"We are going there too. I have two boys with me. My nephew and a boy I found hiding in a bush." Kuany motioned to us. "Get up boys, let's move on."

There were seven people in the group: two women and their husbands, two younger men and one old woman. The two women were wailing that their daughters had been on their way to the dancing ceremony when the shooting started. "God, please protect our children wherever they are." The older woman kept saying, "Didn't I always say, dancing at night is a curse? Curse easily follows today's teens' free spirit because they won't listen to anyone."

"Why do you say that, Mama?" one of the weeping women asked. "Did you cause the spell to curse us?"

The women began to argue until another explosion thundered through the air, silencing even the singing insects. Shooting started again, louder and nearer. Kuany grabbed Anei and me and led us in a different direction. We walked bending low, like crooked old men. I protected my eyes by sweeping the grass out of the way with my hand. A cock crowed from a distance. Suddenly a shooting sound came through the bushes. All thoughts of sleep were forgotten: I just wanted the shooting sound to stop. After a while, the sound of the gun faded and there was only the sound of an owl screeching.

Then a great commotion came from close behind us. We moved to hide in the bush again. A large crowd of people arrived, all Dinka, carrying chickens and driving goats. Tied together, their pots and plates shook and rattled. Kuany greeted them.

"Are you well?" a man with a baby on his shoulder asked us.

"Yes," Kuany answered. "It is only us three, but we are looking for our relatives and families."

We joined that group and walked on. The sun began to shine. When we reached the village of Biong, our group scattered to find friends and relatives. The women of Biong came out of their houses and watched us like outcasts or intruders in their village who would lead the enemy to them. I hoped to find someone from Juol but I didn't recognize anybody.

"We have to find a chief's home," Kuany said.

Everybody had gathered at the chief's home. Even though the crowd was large, the chief was a kind man who allowed us to rest in his compound. The chief's family was preparing to evacuate too because the government troops were slaughtering Dinka village chiefs who would not identify the rebels.

We left the chief's home the next morning with a larger group of people and walked to a place where the SPLA (Sudanese People's Liberation Army) camped. The rebel soldiers were singing and cleaning their weapons. The SPLA captain said he was expecting attacks by the government troops; this place was for his forces and that it was better for us boys to go to a refugee camp in Ethiopia. He thought we would be safe there while they fought to stop the government from killing all the Dinka people. The captain gave us a cow and told us to leave immediately to catch up with another group that had left just that morning. Ethiopia sounded so far away from my parents and from Juol. I didn't want to go.

We walked two days and nights but found no one. I was exhausted and weak. We stopped at a river where we killed and roasted the cow. We ate the meat and drank from the river and afterward we moved on. All of my body was sore, not from tiredness but from sickness. My chest pained and it made me slow. My body was sick of walking. I fell asleep on a mat by the side of the road and stayed there all the next day. I could no longer think much about my family except that I was alone and without them.

Gunmen in the Garden

BENJAMIN

The sun was setting when the men came by carrying guns. I was taking care of goats outside our field of maize when people of different colors—brown and white, not all black like us—stared at me like cobras looking at mice. One talked. I couldn't understand his language. Another said something like, "Leave him alone, he's a kid, he don't know about it." They left and went on toward my village.

Before they reached my house they began shooting. People scattered everywhere. Roofs went up in flames. I left our goats and ran to join my parents, but I couldn't get past the gunmen who stood in the middle of our yard. The village was destroyed. I hoped my parents had fled. I ran back into the bush to hide, afraid that the gunmen might come back and capture or kill me. I watched them kill our cattle, set the millet and sorghum fields on fire, destroy all the things that human life needs to survive.

Darkness fell and everything grew quiet. I didn't know if it was safe to leave my hiding place. I waited until I heard the sound of people. I wanted to find my parents, but I had to be careful. Step by step I went out onto the road.

"Where are you going, little boy?" They spoke my language but they looked like soldiers. Not knowing whether they were rebels or government men, I was ready to run back into the dark.

"I am going nowhere."

"Where are you going?" they asked again.

"I'm going nowhere. I don't know where my mum has gone and I don't know where my dad has gone."

"Go that way," they told me. "You will find people over there."

They let me go and I followed their directions. Soon I met people moving along the way on the main road. I watched them one by one. There were lots of children, some my age, and I asked them, "Did you see my family?"

They said, "No, we are searching for our parents too."

After a while I found my cousins Lino and Emmanuel in the crowd. I was happy to see them but I really wanted my parents. Lino and Emmanuel were crying and searching for their parents too. I joined them and we walked together in the dark. When we rested after a few hours, the elders came and told us, "You kids, we have to leave right away. It's not safe to return to your homes. You must come with us."

We agreed because we had to.

Everybody walked day and night. I was so tired that I cried all the time. Nothing else was possible. I just staggered forward, walking with Lino and Emmanuel and friends we met. Everyone wept.

After two days we came to a town called Tonj. Crowds of people were moving around. My body hurt from walking for so long. Just when I most wanted to lie down in my house and be with my parents, I saw, far down the street, a boy sitting on a mat who looked like my cousin Benson. I was happy to see him because he was a little bit older than me and I thought he would know what we should do.

"Benson!" I called out. He didn't hear me. He was sitting alone thinking too much. Thinking of his family. I yelled louder, "Benson!" He looked around once and didn't see me waving. He looked shocked.

The River Nile

BENSON

That afternoon, sitting by the road in the Tonj region, I heard someone shout my name. I looked around but could not see well through my blurry eyes. I heard my name again and saw Benjamin pushing his way through the crowd. He had no shirt or underwear; he was bare naked.

My cousins Lino and Emmanuel were with him. I was happy to find them but I was too sick to see or talk well. I could only sit there. Benjamin joined me on the mat and I could see that his eyes were dripping with tears. It made me sad, but I didn't want to cry because then my chest hurt more. We rested together for a while. Even though I was glad to have them there beside me, my pain wouldn't allow me to talk.

Kuany took Emanuel and Lino to help him dig cassava roots in the field.

Benjamin asked, "Did you see anyone of our family?"

I shook my head.

"I don't know where they went," said Benjamin. "I couldn't get home because of the people shooting. I don't know if my parents died or if they are alive."

As soon as I could speak, I told him that everyone could not be okay. "Nobody is here. We have lost them now."

"What can I do?" Benjamin asked as if I were an elder and knew what to do. "Can I go back home?"

"I have no idea about that. We might have to go with these people. Perhaps we will meet some of our family ahead."

Kuany returned with Lino and Emmanuel and boiled the cassava. They ate, but my chest pain kept me from feeling like eating.

The next morning we walked on. All I could see was a hole in front of me that I felt like I was going to fall into because of my sickness. I sat down, wanting to lie under a tree and forget walking, but Kuany took me by the hand to see a rebel captain in the village.

"The boy is sick," Kuany told the captain. "He needs a place to stay."

"We live nowhere," the captain said. "We move from one place to another, and can't take care of anybody. It's better if he walks to the refugee camp in Ethiopia with the other boys."

I'd heard the name Ethiopia before, but all I knew was that it was foreign land far away from my home.

The captain leaned down to me. "That sickness will go away if you start walking and get stronger and do not think of your family. If you are thinking too much of your family, you will die before you reach a safer place. This war will end soon. I know you are sick because of it but I will give to your uncle a medicine for you so that you will get well and can walk like other boys."

I didn't want to listen to him. I wanted to stay there and stop walking farther away from my home and parents. I thought it would be better if I died.

"That is a penicillin," Kuany said as he injected me. "It will make you feel better."

I'd had an injection once before when I was sick in my village and my father brought a man from town who gave me a medicine that made me well. That was only a pinprick and didn't hurt. When Kuany injected me four times in the following day, the pinprick was the same, but the medicine hurt going into my arm.

We traveled on. I felt bad that I couldn't help Benjamin or Lino, who were still little boys, just five years old, but I could barely keep going myself. We came to a river with a broken bridge. All around were burned-out trucks. The ground smelled of burning oil. My stomach was not strong. The stench made me vomit.

We found metal cans spread across the grass and sand, and on the bank of the river. "What are those?" the boys asked.

"Ammunition shells," Kuany said.

To the side of the road a big green round metal thing leaked grease and all the boys wanted to stand and watch it. "Move away from that thing," a man warned. "It's an unexploded bomb."

Kuany told us the SPLA rebel forces had destroyed a government troop convoy here earlier, and that was why the government was sending troops to destroy our villages. I kept quiet, wondering if that was true.

We crossed the river at the shallow part by following a man ahead of us who had a stick to detect what was below the surface. If there was a metal fragment we had to divert our route. Climbing out on the riverbank, a boy stepped on a sharp object that scraped the skin off the sole of his left foot. We had to leave him in the next village because he could hardly walk.

We entered a huge forest and walked all night. Even though we'd left it far behind, I could still smell the oil and ammunition and my stomach was weak with nausea. In the cold night breeze my chest hurt more and made me cough. Early the next morning we found blood covering the path, which led us to a man who had been shot while running away when his village was attacked. His leg was broken by the bullet and he'd bled everywhere. He'd been crawling for two days. He said the hyenas had been trying to eat him and he had been fighting them with a stick all night. "Don't go on this path ahead to my village," he said. "Find another way."

A group of men decided to tie him in a blanket and carry him. One man said he knew another way to the village so we followed him for some hours but we did not find it. We returned to the tall grass and found a hut. We asked the people there for directions to the chief's compound but they were cunning. They misdirected us and we walked for another night without finding shelter.

As we became exhausted, our long line of walkers broke up. At times people sat down to rest on the grass or find a dry place to sleep. Sometimes I became separated from Benjamin, Lino and Emmanuel and we found each other at resting points.

When we had to cross a large, swampy area many people were bitten by snakes. Every time anyone was injured, he was asked if he preferred to remain in a village or continue walking. Most people tried to keep walking, but many were left behind and many died.

After almost two months of walking and living off wild food or gifts from generous villagers, we reached the Upper Nile region, and there our problems multiplied. Before reaching the River Nile itself we had to walk for two days in muddy water. Night there was so cold I didn't feel anything. Warm breezes came and then cold ones that made me shiver and my teeth chatter.

When we finally found the riverbank at Shambe, I was amazed to see such a big river, so wide I couldn't see the other side. I couldn't see how we were going to cross it. Hippopotamuses floated open mouthed, showing us their sharp teeth, while the crocodiles moved in close along the bank. When we were told we would be rowed across on a boat, I thought we were sure to die because there was a heavy current.

We had to wait for the wooden boats in tall, swampy reeds. I was so hungry that I picked up some bones of a fish that had already been eaten by a fisherman. Although there was no meat on them, the bones kept my mouth busy so that I wouldn't forget how to eat.

The crocodiles didn't eat us but the mosquitoes that infested the reeds did. Night was the worst. They all came out, big ones, little ones, even their babies. When I swept my hand across my back, smashing five or ten mosquitoes at once, my palm was wet with blood. Even by day the hungry ones fed on us. Sometimes I could feel one biting, so I'd hit it only to discover four or five others already sucking my blood.

On the morning of the third day, the boatmen arrived with rebel soldiers. I was scared when I saw soldiers, but they greeted us politely and gave us some biscuits. They told us to climb in the boats and warned us to be careful on the water. Ten of us crammed into the bottom of a little boat by sitting between each other's legs. The boatman expected us to pay, but of course no one among us had any money. The soldiers ordered them to take us across without charge, which made the boatmen angry. Before we took off, a boy of about twelve who was sitting behind me leaned over the edge to look straight down into the water. He lost his balance and grabbed the side of the boat. It tipped and water poured in. The boatmen straightened the boat, but now they were even more upset with us. The one in the rear raised his big oar and struck the boy who had tipped the boat on the side of his head. Blood poured out and he held his head in his hands as we left the shore.

We were sitting in river water, which turned red from the blood pouring from the boy's head. As the boatmen paddled, the soldiers advised us to not think very much of our parents or of the difficulties that faced us on the way. I tried to follow their advice but it only made me think more. I turned to glance at my homeland as it disappeared from view. My thoughts were on my village that I was leaving behind. Had it been attacked? What had become of Akoon, Alepho, Nieu-nieu and Angong, and my mother and father? If they were still alive, would my parents ever find me on the other side of the Nile? Was there a way back?

As we crossed, the soldiers began calling us the Red Army because even though we were just little boys, as we grew older they expected us to join the military and fight for freedom.

They taught me this song:

> My dear Mama,
> I'm going to leave you now!
> I'm going to the school,

Never think of me again.
My loving Daddy,
I'm going to leave you now!
I'm going to where no one knows.
Never pray for me anymore.

The Ajakageer

BENJAMIN

After we crossed the River Nile, the SPLA soldiers led our group. When we came to villages they said, "We are here with a lot of children. They need something to eat." People believed that when they saw us. Sometimes they cried and gave food to us. But after a few days there were no more towns, and we didn't know the wild foods that were safe to eat. Hunger forced me to try things I'd never seen before.

Soon there were no trees; sunshine was everywhere. In the night we walked with nothing to eat. In the day we sat in the shade. People began dying from hunger. There was nothing to eat at all. I asked anyone who had water if he would give me some. The adults gave their little bit of water to us boys. When adults peed they drank their pee. I was sure that I was going to die.

When we reached a town called Macdeng, we found many people from faraway places crowded there. The townspeople knew that we needed something to drink and eat. A lady came to me and asked, "How did you make it to here? It is three months from your home."

She gave me some water and led me to her house and let me rest there. All I could think about was how much I was separated from my family now. They could never find me so far away. I knew it was up to me to make it back home. Wherever we went I would think of how I could return. I had no idea where we were going, but I was determined to remember every place along the way so I could one day find my way back home.

I rested in the lady's home for two days, and as everyone was preparing to leave, she asked me, "Do you want to stay here as my child?"

"I want to go with the people," I told her. "My cousins are with them. I must be with my cousins."

"You will go and be safe," she said.

I found Benson. He was still weak and sick. His eyes were watery and red. We left the town and found ourselves in a horrible situation again. No rain, no trees, just desert as far as we could see. The adults said this was the Ajakageer, a desert that was worse than anything we had already crossed. We just hoped it wouldn't kill us.

The Skulls Tree

BENSON

In the days after we crossed the River Nile, water became precious. It was the dry season: the grasses were brown and the rivers dry with dust. Nearly all the animals were gone except lions, snakes and the vultures that always hovered above, waiting. If you sat in the grass to rest, they thought you were dying and they'd come down and sit close by because they were used to finding corpses in the grass.

The villages were far apart and as we walked without water and food, my vision blurred. I'd open my eyes wide, but everything surrounding me would turn red and then colorless dark with dim stars that made me dizzy. When I wanted to forget walking and sit down, someone would say, "Carry on. I can hear a cock crowing from the next village." I'd force my eyes wide open but all I could see were little boys like me, only heads and hips, staggering along.

We passed through a village one afternoon and came upon a little boy sitting under a tree crying miserably.

"Who is this little boy crying?" Kuany asked a soldier standing nearby.

"He wants to go to Ethiopia with the other boys. He has nobody to look after him."

"Where are his parents?"

"Two years ago a bomb blasted his house. Both his parents were killed but we pulled him out of the burning house and brought him to this village. He was so small he could not yet talk. He doesn't know the name of his parents or if he has brothers and sisters."

Kuany bent down to the little boy. "What is your name?"

"Monyde," he sniffled. "I come with you?"

"We can't look after him," the soldier said. "We're leaving here and he's too little to walk into the desert."

"I can go," insisted Monyde. "I want to go."

I was surprised at his boldness for such a young boy.

"He's not taken care of in this village," said the soldier. "He's always beaten by other kids who have parents. He's tried to leave with a lot of passersby, but they said he was too young to survive the journey across Ajakageer. He's been left in the world without hope of anyone caring for him."

We took Monyde with us. He was a funny, talkative little boy, happy and courageous even when the walking became bitterly hard at the day's end. He made people laugh with childish questions. He was a little comedian.

That night when we camped, he said, "I want to go to toilet."

"Sit in the grass," we told him.

"I'm afraid of the vultures."

Kuany went with Monyde to the grass.

———

I began to suffer from pinkeye going through the desert. Walking in the hot sun made it worse. By midday we walked like sick dogs, with our steps zigzagging down the road. We could feel our bones trying to exhibit themselves to the world. Everything around us looked ugly and wild. We couldn't find happiness in ourselves, and no one could put it in us.

We thanked heaven one day when we found a few mango trees with small green fruits. I got two little ones that were the size of my thumb tips. Although they were bitter and sour, I chewed and swallowed them raw. When there were no more fruits, someone said, "We could chew the newly grown leaves. It will be like a drink of water."

Everybody was bending the branches down and plucking the leaves. I tried the leaves but they made my tongue and throat itchy.

That day I became exhausted and fell back. I couldn't keep up, although there were still many people behind me. From out of nowhere many antelope ran toward me in a cloud of dust. I was scared and stood still, not knowing what to do. A voice behind me yelled, "Move out of there." But it was too late to move. As they were about to run me over, the leading antelope saw me standing there in my red underwear and skipped aside just before knocking me down.

"That leading antelope saved your life," said a soldier. "They could have danced all over you."

"Go after them," I told him. "Shoot us some animals with a fire eye from your gun. Even monkeys. Go shoot."

"I have only five fire eyes," he said. "And those are to protect you. There are bad tribes on the way who like to attack the walking people. They kill them and take away their belongings. They'll kidnap the young boys."

The only talk among us became the huge desert that lay

ahead. More than halfway to Ethiopia, everyone feared and dreaded this most dangerous part of our journey, the desert of Ajakageer.

My eyes grew worse every day. At midday, when it was hottest, I sweated. My eyes burned and my skin was slippery and irritated. At night, I was desperate to have a good sleep and gain strength for the walking but I couldn't because it was cold in the desert. We used the middle of the road as our bed and all you could see was all the different colors of people's clothes lying there. My skin was crusty with dirt and sand from sleeping on the ground without a blanket and my underwear tingled with lice. At dawn, when the soldiers blew the whistle, a murmuring sound traveled all along the road. It was time to get up and walk again.

A day after we entered the Ajakageer we met with some luck. Six thousand men, going to the army training camp in Ethiopia, were being escorted by SPLA soldiers with a large water tanker. The youngest boys were selected to ride on the tanker.

I had never ridden on a vehicle before. The first one I saw in the village came so noisily, running fast and raising clouds of dust, that I ran from my goats. I came out of hiding after the dust clouds subsided, having forgotten my goats, and printed my feet along the tire tread marks. I kept my eyes on where the vehicle had gone, amazed by how fast it ran and knowing that if it returned, I couldn't outrun it and that it might knock me up into the trees.

The only thing that scared me about riding on this water tanker was how smooth and round it was on the top, where we sat. The soldiers put several logs of wood on the edge to prevent us from falling off. When the tanker started moving, I saw that the trees were running backward. I was so scared from the rocking about that I grabbed a soldier's clothes to keep myself from falling, which annoyed him.

That night, in the desert of Ajakageer, Benjamin and Emmanuel fell off the tanker and we had to shout loud to get the tanker to stop so they could climb back on. An hour later Monyde fell off. We shouted again but this time our weak voices from the back of the tanker were not heard by the driver, who was plunging in and out of the desert holes made by the mud during rainy seasons. The soldiers banged and banged on the cab, but the driver was drunk and he did not hear for a very long time.

Luckily Monyde was a very smart boy. He knew that surrounding him were lions and many wild animals, so he hid under the tall grass and waited. When eventually the tanker turned back, searching for him with its lights, Monyde came running from the grass.

The soldiers told him, "You are a clever and brave boy for hiding and not crying."

"Something was shaking the grass," Monyde said. "That's why I was hiding."

The soldiers lifted him up and put him in the cab with the driver.

In the middle of that night, after we had passed and left far behind the long marching line of men, the tanker stopped in the desert to wait for them. Everyone climbed down. It was very dark. A soldier stepped on something with his boot that broke with a cracking noise. He lit a torch. It was a smashed human skull.

"Shit!" he said. "This is a bad luck."

Our eyes followed the torchlight into the grass and saw

many more skulls. They seemed to be smiling but were scary with teeth missing. "From the people who died of thirst," explained the soldiers. Some of the skulls were smaller, like children. Emmanuel looked at me, his eyes full of terror. A light sweat broke out over my body. It was midnight and very cold. I tried to put the skulls out of my mind. We needed to get warm and we had no blanket or clothes. My underwear, horrible with countless lice, was all I had. So Emmanuel and I went down to sit under the tanker where the engine was still warm. The warmth felt so good to me that I fell deeply asleep, even though it was in the middle of a grave-yard.

But the driver changed his plan and told everybody to prepare to leave. Everyone got up on the tanker and the driver started the engine. Emmanuel called my name to make sure I was okay and instantly knew that I was not there because I did not respond. He screamed as the driver let go of his brake and was about to pull out. The soldiers slapped on the truck cab to try to get his attention, yelling, "There is a boy down under the tanker."

They found me there snoring and a soldier poured cold water into my ear. That startled me awake and I banged my head on the axle.

When the sun came up in the morning, we saw that the tanker had stopped again in the middle of the desert to wait for the walking crowd. Everything was quiet and calm. Nearby many skulls were clustered under a huge tamarind tree. A soldier told us, "That is a skulls tree where you can see all types of bones from a lot of people who went to rest in the cool shade and never got up to continue their journey."

When we started out, the driver told me not to ride on

his tanker again. "I don't want anyone to die and blame me. If you want to die, die on your own, not by my truck."

He wanted to leave me in the middle of nowhere beside a tree with countless skulls and bones! My eyes were so sick that I was afraid I couldn't make the walk. I ran to the other side of the truck and tried to climb up with some other boys. A soldier struck my shoulder with his whip and I fell off. I pleaded with the driver not to leave me. He drove off anyway.

I found Kuany in the crowd that was following the truck and walked all day with the very hot sun burning the whip's welt on my back. At three in the afternoon, when I reached the place where the tanker had stopped again, all of the water had been finished. Kuany tried to find me some without success. I was too thirsty to cry. I had no saliva in my mouth or tears in my eyes.

The same soldier who had whipped me earlier that morning saw me and kindly offered me the little water he had left in his container. Kuany didn't get a single drop.

That evening the driver let me back on the truck because there was a night and a half day's walk until the next village where we might find water. The road narrowed and the driver had difficulty following what was a footpath. Sometimes he lost his way. Then he would turn round to find the track again and begin following it once more.

In the middle of the night we ran into three lions. The driver blew the horn to scare them, but they didn't move until the soldiers fired their guns. They ran into the grass, but a few minutes later one lion jumped onto the tanker and nearly pulled a boy off.

The next morning the tanker dropped us at the village of

Gumuro, with thousands of people trailing behind in the desert. Kuany arrived later with a few strong men. The soldiers escorting the walkers came with the news that twenty-five people had died of thirst that night alone. Many were those who carried peanuts and sesame in a small calabash. They died because eating this food increases thirst. Among the dead was a huge man, a cook, whom everyone knew because he carried a large metal cooking drum with extra food and water.

After dropping us off, the tanker returned to repeat its journey. We only spent one night in Gumuro because the local people there, who received weapons from the government, hid in the bush and shot at trespassers. Even the SPLA soldiers guarding us were afraid of them.

And so, with just one day's rest, we had to continue on foot. Eating became a big problem because of the number of people. Whenever we camped it was hard for little boys to get food. We were like gazelles among a herd of buffalo. But in this crowd there were a few good men who cared for us first. They contributed what little we ate and that kept us strong. They told us that nothing could befall us while they were around.

Monyde, who had been given a bowl of water, brought it to me so that I could drink and wash my eyes. I was so grateful for that.

At night I usually slept on the gravel road because the wet grass made my skin itch. When we were told we had to walk three more days to reach the last town in Sudan on the border of Ethiopia, I fell asleep wondering if I could make it through the rest of the desert, or if I would be one of the ones to end up under a skulls tree.

Falling Down

BENJAMIN

In the town of Pibor Post we found people waiting for us because they had been told that the boys were coming. Our leader asked the people, "Please, can you offer them one cow so that they can come and eat the meat." They agreed to cook us a cow. We ate the meat and found good shade next to big buildings. I just wanted to sleep for nine hours.

I awoke when the sun was about to set. People said that we had to leave for Pochala and it would take three days to cross the desert. We worried how we were going to endure so many hours walking again. I told myself that if I worried I would have no hope of avoiding disaster. I made myself strong like an elder. I made my heart strong. I told myself I was going to make it.

I walked through the desert with a big group. Sometimes people fell, just like that. At first we thought somebody who fell would wake up and follow us again. But when a person fell down, the elders told us, "Okay, come along. Now that he's fallen down, he's not going to wake up. That's it. He's dead."

An elder told me, "You just take care of yourself and don't fall down like him."

I said, "How am I going to fall down? I feel I'm strong."

He said, "Okay, if you're strong like that, let's keep going."

But after a while, as I was talking to him, he fell down too. I tried to wake him up but he didn't answer me.

Some bandits in the area started shooting at us so I took off my clothes because my shirt and shorts were white. I rolled the clothes under my arm and then I was a dark person, dark as nighttime itself. Nobody could see me anymore.

We reached Pochala on the border of Ethiopia early in the morning. People waiting there said it was good to receive us but that we were not the number they had been expecting. Our number had been greatly reduced because a lot of people had been falling down.

One of the SPLA commanders said, "Now you are in Pochala. Tomorrow is your rest day. But the next day you will prepare to cross the border. It is seventeen hours. You guys are going to Ethiopia!"

We were too tired and skinny to walk seventeen hours. But the commander had some good news too. "All the kids will be taken by armed truck." I was so glad because I couldn't walk anymore. I was so tired of walking. I felt like I'd spent a year walking. For so many days I had only been thinking of how to survive. Now I thought of my parents again and all the kids who had died along the way. When I saw the few kids still with their parents, I hoped to see mine.

Monyde

BENSON

After Monyde gave me water at the river we became best friends and traveled together in the following days. I believed that he would be a good leader when he grew up because even though he was very young, I got courage from him because he never complained of any difficulties. When we became thirsty, hungry or tired from the long walking, he just kept quiet. Adults praised him for being the bravest and strongest of all the boys on our trip. I think he was.

At Pochala, after walking three days, Monyde suddenly became sick. They said it was yellow fever. Kuany did everything he could to help Monyde, but he died in only two days. He'd crossed that whole desert, even though they said he couldn't do it. He'd survived when many big people died. But we buried him just a half mile from safety. I was so sad to lose my brave friend. I knew I would never forget him.

We suffered another sadness in Pochala when the SPLA conscripted Kuany, who had been caring for us. Without our uncle, it was really not safe for us, little boys alone. Without Monyde and Kuany, I was beginning to give up hope that we could survive.

At least the soldiers put us in a lorry to take us to the

refugee camp of Panyido in Ethiopia. The lorry, though, was full, with a lot of people who spoke different dialects.

For the first few hours out of Pochala, Ethiopia was flat and the dark mud had dried and cracked like an old woman's skin. It was the dry season and the Gilo River was low and slow. After we crossed the river, the land became hilly and the lorry dipped and climbed. I don't know what made me sit next to a Nuer man and his wife that day, but when the movement of the truck caused me to fall across her legs, the man grabbed me by my belly with his right hand. His fingers dug into my tummy and he shook me up and down, hitting me against his knee.

I cried but nobody cared. He was breaking my intestines. Emmanuel tried to help me by grabbing the man's hand, until the man let me go, clenched his fist, and hit Emmanuel on his nose. It was serious. Emmanuel fell unconscious. Still, no one cared. They just pushed Emmanuel away as if he was a dead body. There was nothing I could do but sit beside him and wait for him to awaken. Was this what it was like in this country? I thought about my home, my mother and father, my brothers and sisters, Monyde, and worried what would become of us in this far off place, the refugee camp they called Panyido.

Emmanuel awoke when the lorry stopped. The driver told us to get down. There wasn't much around and I thought it was just a place to rest before we continued our journey. "No," the adults told us, "this is Panyido."

It was not what I had expected. The elders had told us there would be schools and thousands of people and that we would be safe. There were thousands of people but only a few shelters made of sticks and branches for protection from the sun. Not one school. The whole place was full of the smoke of small fires that mingled with the dust. People were everywhere. Chopping trees, burning new clearings, coming and going from the river with tins and gourds of water. Sick boys lay quietly on the ground. It had been the dry season when, three months earlier, I had left my village so I was surprised to see new shoots of maize and sorghum sprouting near the river. The rains had begun and green grass leaves were emerging from the withered soil.

We were left in an open place and told to wait for the corn to be distributed. Emmanuel, Lino, Benjamin and I found a tree to sit under, but I was overwhelmed by thirst. My stomach still hurt badly from being squeezed by the man on the lorry. When I asked someone for water they pointed the way to the river. In spite of my painful stomach, I didn't hesitate and went alone following the path made by the people who were carrying water.

I don't know what was wrong with people that day. I tried asking everyone on the way with water to give me a drink but after five people refused I gave up and didn't ask again.

On my way to the river I encountered dark brown skeleton boys swarming everywhere and making a lot of noise. Fighting had broken out between the Dinka and the local Ethiopian Anyuak people, a small Nilotic tribe who spoke a different dialect but had the same custom of removing the six lower teeth. Some of the Dinka boys had stolen corn from their fields and one of the boys was shot dead by an arrow. The other boys were fighting back for their dead brother.

When I came out of the cornfield, just near the river, I met a man on the path holding a club. There were many other people, some carrying dirty clothes going to the river to wash and others returning with water containers. But this man thought any boy walking bare-handed was a fighter and he struck me with his club on my right thigh. Ah, the pain! I thought he'd broken my leg. I fell down and he left me alone as he went to attack other boys who were not carrying water or clothes.

Once the pain subsided, I got up and limped down the dry streambed away from the man with the club. There I met three girls dressed like Dinka and carrying water pots. They were talking when I first spotted them coming out of the grass but they stopped when they saw me.

"I'm thirsty," I said, thinking they spoke Dinka. "Can you give me some water, please?"

They fixed their eyes on me and set their pots down so quickly my heart went beating. Putting a hand on each hip, they walked toward me throwing words I didn't understand. I staggered backward and when they began to throw stones, I turned and ran. What would have happened if I had met men? Panyido didn't seem like the safe place they had told us we were going to. Even the girls were aggressive!

When I finally arrived at the river, it was full of people washing their clothes and swimming. Soap foam leaked along the bank yet people still took drinking water home in their pots and gourds. Across the river, the clearing fires had licked off every leaf leaving only gray tree skeletons and dry grass. People swam across and strolled in the charred ground scavenging for charcoal. I stared at this ugly place where no boy seemed safe. This was Panyido. Every boy was on his own.

At first Panyido brought tears to every boy. The Ethiopian people were peaceful and didn't seem to like wars when we first came marching into their land. They called those of us in the camp Little Sudan and made fun of Sudanese, saying, "Big Sudan knows only wars. Small Sudan knows only stealing. Sudanese people are crazy." We were starving and the Ethiopians were experiencing hard times because we were stealing their food.

There were thousands of people, many of them boys, but no houses or latrines. Everyone in the camp, ten thousand boys already and more coming, went into the bush for latrine. Swarms of flies followed us wherever we went. They liked to sit on us, and bite and pick and spread the common killer diseases dysentery and diarrhea. Many boys became very sick. There was little food or medicine. Many died. To survive we used all of the little strength we had to scavenge for food. We were so hungry we went into wet grasses, with frogs and green snakes spitting all around us, to collect the kind of grass leaves that we could cook for soup. To do that, we first had to sneak into the Ethiopian market to search the trash heaps for rusted Ethiopian beer tins in which we could cook our soups. The market was forbidden to us because many boys were tempted to steal. The grasses made my skin bumpy and when we cooked them for soup my throat itched. Many of the boys got sick and died from eating grass soups, but it was often all we had.

Older boys who knew how to swim well went up the river into the Anyuak village lake with their fish spears and brought home fresh fish for themselves. They sold some of their fish to Ethiopian locals and did whatever they wanted with the money. Some bought clean-looking clothes while the youngest of us scuffed around in rotting rags.

My red underwear I had worn crossing Sudan and an old shirt I'd found in the trash heap were my only clothes and I shared them with all the lice I picked up on the way. When I went swimming I'd put my clothes in the hot sand by the riverbank but it was difficult to get rid of the lice entirely because the pure white nits wouldn't die in the sun. The lice tingled me at night and kept me scratching while sleeping. I became so weary of the itching that one night when they wouldn't let me sleep I took off my clothes and put them by the fire to warm them up. When I put more sticks in the fire, there was smoke and then flames. I was enjoying the warmth, holding my clothes up to kill the nits and lice, when a tongue of flame touched my red shorts and melted one side. I tried to put them on again but there was a hole right through one side. My favorite piece of clothing, the only thing I owned that was from my village, was nearly destroyed. In the morning I searched the garbage and found a green rag and used a thorn and sock thread to sew up the hole. Dirty, torn, patched, full of lice and nits, my red shorts were still precious to me. A hundred times a day I looked at them and remembered that they were a gift from my father.

My hair was a lice kingdom too. We had no scissors or razor to shave it off. You could buy a razor with only two biir, the Ethiopian currency, but I had nothing. So the lice came. One hot day while I was swimming in the river, my head tingled so badly with things crawling and biting that I felt like going crazy. I picked a rusted piece of tin from the trash and bent it and broke it into pieces. I asked my friend Nicodimus to cut my hair and offered to cut his in return.

We sat under the mango tree. As he cut, big lice dropped on my shoulders and crawled away like fat sesame seeds with my blood boiling in their abdomens.

We had scabies across our bodies, even on our hands and buttocks. Some boys walked around with hundreds of flies following them and sitting on the white wound spots created by ringworm. No matter how tall their hair grew it couldn't be shaved while those wounds were open.

One day we were informed that white people were coming from Addis Ababa to look at our situation. Many boys gathered to welcome two men and three women visitors. Curious to see a white man for the first time, we shoved to get a close view of them.

"Look at them," one boy said. "Did their skin melt off from flying near the sun in the sky boat or what?"

They walked around the camp and the women cried bitterly as they saw a naked little boy, his anus running with bloody diarrhea, struggling to cook a kind of grass soup by himself, who looked like he would die that day. One woman took something from her pocket and gave it to a boy sitting in the front. More boys gathered around her and touched her hand. She cried and rubbed her hand on them. The two white men began talking but we couldn't understand them. An adult translated for us: "They are UNHCR and they are coming to look at your situation. The women are crying because they feel sorry for your suffering. 'Be strong,' they said. They will bring some more blankets, food and medicine for they have seen enough suffering out of you. They will help you."

We clapped our dry cracked hands and saw that the white men moved their heads up and down like happy salamanders. They began giving out small pebbles to the boys in the front and those who got the things put them in their mouth and said they were called sweets. The adults did their best to keep us from getting near them, but we wanted to hear the white skins telling us that good things would come.

It was months later before the UN came to rescue us from hunger, but even this caused many deaths. Not because the food was insufficient or bad, but because a lot of boys tried to eat their fill without grinding the grain. They died of tummy swelling at night, and nothing could save them. Also the vegetable oil brought by the UN made boys more likely to sicken and die from yellow fever.

At Panyido we used empty metal ammunition boxes to carry our food. With five boys to one ammunition box and each group of boys called a circle, we put the box in the middle and started with each boy taking his turn of one scoop until we came back to the one who had started. When the time for the food distribution came, the cooks announced, "Ammunition tins! Bring the ammunition tins," and a boy from each group went to collect the food.

Life did not improve much with the UN food. The powdered milk was diluted with so much water that it didn't taste like milk. All the Dinka boys had either come from a fishing area or were used to meat from the hunters in our village. A lot of the boys could not eat the grain. It was hard to get meat for them until we discovered a spot in the nearby river where we young ones could fish. A few boys were taken by crocodile; but still no one gave up fishing because it was the best source of meat.

Other boys were bird catchers who used small threads from nylon food sacks, stones and long sticks to build clever traps. Crowds of beggars followed whoever killed a lot of birds. "Give me one bird, Chol. I am so hungry and caught nothing. I will pay you tomorrow." "These are for my sick brother admitted in the clinic." "You were my friend, remember?" "What about me? What about me?"

One boy, Baak, became crazy about birds. He woke everybody in the middle of the night with his shouting. "Who is going out to catch the birds with me? My traps caught four birds. One for me and one for my father if he comes. One for mother if she comes and one for sister if she comes too. My twin brother, he could have mine if he wants. There! I want to go catch the birds. Who wants to go with me?"

Even though Baak's twin brother had gotten sick from eating the grass soup and died in the clinic, Baak never gave up catching imaginary birds for him.

"Baak, Baak," we'd say. "It's the middle of the night. No birds out at night. Go to bed and we will go catch them tomorrow." We held him and told him to go back to bed, but he'd say, "No, no, I can hear the birds flapping their wings on my traps. My two traps have caught some birds. You want to steal my birds?"

Sometimes an adult came out and said Baak had to be tied up until morning. They would take him away.

There were many boys who lost their minds because of sickness and thinking of their parents. They were put together in the place called the crazy people clinic. It was bad because they ran around putting plastic sheets on their shoulders and beating themselves with large sticks. They would beat anyone they saw near them. Some got hurt and died of injury. Some could not feel the pain.

In the middle of one night, I heard a rapping noise under my bed. Then a voice said, "Hiiy! People with plastic bags!"

Under my bed I had a plastic bag with the soap I used to wash my scabies wounds. There was more ripping of plastic noises from under me. I was scared and jumped from my bed to the bed of Ater, the boy next to me.

"What you doing?"

"There is something or someone under my bed. Listen. Can you hear that?"

The guy under my bed heard me and said, "Hey there! Is that you mama? Answer me. Are you chewing UN plastic like me?"

"He is a crazy one," Ater whispered. "Be careful."

We kept quiet and didn't answer. I sat on the edge of Ater's bed until morning. By then the crazy boy had gone but he'd torn my plastic bag and soap into pieces with his teeth. I swept up the plastic bits and soap particles and scratched the new sores I could no longer wash. I thought of my mother and how she'd wash my body in the cool river. I thought of my father telling me no harm would ever come to me with him by my side.

Back in the Village

ALEPHO

When Benson disappeared during the attack on my sister's village, everyone went looking for him. My older brothers, my mother, and my father all searched the area. They were away for days. But they found nothing. Nobody had seen Benson.

A year later, in our village, people had begun to put their lives back together again, rebuilding their houses and planting crops. But the fighting was not far away. When Toch, an area three days walk away, was destroyed by new attacks, people from there moved to our village.

During the year the village was getting back in shape, my father never stopped looking for Benson. If he visited nearby villages, I went with him. He asked everyone he saw if they'd seen his son.

Now that I had grown a little bit and was six years old, my mother sent me to Angong's house to take care of her goats. Angong's little boy was still an infant and she was being driven crazy by all the goats because Benson was the only person who had been helping her.

It was there, a year after Benson disappeared, at Angong's house, that I found out Benjamin was missing as well. His parents had no clue where he might be or if he was even alive. Because he was so young, they had little hope.

I didn't do so well at Angong's. When I took the goats out, I'd sit down and play and then the goats would disappear. I was scared to go after them because of the lions.

Angong had one or two hundred goats and sometimes I came home at the end of the day with just three. The rest had scattered and were eating other people's crops and people didn't like that. Everyday there were reports coming to my sister's house. "Your goats ate my sesame!" "Your goats ate my sorghum!" She'd say, "I'm so sorry. My younger brother, he's new to the place and he tries so hard." She was very understanding and she didn't get mad at me.

I was so embarrassed to come home with my bare hands. "I'm not able to take care of the goats," I told her. She said, "Just walk with them. If you see a lion just try to scare it." But I knew there was no way a lion would be afraid of me.

I told Angong that I really wanted to go back home to my mother's house.

---

*O*ne day we were at the well. Angong was drawing water and pouring it into a small hand-carved boat until it was full. Then I would lead ten goats to drink. She would fill again and we alternated like that until all the goats had enough to drink.

A little girl hobbled up to us like a weak and wounded gazelle.

"How old are you?" she asked.

"Six and a half years."

"I'm five and a half years."

"I am older than you," I told her.

I started playing with her and I forgot that I was helping my sister.

The little girl's mother came to the well. "Don't hurt my daughter," she said.

I didn't understand what she meant by that.

"Don't insult her or make her upset," said Angong. "Don't ask her any questions."

Later we took a bath together. I didn't know what had happened to the little girl; I thought she was born with a deformity. Perhaps where the legs joined the hipbones was crooked and gave her the limp. I was curious to ask her about that but I remembered my sister's warning so I kept quiet about that and complimented her about how beautiful she was and that when we grew up we could get married. I was joking to make her feel good.

Later in the evening, when the little girl and her mother left, I asked Angong, "What happened to her? Why were you warning me not to say anything bad?"

Tears came to Angong's eyes. "I've never witnessed more inhuman activity in my life. When the village was attacked, that little girl was raped by a grown man."

I still didn't understand how it made her like that.

"You are nearly a man, and this is a time of war, you should understand these things that happen." The tears stopped flowing from Angong's eyes and she looked angry. "The men had guns. One of them wanted to take the little girl with him but she clung to a small bush screaming in terror so it was difficult for him to remove her hands. 'You a little stupid girl,' the man shouted. 'I will give you the medicine you will never forget.' He stooped over her and pulled out his penis. We screamed but there was nothing her

mother or I could do. They had us tied lying on our stomachs and held us back with guns. The man tried to dig his
penis into the girl, but he couldn't get it in while he was
holding her down too. He got up and tied her hands to that
small bush. He pushed it in and pushed and pushed on her
with his full weight. At first she struggled and screamed, but
a few minutes later the loud cries stopped. The little girl
had passed out.

"I couldn't look at this act one more minute. To my dis-
grace, all I did was lie on my belly and cry.

"The man raised his gun to shoot the girl in her head,
but another man argued with him. I couldn't understand
everything they said; my Arabic is not that good, but it
sounded like the other man was upset about his inhuman
act. They didn't shoot her and left."

Angong didn't say anymore about that again. I didn't understand all of the things about rape or what she said about
it being a time of war, but I never forgot that little girl and
what I'd seen it had done to the bones inside her.

---

*W*eeks *went by at Angong's.* Every day I had more problems
with all those goats. I told Angong, "If you don't take me
home, I'm going by myself." I don't think she believed me.
It was only a two-hour walk, but even if it had taken two
days, if I said I was going to do that, I would do it. I didn't
like anyone telling me what I couldn't do.

When she still didn't take me, one morning, without
telling her, I started walking. The path had high African
trees over it and bush taller than a grown man. No one

could see me moving down the trail. I'd heard stories that people disappeared on that path, eaten by cannibals or something, but I got so tired I forgot about it and sat down to play. When I got hungry I climbed into a tree called *cum* (shoom) and picked some fruits like grapes.

As I continued wandering down the path, I nearly ran into a mother warthog with her babies. We surprised each other. She snarled. I was so scared that even though there were no branches until way above my head, I climbed a tree. Went straight up like a monkey. The warthog wasn't scared. She and her babies didn't run; they just stayed under that tree eating and talking warthog.

I moved through the tree branches, wanting to climb down and be on my way, but the mother warthog did not move. I was stuck. Warthogs can cut you badly: they can kill a grown man with those teeth.

After a while, when I looked below the tree again, I couldn't see them. I went down quickly and jumped from the lowest branch, which was high above the ground. I landed noisily in the bushes. The warthog was still below with her babies but I scared the hell out them this time and we both ran.

I got back to Juol just before dark. My mother was very surprised to see me. She hugged me but then looked at me with a questioning face. "Does Angong know you came home?"

I think Angong got very worried because the next day she walked the two hours from her village to ours to make sure I was there.

Around that time my father began trying to get people to build a school in our village for the kids so that they could learn about the world. I thought my village was the world, but my father told me, "There is another world." One day he pointed to an airplane going across the sky. "See that sky boat. A girl is flying it."

I wanted to go and fly that airplane.

"Those are white people going to America," he said.

———

About a year after Benson disappeared, my father said he wanted to go to Toch to find out if Benson had fled there. My mother told him she wanted to go with him once she finished mending the roof to the big cattle house. But my father didn't wait and went alone. A few days later a man came to our house and talked to my mother. She started crying.

A week later they told us my father had died. I still don't know why he died. Maybe he was killed. After I heard the news I got sick. Terribly sick. Vomiting and fever. So hot. Things came in my head like people flying and talking to me. My poor mother. She'd lost Benson, lost my father, and now I was dying, until my brother, Nieu-nieu, brought home a small tree whose leaves looked like a tamarind and produced a really bitter tea, more bitter than chloroquine. He ground the leaves and roots and soaked them and sieved the water. He held my mouth and poured in this medicine. I threw up green and yellowish stuff.

My body was better after that but my heart still ached for my father and my brother, Benson. So I stayed in the village and watched our own cows and goats with my brothers. My mother didn't send me back to Angong's again.

Why? Because

BENSON

In Ethiopia, a year after we arrived in the camp in Panyido, we finally started primary school under the trees. Our teachers were Sudanese adults who used charcoal to write the alphabet on the empty oil cartons brought by the UN. As we copied the letters in the sand, the teacher walked behind us looking at our handwriting. If he was unhappy with our work he grabbed our fingers and rubbed them harder into the ground until they were nearly pink and we felt the tingle of blood trying to jump out.

In first grade, I learned the English alphabet and how to add and subtract. The first English word I liked to say was "because." I didn't know exactly what the word meant, but our English teacher said that you always answered the question "Why?" with "Because."

During the second year the UN sent us a few exercise books and pencils. We cut the pencils and thirty-two-page books in half so there was enough for everyone. Our new English teacher was kind and always treated us like his own children as he taught us spelling and reading. But our math teacher hit our fingers with his big thick blackboard ruler if we missed narrating the multiplication tables. The number of hits depended on how many you missed.

We were only given minutes if we wanted to go into the bush for toilet. I was late one day. "You are late!" he said. "Why?"

I heard the word "why" and remembered my English teacher had told us that good English speakers always answered "why" with "because."

"Because."

The math teacher kept looking at my mouth and repeated, "Why?"

"Because." I repeated. That was all I knew how to say.

"Come here and show me your dirty fingers. I want to shake the dust out of them."

I knew he was going to hit my fingers even though I'd answered his question. I held up the back of my hand and he hit across my fingers with his big blackboard ruler. My hand was numb with pain. He hit me again harder. I grinned with pain, showing all my teeth.

"Uh! I see you are even smiling at me. That didn't hurt at all. You should have spoke more English after it. You must learn that the word 'because,' by itself, is insulting."

I didn't know that. But his punishment almost made me give up trying to speak English.

Mostly what we did at Panyido was wait. We waited for the war to end so we could go home. We waited for more refugees to come and give us news morsels from Sudan. When we weren't looking for food, we waited for food to come. Once in a while when we saw planes going overhead, we'd yell out, "Look! The white man can fart white smoke into the sky."

Once a white man came to the camp in a car. He sat in it holding a beautiful twisted black rope to his ear and talked to it. My friend Nicodimus and I went close to listen. We understood some of the English words the white man was telling into that rope line. That thing talked too. It asked, "Where do you reach today? Over." The man answered, "Now living in Gambella today. Over."

We memorized that. Sometimes I pretended to be a vehicle and asked, "Where do you reach today?" Nicodimus would answer back, "Now we are living in Panyido today. Over." Anytime we were near girls, we'd tell them, "We saw the white man talking to his vehicle. That vehicle has big white glaring eyes. It saw strange people at a strange place, so the vehicle wanted to know where they were. The vehicle asked the owner, 'Where do you live today?'" The girls thought that we spoke English well, but in fact that was all we could say.

The camp at Panyido grew steadily to over fifty thousand people. Our area was mostly boys and only a few adults. Night after night, more adult men disappeared from the camp. People said they went to join an army training camp called Bongo somewhere far off in the hills. They left at night because they didn't want their family or the boys to see and cry after them.

In that time I met only one person at the camp who knew my relatives in Juol. His name was Kuot, and the army had no use for him because his right leg had been amputated. As it was difficult for him to carry his water and rations, he asked our teacher if I could stay with him for a while. I moved to his house, helping with chores and attending school in the day. I was happy doing that.

Kuot liked to talk and tell me stories. I'd been curious about his amputated leg but didn't want to be rude and ask. He told me that he had lost it in a place called Torit town. "It's an important town," he said. "That's where the first war began in 1947 when the students rebelled and were massacred by the government troops. It's been fought over many times since then. That's where I was fighting in 1985 when I was shot in the leg with a machine gun. They couldn't save it." He pointed his walking stick at his stump. "And cut it off."

One day Kuot asked a neighbor woman, an Anyuak, if she would cook something for us. According to Dinka and Anyuak culture, a man may always ask a woman to cook if he is hungry. This woman lived with her mother-in-law because her husband was away mining; it was dangerous work.

———

Kuot knew this woman was a good neighbor but he didn't know much about her mother-in-law. The woman put the white beans on the fire outside and added some meat. She left it with her mother-in-law to look after while she went to pound some maize grains in the neighbor's mortar to make flour. I could see that the mother-in-law was angry or jealous that Kuot had asked her son's wife for food. Maybe she thought Kuot might like her son's wife.

The woman returned with the flour and cooked it with some water. Later, when it was dark and the food was ready, she brought it to us and apologized for being slow in preparing it. We thanked her for her kindness.

I set the table and we were ready for a supper that smelled delicious. The woman placed the *injera,* a soft thin bread, on the table. We would use the *injera* to scoop the soup, but Kuot liked to use a spoon because he'd lost two of his fingers.

I waited for the older people to start first because we were eating from just one bowl. Before I dipped my *injera,* Kuot found something heavy in the soup with his spoon. He struggled to get it out thinking that it was a piece of dry meat.

"Look what I found in the soup," he said and lit the torch so that we all saw the creature with four legs on his spoon. A salamander! At first we all poked at it and threw it away but then we picked it up again and called the younger woman to come and see what was going on. She was so surprised and pleaded with us that she'd covered the soup and she didn't know how it had happened. The old woman was peeping out to hear what was going on. At that minute Kuot started vomiting.

We took Kuot back to his house and left him in the bed sleeping. When I left for school the next morning he said he was cold. When I came home that afternoon he had been admitted to the hospital in a coma.

While Kuot was in the hospital, that old woman tried to run away. She wanted to get rid of Kuot and killed a salamander that was clinging to the wall by hitting it with a stone. Then she threw it into our soup while it was still bleeding. The salamander's blood is poisonous. They arrested her and put her in jail. Three days later, when Kuot came out from the hospital, he told the police to let her go, saying that it was his fault to ask her son's wife for the food.

We boys were not living according to our own free will. Each group of boys had two head boys and the teachers and headmaster in charge of all the boys. One head boy gave us work orders and the other organized what we ate. At the end of the year the teachers and headmaster ordered us to rebuild our houses because they wanted them to be strong and safe for the rainy weather.

After a year at Panyido we had become more adjusted to our environment in Ethiopia. Life had improved with the food and the education, but, always, I only thought of home and waited for the day the war would end and I could return to Sudan.

Not in Our Mama's House
No More

ALEPHO

The month before the attack when Benson disappeared and Achol was killed, the *wella wella wella* of helicopter propellers brought us of out of our houses. It had slowed down overhead, as though getting tired, and black smoke trailed against the sky behind it.

One year later, it happened again. This time the helicopter was smaller and very close overhead. The people inside were looking out of it. I didn't know what they were looking for.

Soon after the helicopter, raiders came to our village. There was no warning. Sometimes the elders heard that the northerners were coming and we would leave the village and take our cows to another place. But this attack came suddenly and horribly. Explosions, horses and camels chasing people, shooting, screaming, crying: it was like the end of the world.

I deserted my goats and ran into the bush to hide with other people. Smoke billowed out from our village and hung over it like a cloud. The roofs of the huts shot up in flames like torches. People scattered to escape the bullets. I watched as the invaders tied the arms and legs of their captives and put long ropes around their necks. They led them from the village on a line blindfolded so they didn't know the place they were going. "Drowning them in the river," a person cried. "They don't want to waste bullets."

That night, I saw my lovely village, Juol, full of palms and coconut trees, fade in a way I couldn't understand.

The survivors told us not to go back to Juol because there was nobody alive except the enemy. We moved in the darkness, skirting the long grass and not minding the snakes. The fear inside us was acute. All I could think of was my family. I wanted to go home, but the adults wouldn't let the children return. "It's not safe," they said. "You'll be captured."

With no food and little water, we trekked a hundred miles, staying away from Toch, where the Sudanese government had its army. After four days walking we reached Tonj County. People were gathering there because it was under rebel protection. The adults were instructing us kids, "Move on, move on, move on," through the street, when I recognized my half brother Peter sitting on the road crying. Peter's mother was my father's fourth wife and they lived with his grandmother in another village. I knew his village had probably been attacked too.

Peter cried even more when I went to him. He was only five and had no clothes or blanket; he had nothing. At least I had a raggedy shawl tied across one shoulder that I could use as a blanket to sleep. I was lucky. Peter stayed close with me after that and we shared my blanket. We were escorted by the adults from town to town. They said to each other, "These boys have no parents. They belong to Sudan and we can't let them die from hunger." But many of us did die, from disease, thirst and starvation, especially the little boys like Peter who cried all the time.

After walking several days we got lucky at a town called Thiet and found an older cousin, Joseph. I cried and begged him, "We have to go back. Take us back home."

"I don't even know the way home," he said. "We might get lost or get eaten by a wild animal or run into those wolves. Let's just go together with this group of boys. Maybe we'll find a safer place."

Joseph was nine, two years older than me. He lived in a village near Juol but I rarely saw him because he was always watching the cows. He had two friends, Santino Akuetoch and Diing Ngor, with him. We came together as a group of five. Joseph was the oldest and the tallest.

In the town of Thiet, the adults divided us into groups of two or three hundred boys. We had to sleep outside. Joseph found a mosquito net in a garbage pile. It was worn out, and dirty and full of holes. He pulled a thorn from an acacia tree, peeled it and made a hole at the dull end. Using thread from a white sock we found, he sealed all the holes in the net. We picked up some clothes from the garbage and washed them.

While in Thiet, we ran into my older brother, Yier. Joseph was the one who recognized him. I'd only seen him a few brief times in the village because he'd been away at the university in Wau until the government killed all the students. Now he was with the rebels and Joseph saw him in a crowd of soldiers coming into town. Yier told us that he'd heard there were boys gathering and he'd come to Thiet looking for us. Peter, Joseph and I were thankful to see someone else from our family, especially someone older who could look after us and give us advice. My heart longed for my parents there to love, protect and advise me. I missed my father every day. When Yier was suddenly called away to the north to fight with the other soldiers, my chest went hollow. Family had become so precious to me. Without it I was like a tree alone in a desert.

———————

We headed south again with another group of soldiers. Every time we came to a new place or met with new people I looked out for anyone else in my family, especially Benson. I'd found Peter, Joseph and even Yier. So, even though Benson had been gone for two years now, why should I not find him too?

All the walking made many wounds on my feet. I wasn't the only one with that problem. We couldn't travel during the day because it wasn't safe. We walked barefoot at night, but in the dark I couldn't see what I was stepping on. The snakes came out to eat at night, and that was when most people were bitten. I got a swollen leg but I didn't know what had happened to me. It was difficult to walk. To keep up, I had to limp along. I was determined to survive and help our family survive. A week later an adult said, "See this tiny hole and that oozing liquid like water. You were bitten by a snake. You're lucky that it was a nonpoisonous snake."

Joseph was our protector and he liked to keep us around him all the time. When it came to a dangerous situation, like when a hyena jumped up and everybody scattered, he knew what to do. He carried a piece of wood as a club. He couldn't protect everybody but guarded quite a few of us that he knew.

Sometimes though we found ourselves so desperate, not even Joseph could help. We wept; even Joseph cried. Just walking for weeks was terrible. Kids were dying from snakebites and starvation. Some of the boys were so depressed they didn't stop crying. Some didn't eat. Many times Peter wouldn't eat even if we had food. I'd find little things but he wouldn't eat them. When Peter cried he made me and the other boys cry too. Usually I was the one who went in and tried to break that up. We didn't want that. We saw that the kids who were crying and not eating were dying.

The first time things seemed all right was when we reached a town where people still had cattle. They gave us five bulls, but we were so many we each had only a very small piece. When they brought the milk, only the smallest boys received half a glass. There wasn't enough for boys like me. That night, as we slept outside near a river, a hyena attacked a boy and took off part of his face. I saw it that morning, the cheek open into the mouth, and I was so scared that the next night I didn't sleep at all.

For a month after we left Juol, we'd slept outside and had almost no food. It was only when we reached the town of Yirol that we were given another mosquito net to share and two hundred of us boys were led to the cement floor of a long building.

The next morning, explosions woke us from our sleep. Our bodies trembled at the sound but then it was gone. We went down to the river. Many mango trees that had been in the area the day before had all disappeared. The soldiers said Antonovs threw bombs at the white birds resting along the riverbanks because they thought the birds were people washing their laundry.

We'd heard adults speak of these Antonovs. "What is Antonov?" we asked.

"They are the planes that the government buys from Russia. They drop bombs from so high we cannot see them. Only hear them."

What is Russia? I wondered.

A captain sat us down and talked to us in Arabic, which was translated to Dinka by a few Nuer boys who were there. "You guys are the tomorrow," he said. "The future of Sudan. We're going to find you a safe place, find you a school, and put you under rebel protection. We know you are kids and you are helpless and we want to help. We don't want any of you to die."

The soldiers taught us about bombs. "Don't run," they said. "Just lie down. The little planes go very, very fast and when you hear them they've already gone by and dropped the bombs. The big ones are the Antonov. You can hear a very big roar but the bombs are already falling by then. You cannot outrun them."

Every night we swept the floor with palm leaves to keep it clean and every morning the Antonov bombed. It didn't miss a single day. We woke up before the sun each day and went to the trenches to protect ourselves. When the UN plane that brought medicine came, someone would shout, "Antonov, Antonov," and we'd run to the trenches. The Antonovs flew so high we never saw them but they saw us. They found the direction the wind was blowing and dropped sixteen or twenty bombs. You'd see the explosion rise up after each one. They bombed Yirol every day so metal fragments were all around. Some people ran and metal cut off their arms and their legs. Even their heads. They ran anyway because they were scared. Lying down, I learned, was how you survived the Antonov bombs.

Occasionally, when people were unlucky, a bomb would land in a trench and no one would survive. Everyone would die, cut down by a bomb full of metal.

One night I heard a deep vibration from very high up. I opened my eyes a little and saw that all the other people were sleeping, so I thought I had been dreaming and shut my eyes.

I was in a deep sleep when the building shook like an earthquake that didn't stop. There were explosions outside. It was still dark but I could hear crying and shouting everywhere. Boys ran out coughing from the dust. I got up and ran out too.

Later, when the sun came up, we saw that a bomb had gone through our roof and landed between our building and the next one without exploding. It was big, the size of a fat man. The up end had a propeller and the other end was stuck tip down in the ground. That would have been the end of us if it had exploded.

The rebel soldiers in Yirol were often sent north to fight. The person in charge said, "We have three or four hundred boys here and they are being killed by Antonovs. This place is not safe for them. We must move on."

South of Yirol we passed through a place where people believed there were cannibals. Boys disappeared, especially little ones. Maybe wild animals devoured them. There was a type of small lion in that area called *nyanjuan* that I had never seen in my village back home. If you were big, over ten years, this lion could only gash your eyes, but if you were five or seven, it would take you and eat you. That small lion ate many of us boys.

One night that lion, *nyanjuan,* came while we were sleeping. It picked up a boy sleeping near me. "Help, help," I cried.

All I saw was a blur of his body and heard his last cry echoing as he disappeared into darkness. In the morning we found the blood and some remnants, his hand, legs, and head. His eyes had been gashed all out. When the *nyanjuan* eats you, it gashes out the eyes, eats the guts and stomach, and only leaves legs and hands so that you cannot be recognized. When you don't have eyes, it is terrible.

I think God protected me or I would have been eaten by that *nyanjuan.*

———————

In some of the villages we went through, people who had lost children would see a cute little kid and wanted him for themselves. In one village I met a lady with some nuts. I wanted those nuts so badly that I asked her for some.

She said, "You are so cute, boy. My baby just died. You look just like my boy. When I saw you I thought you were him. Where are your parents?"

I said, "I don't know."

"Where are you going?"

"I don't know."

I was giving her all the answers but she wasn't offering me the nuts.

"Just stay with me," she said. "You're going to be happy."

"Give me some nuts," I demanded.

When she gave me the nuts, I ate them.

She asked, "Are you going to stay with me?"
I said, "No. I must be with my family."
She looked sad. I walked away.

Walking was hard for little boys like Peter. He stuck to me because he was my half brother. We walked off-road for three days with no food, only water, and were very hungry when we reached a small town. But the villagers wouldn't spare us some food. I had never begged in my life, but I wanted something so badly that I begged for peanuts from a woman. She refused and said, "If you keep asking insistently I will beat you!"

I kept quiet and walked away. We found a few grains on the ground and some of us boys started picking them from the sand. When I raised my head, I saw that Peter was just sitting. "Peter," I said. "Come and pick some grains."

"I am not a hen," he replied. "I can't pick from the ground."

When we finished, I had a little pile in my palm. It was worth a lot to me. We combined our grains, fetched some twigs, made a fire and cooked them in a tin. Each person got a mouthful. Peter got his share too. That one bit of cooked grain let us talk cheerfully for a while.

When we were done, I went to where Peter was sitting. "You are not in your mama's house anymore," I told him. "You have to think about what brought you here. You can't complain about being a hen; you have to do everything to stay alive. You've already seen that boys like you are dying. They always cry and they're always depressed. I'm not saying

I'm a grown adult, but this is the situation. To live, this is just my thought. Whatever you think is up to you. If you want to die, just go ahead and die. I don't care. We will all die. No problem." I did care. I didn't want Peter to die. He was the only brother I could be sure was still alive.

Peter went quiet. He was so homesick. But he listened to me like an elder. He knew if it wasn't for me and Joseph he wouldn't be alive.

We moved on again and came to the Upper Nile, where a ship would take us across to the Equatorial region. I wondered if Benson traveled this way. I was told many boys had been through this region before and traveled eastward toward Ethiopia. We spent two days there entirely without food and I became so miserable and hungry I couldn't talk. I shut down like a car without gas.

We crossed the Nile on a big motor ship. It was a sad crossing. I could only think of my family, my village, and the Dinka land I was leaving behind. The adults said we had to find a safe place and wait for the war to end. But all I wanted to do was go back home.

On the east side of the Nile, the Aliab Dinka offered cows to us. The commander assigned ten boys to each soldier. When they killed a cow, the soldier went to get the meat and cooked it for us. It was our first good meal in weeks. But that night, we were discovered by the mosquitoes, which swarmed so thick they sounded like many cows crying. None of us could sleep. Ten of us shared the mosquito net and one pulled one way and another pulled the other way. All you could do was let the mosquitoes eat and when you wiped your hand on your body it would be bloodied. We wondered how people lived there.

In the morning we were so weary, so sick for home, so miserable, we cried. The adults told us to be quiet.

"We want to go home."

"You can't go home. There is nothing there but the war."

"Where are we going?"

"We are taking you to a place where all the boys are gathering."

"Are we going to Ethiopia?"

"No, we're going south. To a place called Palataka."

"Palataka? What is this place Palataka?"

"There is a missionary school. You will be safe."

Palataka sounded like a good place for us. "How far is that?" we asked.

"Not far now. Only a few days beyond Torit. We'll be in Torit in a couple of weeks."

They told us we'd already traveled four hundred miles. Torit was only two hundred more and Palataka just a two-day walk, less than a hundred miles beyond there. When we heard how far we'd come we were encouraged and we wiped the tears from our eyes and decided to be strong.

But we weren't strong. Some of the boys went crazy. They did things a normal person cannot do, crazy things. One boy urinated and sprayed the rest of us with urine and said, "It's raining." Some boys wouldn't talk. They couldn't. They just looked at you. I found myself also not talking sometimes. I did silly things: got angry over nothing, fought. It was my way of dealing with our situation. Then I began to understand that if we were strong enough to fight each other, why not fight the people who separated us from our parents? I told the others, "We also have to fight for anything that comes our way. As a group, ten boys are equivalent to one adult. Because each one of us has a brain we can come up with a better idea to defeat anything." That was another way of surviving, making ourselves strong as a group.

Some boys were selfish. When they found food, they'd eat it themselves and they wouldn't share. I learned a lot from sharing. If I found a small thing and I looked at another boy, I felt so bad to not split or give him a little. I'd break it up; give him a piece and eat a piece. When I needed it, somebody gave me a piece.

We followed the Nile south to Gemmeize, where we stopped to rest for the night. The setting sun was leaving behind rays that were red like poking embers. I looked up at the clear blue sky and called to the other boys, "Guys, why is it so clear up in the sky today?"

"Maybe it's going to rain," Diing said.

Diing had the same prophecy as me.

The other boys gave mocking laughs. One boy said, "Do you think you are prophets?"

They broke into another long laugh until their eyes were wet with tears. Diing and I withdrew and kept our mouths shut. As night fell we broke into groups and went under the mosquito net cuddling ourselves together like puppies to their mother. Most of the boys fell fast asleep. I was gazing at the starry sky and thinking back to my mother and my home where I used to sleep softly like a little baby, with warm blankets and peaceful coverings to keep my body from cold. One boy started snoring like a frog in the rainy season. Someone broke into a chuckle, breaking my train of thought.

I raised my head above the long line of boys. "Who is that?"

"Me, Santino."

We had a little conversation, then he slept too. As soon as I fell asleep, a gusting wind woke me abruptly. I jumped up like a small child who steps on a hot coal. Soon a heavy wind bent the trees, a gale, creaking and breaking the dried twigs, moving dead leaves and old stained tins. With cloudy eyes I stumbled into the darkness with the other boys. I'd taken a few strides when rain began to fall. It hardened into dark particles, turning to heartbreaking rains, beating the sun-baked, cracked ground thoroughly, sealing up cracks with big pools of water. The boys broke into shrill cries, sounding like sweet-voiced musicians. The rain beat down more heavily, like the *adougo* drum. I'd never seen such rain before. I waded through the dark, wet earth, my feet making a *sholob, sholob* sound.

Santino called out, "Wow!"

"Nhiallic," God, I mumbled. My chin trembled and my teeth chattered. A tongue of fire flashed as lightning struck. Every boy ran in a different direction. I headed for some thatched houses roofed with yellow elephant grass. I poked my head in to save myself from the freezing cold. It was already crowded. An older boy placed his heavy hand on my head and pushed me back. Everybody roared, "The fire is small."

I stood motionless in front of the door, then I tried another hut. My shivering body felt on the point of death. Was this to be the end of my life?

No! I was determined. I threw myself inside, sprawled on top of them.

At least the rain reduced the mosquitoes the next morning.

———

That day, long trucks began arriving in Gemmeize. They had three trailers as big as houses with sheets for roofs and were empty after returning from delivering food to Bor.

The drivers parked their trucks and started cooking. The soldiers went over and talked to them. "Look at these young boys walking. We soldiers can walk, we are grown, but these kids, they have suffered badly. We need your help to take them to Torit."

One of the drivers shouted something back in another language and jumped in his truck. As he started the engine and began to drive away, the soldiers shot all his tires flat. The driver jumped out and yelled at them. The soldiers grabbed the drivers, beat them up, and forced them back into their trucks. Now the drivers looked scared.

The soldiers yelled to us, "Jump on the trucks." The engines started up. I tried to climb up, but the tires were taller than me. Then a guy came along and helped us all up until the first one was filled and they started filling the next one.

Thirty of us sat on the floor of the trailer. I was excited. It was my first time in a vehicle. The truck began moving and I looked out through the canvas sheeting. Except for the one with its tires shot out, all of the trucks were following. When the trees began running backward very fast, I got scared and sat down. It grew dark and we were bouncing everywhere. Other boys grabbed and held on to me. We were shaking and swirling side to side. All we could smell was the smoke of the truck. I was fine, but many of the boys got sick. A lot started throwing up. Puking everywhere. It was so dark, no light and *aaahh* it smelled so bad.

During the rainy season it is very hard for vehicles to move in southern Sudan. Our driver saw that the road was covered with dirty water and other trucks and cars were stuck there. He tried to make a detour around the trapped vehicles until we got stuck too. All the soldiers jumped out. I was curious and put my head outside the vehicle to see what they would do. Destroyed vehicles were everywhere and all around them were human bones. The skulls seemed to be smiling up at me. The soldiers pushed for an hour before we got the truck out of that mud.

Government troops still held the town directly on the other side of the Nile. When we stopped and the soldiers got out of the trucks and made fires, they told us to be quiet. We were so hungry. The soldiers were taking care of themselves but nobody looked out for us. "Boys," they said, "you're not in your mama's house no more!"

Joseph had brought some grain. We got out to make a fire but a few minutes later the soldiers announced we were going. We traveled all that night through a beautiful green area with hills and trees. We came to a village that the Antonov had bombed a week before. The homes, hospital, and schools were destroyed. Many people had been killed or were badly wounded, with no help.

We rested there but the soldiers told us not to walk out of the town because there were land mines. Joseph started to a cook. A few minutes later the soldiers announced, "Okay boys, we're going." Once more, we didn't eat.

We passed more towns. All ruined. Wrecked buildings. Wrecked cars. They looked like battlefields and smelled of human blood.

Seeing destroyed towns changed our mood. They didn't

even look like villages anymore. I thought I understood why the Murahaliin attacked our village. They wanted our cattle, our things and our kids. But I didn't understand this complicated war, how it mortally devoured the land and left it so full of skeletons. The adults talked of the war all the time. They discussed slavery, apartheid, racism, segregation and tribalism. They called it a religious war. A jihad. I heard all the words but I didn't understand them. I think kids feel differently about things than adults do. From what I could see, men or women, children or adults, young or aged, rich or poor, war was making everyone equal.

Through all of this, Joseph was serious and caring and worried and he always looked after us. Peter was always miserable. He didn't eat and cried over little things. If anyone took a little thing from him, he would just break into tears. He'd say, "If my mother was here, I wouldn't be like this." We'd say, "Shut up boy, you're not in your mama's house no more." We said that a lot. As children, seven or eight years old, we knew nothing about the world, just that we were not in our mama's house no more.

Palataka

ALEPHO

It was night when our line of trucks entered Torit. We were the first group of small boys to arrive there. The rebels had just captured Torit back again from the government, after months of fighting. The whole city stank.

We awoke the next morning to destroyed buildings, bullets, shells, and bones and skulls lying everywhere. The city had modern buildings and even some paved streets. I could tell it had been a nice place before the battle. There was a mission station with high buildings and a very tall Catholic church. The area was a little hilly and green with mangos, guavas and lemons. Many cars and vehicles were still there, but all destroyed and smeared with blood and smelly with bones. It looked like there had been fighting for years, not just three or four months. We were taken to a deserted school facility that was partially bombed. The water system had been destroyed. They had flush toilets, the first ones I'd seen, but they didn't flush. The soldiers had been using them anyway; all of the bathrooms in town were filled with shit, some of the houses too. The place smelled terrible. The city was big and we couldn't go far because it was ringed with land mines, so we couldn't get outside to relieve ourselves.

We slept outside under blankets. My blanket was the strongest, the most beautiful and the best thing I had ever owned. It had yellow, blue, red and gray stripes alternating all over. When I washed it, I had to sit all day and watch while it hung from a tree to dry so that no one stole it. I loved that blanket. It stayed thick and strong and when it was wet, it smelled so good it almost felt like I was back home in our village with the sheep.

We wandered around as much as we could. Inside the city we could see a marketplace with food, but there were bombs and mines and they wouldn't allow anyone inside until it was cleared. The soldiers were always telling us, "This space is cleared of mines. Don't walk far from here. Don't ever go there." They showed us the distance we could go. "There are a lot of mines out there and people are getting blown up everyday. They must go out there to do things, but you don't. For your safety, don't go out there."

We didn't listen. Even though there were mines we had to go out and get food and firewood, which was very dangerous. One boy brought back a bomb and laid it down. *Blamhh!* It blew up just like that. "Don't do that! Don't do that!" we told him. "That can kill people." "It was fun," he said. He did it again and was blown up. He almost killed other boys.

For fun, we'd play with the bullet shells we found lying around. Each of us took a few and lined them up. "Okay, we are Arabs and you are rebels. *Bam!* I knocked your shell down with my shell, I've killed your soldier." In the mornings we watched the soldiers shoot the real guns.

An open-air market grew up where people traded money, food and little things. Joseph and I started a business too.

When the river in Torit overflows, no one likes to go out and pick mangos because the fire ants are very bad. Once you go up a mango tree they crawl on you really very fast and their bites hurt so badly that many people fall from the trees that way. But I loved to climb and Joseph loved to climb too. I don't know how he did it, but Joseph figured out that if you smear your urine on your legs and your hands and climb the mango tree, ants will run away from you.

That way, I'd climb the mango tree and eat my fill then take mangos to the market and use the money to buy cooked food. It tasted so good.

That first month in Torit, the Antonovs bombed the market twice, killing more boys. The second month a lot of boys came all the way down from the Nuba mountains. They were starving. So thin. So sick. They hadn't showered for months and smelled awful. They had so many lice that if you sat next to them, armies of lice moved toward you. The Nuba boys killed lizards and roasted them. That smelled terrible but those Nuba boys didn't care. They just wanted something to eat. The body is like an engine. When the engine is shut down, there is no way you can even think of taking care of yourself. When you have food, the mind can take care of all those things.

Joseph protected us in Torit. When older kids, ten or eleven years old, beat us up, Joseph defended us. Once he confronted three bullies who liked to bully every boy. They attacked Joseph and beat him up. I felt so bad that I beat up one of the bullies. The bully shouted at me, "I'll kill you, boy."

An adult came with a stripped stick and beat that boy. He had a gun and he said, "You guys just came from a lot of killing; I don't want to see you fighting each other. You should start liking each other. You have so many things to deal with now. You're fighting hunger, you're fighting people that want your life—the people you escaped from to hide your life. And now you're starting to fight each other. You try to bully or fight another boy and I'm going to shoot your head off."

We'd never handled guns so when we saw a person handle it and it went bang, we knew that thing killed. We called it the harmful stick. We learned quickly that if somebody points the stick at you, you die.

Some of the boys, like ten-year-olds, didn't listen. They'd seen a lot of killing and they also wanted to kill. They wanted to be warriors. They didn't want to have mercy. I think it is because they were worn out by so much killing.

After two months, the adults announced that we were leaving for Palataka and that we would stay there until the war was over. It was in the southernmost part of Sudan, away from the areas where the government troops were attacking. We had no choice. We couldn't go back home. We followed, hoping Palataka would be good.

It was still the rainy season when the soldiers escorted us across the bridge over the bursting river at Torit. Under cloudy skies we headed south toward the hills through grass over my head. Everything was taller than me then. With the boys from Nuba mountains, there seemed to be over a thousand of us, maybe two thousand, escorted by just five soldiers.

The second day we reached a small town called Khartoum—same name as the capital of Sudan in the north—where they gave us beans. We hadn't eaten since we left. We cut the top off of a gas can and cooked the beans. Even though they smelled like gas we pushed and shoved and dug our fingers in. The Nuba mountain boys thrust their fingers in there and picked up those hot beans. I'd taken only two pinches before my fingers were burned and the beans were gone. I was so upset and angry I fought with those Nuba.

That night many boys claimed the adults were lying. "We heard Palataka is a deserted place filled with chiggers. Most of the boys went to Panyido. Panyido is better." They slipped out and headed toward Ethiopia.

Even though we thought there might be a chance that was where Benson and our other cousins Benjamin, Emmanuel and Lino might have gone, Joseph, Peter and I stayed. What did those boys know? Rumors were always flying. The adults said we were going to a safe place. A missionary school. A place where we could live until the war was over. We were tired of walking. We were tired of being scared every night when we slept and tired of wondering if we would live another day without food and water.

We first saw the red brick buildings of Palataka from a distant hill. Looking down on our destination, I felt strangely good. The closest thing I'd seen to a home in many months was only a few more steps away. I hadn't been bitten by a poisonous snake, eaten by a cannibal, sickened, starved or died. I had endured the terrible trek. Anything that came my way now I felt I could survive.

We were not the first to arrive in Palataka. A smaller group of boys was already there. They were dirty and thin.

Really thin. Most walked around on their heels and sat and picked at their infected feet. Chiggers!

The first week they separated us into different buildings by age. I was with Peter but Joseph was moved away. The first day Joseph was gone I fought fifteen times with boys from other regions like Bor and Nuba. Many other boys were getting into fights too. When I kept fighting the adults said, "You need discipline," and put me with the older boys to do what they did—cut wood, clean, build the commander's house. I stopped fighting. I was happy that I was with Joseph. I got discipline.

Ever since I'd left home, until I arrived in Palataka, I'd been sad or angry. I'd just been staying alive. But once I was with a group of boys, many of them, in a settled place, I saw a change in myself. I tried to fit in. We would go out and play soccer in a group, shouting, "We are the best team! We are the strongest team!"

But Peter wouldn't do that. He would cry and sit by himself. He still didn't want to eat and he wouldn't play with any other boys. He didn't change. He was set apart from us, in the group for the little boys, but I would see him like that and it made me feel very bad for him.

At night I slept on the floor on a sack. My feet were still cracked and cut from the long walk and the place was so dirty I soon had chiggers too. Chiggers are very small, dark red things that enter the cracks in your skin at night when you're sleeping. They suck your blood and become fat, round and white. They itch. If you scratch at them, they urinate. If you got one, another went in beside that wound the next night. If you tried to remove them the wound expanded until the whole foot was infected.

Some of the boys got them on their penises and their be-hinds. I couldn't even look at them. The doctors had to take the chiggers out and their penises swelled so huge. The next day another chigger would enter inside the soft wound.

I learned to go to a small stream and leave my feet in the water. Because I had no shoes my feet were all cracked and the chiggers liked all those cracked areas and dead parts of the skin. If I kept my feet smooth and soft they couldn't find those cracks. So every morning I went to the stream. The water was cold, but I had to keep myself clean. Soon the chiggers were gone from my feet.

Each week a little grain was distributed. We pounded it and cooked it and ate it only every two days so that we didn't starve to death. The day we didn't eat there was nothing to keep the time moving.

More starving boys came down from the Nuba moun-tains. Food became so scarce, we'd eat almost anything. As I watched boys eat stuff they'd never eaten before, get sick and die, I only ate what I was sure wouldn't kill me. There was another large tree called *kunyuk* with a dark fruit. If we ate it we got full, but it didn't nourish us. Sometimes it gave us constipation and many boys who climbed those trees to get it, broke legs, necks and arms. Other times we'd be so de-lighted to find a beehive that we didn't even care about be-ing stung when we went after the honey. The Nuba boys introduced us to a root called *ajaamer*. It looked like a pineapple but smaller, with juicy stuff inside. It tasted like sour milk and it wasn't poisonous. We trapped a small ani-mal, a cane rat called *parboos* that was the size of a squirrel, and roasted our catch.

Sometimes if no food came and I'd caught a *parboos*, the

older boys would take it from me by force if Joseph wasn't around. We heard stories about Ethiopia that made us so sad we were in Palataka. They said that the UN had discovered all the boys in Ethiopia and was giving them food and clothes and that everybody was fat and enjoying it. But the UN didn't come to Palataka. We had no clothes, just rags. Everything about Palataka was like a survival contest.

Some boys got so desperate they just sat around in the dirt and wouldn't do anything unless they were forced. They hadn't washed for so long that a committee of grown boys was formed to make sure all the boys took a bath in the river. The worst ones had to be forced into the river. The water was really cold and the boys would tease each other because some were circumcised and others weren't. Nuba and Bor boys weren't circumcised. We made jokes about each other.

The elders said that if you want to live, the best way is to work. So we worked hard. We dug open holes and built latrines with boards and put ashes on top because the flies breed a lot. We were sent to chop trees and two boys carried the heavy poles back for miles. We built a house for Kuol Manyang, the commander. They were teaching us how to work when we grew up.

At night we were tired, but we couldn't sleep because of the bedbugs. Every morning we'd get up and have bumps all over and smeared blood from scratching ourselves. Those bedbugs were small and dark, like the small tick, not like the big tick, the one the size of your big toe. Some were red and all had six legs. We couldn't kill them because if you did it could fill the whole building with its bad smell. Worse than a skunk. If someone squashed one, the boys would come in, "Oh my God, you killed a bedbug."

The second year they opened a school and two white ladies came and brought supplies. We cut the pencils and books in two so we'd have enough to share. We began learning ABCs, but there were only six teachers for a thousand boys. Learning another language was really difficult. They'd say words but if we didn't know them the next day they'd hit our hands with rulers. I had sore swollen fingers the whole time. From the moment they hit me I didn't learn anything from their teaching. I didn't want that beating. I was so dumb in school. If this was school, I was going to hate it.

The teachers said we needed discipline. They would tell us to go out, even when it was raining hard. They called it *gymbast* and we ran and marched. Our clothes were wet, we were wet and it was so cold. They had these boys they called *churta* who liked to beat people up if they stopped running. It didn't seem like discipline, more like punishment or revenge.

The adults told us, "We have been fighting for too long. We are old people. You are the boys and we want you to be educated and be the boys of the future. You will take over and be the leaders of this country. Don't hate us because we beat you or force you to do something. We do that for your own future, not for us. We don't have a future anymore."

After two years in Palataka, by the time I was nine and Joseph eleven, Joseph whispered to me one night, "We have to escape."

Those words sent my heart racing. I'd seen too many boys beaten for running away.

"They're taking the older boys to a camp called Gromlee and training them as soldiers."

I didn't say anything. Some boys wanted to have guns, but

that scared me. I didn't know if it was true, but we'd heard they always sent the boys to the front lines.

"We'll go to Torit. Yier is a soldier; the post office can tell us where to find him. Yier knows what to do."

Yier! We hadn't seen him in two years, since that day in Thiet. Still, my heart soared at the possibility of seeing my oldest brother, of being with an elder from my own family, someone who cared about us and would know what to do. "Will Yier take us home?"

"I don't know."

"What about Peter?"

"He's only six, he can't go."

"I can't leave without Peter."

"He will be fine. He's too little to be trained as a soldier. They'll keep him here in school. He can't make it with us."

It still didn't feel right to leave Peter behind. "When will we go?"

"Don't talk to anyone."

I knew better than to do that. Sometimes if five boys were seen sitting together and talking they'd think they were making a plan to escape and those boys were punished.

"But when?"

"I will let you know."

Poisoned Trees

BENJAMIN

For the first eight months in Panyido refugee camp Benson, Emmanuel and I faced a lot of difficulties; we had no food, no shelter, and no one to depend on. We fended for ourselves. We went to the river and hunted fish to eat. But the river was really unsafe. Local people called Anyuak sometimes attacked us and took away the clothes we were wearing. Other times they shot people and took everything they had.

The government of Ethiopia talked to the UN high commissioner of refugees about coming to see how the situation was with the Sudanese on their border. When he came and saw that the situation was really bad, he sent us maize, beans, oil and salt. He opened schools. If you were eight years or under you went to school, but if you were ten, twelve, up to twenty years old, you would first work in the forest and cut poles to build a shelter. You could not go to school without working first.

I lived with seventeen friends who were my age-mates. One day my friend was told by the elder to collect some firewood. He asked me to come with him to help. I said, "All right, let's go."

He told me to go up the tree and throw down the firewood. I said, "No, I don't know how to climb. The tree is wet and I can't climb it."

"Okay, you stay here under the tree and I will collect the wood and throw it down."

He broke off dried branches and dropped them below the tree. I put them in a pile. I was in the middle of the pile when he shouted, "A lion is coming."

I started running across the dry wood, which clawed me on my right leg. A large piece entered my flesh and stuck into my right leg bone.

I made it back to the camp, but after a few days my leg had gone really, really bad. My friend felt bad because there was not a lion. I went to the clinic but the medicines did not help because they said that every tree in Ethiopia had been poisoned by the bombs from the big war. With that poison in it, the wound in my leg got worse.

The Gilo

BENSON

The summer of 1991 began with heavy rains and screeching wind. There was so much rain in Ethiopia that every green plant blossomed. The maize and peanuts planted near our huts bloomed their yellowish flowers. We'd planted crops and in a few months expected a good harvest. After three years in Panyido life had become tolerable. Our only suffering was not knowing what had become of our families in the war in Sudan. Every night I longed for my safe warm bed back in Juol. I wondered about my mother and father, my brothers and sisters. What had become of Nieu-nieu and Angong? Akoon and Alepho? I even missed their teasing. I hungered for everything I'd lost.

Then war found us once more. The Ethiopian government had been overthrown by guerrilla fighters called the Ethiopian People's Liberation Army (EPLA). Before we could harvest, the Ethiopian people warned us to leave their country. We had to evacuate the refugee camp in a week. We were frightened. The Sudan war had grown worse and spread farther. I longed to go home, but not like this—not running again, not back into the battles. My beautiful homeland wasn't a home in wartime. But to avoid conflict we agreed to leave their land and our lovely crops behind us.

But where would we go? Leopards were chasing us into the jaws of the lion.

I have many bad memories that I will never erase from my brain, but witnessing how the River Gilo gulped Sudanese underneath to their deathbed will always prevail.

We trudged from Panyido back toward the border with Sudan. For two muddy days we made our way to the Gilo. We prepared our camp on the Ethiopian riverbank in tall grasses infested by buzzing mosquitoes and tsetse flies. The weather was tranquil and everything was quiet except for the murmuring of fifty thousand refugees, the smell of cooking fires and the wailing of infants. The situation seemed safe; we only wondered what we would eat.

Late in the afternoon it began to drizzle and clouds shaded the sun. We scattered under big trees for shelter. Some people huddled under blue and white plastic sheets, little mounds in the field. I sat near one of the many fires that sent smoke wafting upward through the drizzle.

The cold, damp night passed, leaving my body itchy again from mosquito bites. In the morning there was a rumor that roaring artilleries had been heard during the night from the direction of Panyido. They said it might be the Ethiopian troops. An SPLA commander arrived and said that he and his army had fought the Ethiopian People's Liberation Army at the camp after we left. He said many of the Ethiopian fighters were women carrying machine guns who shot at SPLA soldiers to stop them from coming to protect us at the Gilo. They shot from their tanks and yelled, "Sudani, why do you run away from women? Don't Sudanese like women? Just stop running and look at us, the most beautiful Oromian women. You would like us." Sudanese men thought women were too weak and cowardly to fight, but any soldier looking back got his head blown off. So the SPLA fighters abandoned the road to Ethiopian tanks and lifted their boots higher above the grass to escape the Ethiopian women warriors. The commander warned everyone to cross the river to the Sudan side before it was too late.

Our teachers began squeezing us into two small wooden canoes. As we shoved off a few of us at a time, we knew there was no going back. The wicked river, not as wide as the Nile but flooded with rainwater and flowing swiftly, rocked our small boats wildly. I was among the first to cross. To get the twenty thousand boys to the other side would take hundreds of crossings a day. By the third day only half the population was across and waiting on the Sudan side for the rest.

On the Sudanese side of the Gilo, there was nothing to eat, but it was calm and all you could hear was the humming voices of the crowds on both sides of the river. We slashed the grass down for our campsite, left a space in the center to play soccer and made a ball from collected rags. We took turns playing to amuse ourselves, each group going on the field after one group was defeated by two goals. Everyone, including our teachers, lined the field to watch—innocent crowds waiting like puppies not knowing the danger creeping nearby.

The sun's rays broke through the dark clouds once and then disappeared. For many it was the last time they would ever see those rays. A gunshot came from the Ethiopian side of the river and all the voices died down—just one shot.

Once its echo disappeared, we turned back our attention to the game again.

Then suddenly: *Boom! Bang! Bang! Taai! Tuuk! Tuuk!* The guns were loud and near. At first we thought it was the sound of the SPLA soldiers. But then more guns were fired together in a blast of heavy explosions. Then there was the wail and the woe.

Those wrapped in plastic sheets threw them from their heads. Bullets flew from the Ethiopian side to our side of the river. A teacher yelled, "Lie on the ground." A big gun boomed. There was a dull thud as the shell hit the ground. Women screamed. My heart pounded at the crying and shooting. On the Ethiopian side, men and women rushed into the river, trying to cross to our side, kicking glass cups and plates and tins as they went. "Oh Mother! *Koc a moc! Koc a moc!*" they shouted. "We are attacked! We are attacked!"

The enemy emerged into view and shot people trying to cross the swollen river. Blood exploded out of their heads as they crumpled into the water. Bullets hissed among us on the far bank. Thousands of people flowed into the river and disappeared like water poured into the sand of Sahara. Those who managed by the help of God to swim across dared not run up the bank or they would get a bullet through them. They had to wait in the reeds among the crocodiles that had been awakened by the blood in the water. One woman crossed on the backs of bodies that had accumulated in the water. She walked ashore without touching the water. A mad Nubian man who had somehow gotten a machine gun yelled at people for crossing and leaving him behind because he couldn't swim. He shot people and when he'd finished firing all his cartridges he jumped into the river and drowned in shallow water. I had no idea where Benjamin or Lino were.

"All of you lie down and crawl," ordered our teachers. Without hesitation, we touched the ground with our hands and knees and crawled like baboons down a grass-concealed road into the bushes. A deafening noise overhead was followed by an explosion right in front of us. My heart almost jumped out of my chest. I couldn't breathe. The women and children behind me were crying. I was confused, not knowing what to do between crawling and crying. The Ethiopians kept shooting after us even when we were a long distance from the river. We listened for its horrible roar, but thank God they didn't have the Russian warplane Antonov or we would have been killed for sure.

When the people who survived the crossing finally reached us, they said that more than two thousand people had been shot, drowned or eaten by crocodiles. It was one of the darkest days for southern Sudanese black souls.

The Gilo killed many that day, but it also saved many. Those troops would have come after us with their tanks and finished every single soul if the river hadn't been overflowing. I bet they were afraid when they witnessed how cruelly it was devouring the Sudanese. Maybe their eyes had enough of what they were seeing happen to Sudanese that day in the river. Maybe they stood in awe of the Sudanese women and children dying. How would they feel when the human bodies floated up, rotten, bloated and smelling? Maybe they still have horrible nightmares like I have had all these past years.

We crawled on for long hours. Our hands lost their skin and those who were wearing short trousers scraped their knees. The sun went down to the echo of gunfire behind us. My few grains and precious blanket were left under the tree by the riverbank.

It was the rainy season and the desert that had nearly cooked us more than three years earlier on the way to Panyido was drowning us now. Three hundred teachers had to help twenty thousand boys. The women and children from Panyido, combined with the Itang and Dima refugee camps, meant our group numbered more than sixty thousand. The front of the walking line could be two days ahead of the last exhausted people who lagged behind with hunger, disease and wounds. If Benjamin was still alive, he would be among them. I worried that his leg wound would get worse from walking in the flood. But no matter how far back the weak ones were, some teachers stayed behind with them. No boy who survived the attack at Gilo was abandoned.

We staggered for three days in flooded plains on nothing but empty stomachs and sore skeletons. The mud sucked up all my strength. My body was surviving on the energy of the boiled beans and corn I'd eaten the morning before the attack. Whenever we were tired there was no place to sit unless we could climb a tree to rest our feet. Some of us were so tired we wanted to give up. We knew only that we were headed into danger.

By the time we arrived at the Pochala River we were a bunch of heads throwing stick legs forward, slithering in the mud like wild boars bathing. Pochala was a shallow, rocky river that was wild with the rainy season current and wanted to take part in drowning the cursed children of southern Sudan.

As we tried to cross over to Pochala town, the current waited for us, wanting to break our fragile bones on its deadly rocks. The river stole some of our blankets as we slid over on the slippery stones. Our teachers came to the rescue and stood where the current wanted to engulf us. Our legs quivered as we held hands from one teacher to another, but many of us were not strong enough to make our skinny feet stick on the those enormous smooth rocks and many slid over. The moment they fell into the water, the current took them along like a paper on a stormy day. The teachers did their best. They stood all day as the twenty thousand of us took our turns. They were our guiding heroes, our crossing bridge.

When we first arrived, Pochala was not a place that would bring a smile. We were given blankets and sent to make a camp two hours from town. Emmanuel was there and we asked around desperately for anyone who had seen Benjamin or Lino, but no one had. I didn't want to think of my worst fear, that they had not made it across the Gilo.

We waited for a big plane to drop the food for us in Pochala town but our hope was no more than an ache. The UN brought some sheets to make mosquito nets, a good deed, as our blood would have normally been gone in few days, but even the mosquito's yellow fever bite can't make you sick when you are emaciated.

Lino and Benjamin were still missing when Emmanuel left on foot for Buma, another town in Sudan where the refugees driven out of Ethiopia were gathering. He accompanied a teacher who was searching for his wife. I was left totally alone, without any family. Twice a day I went into the woods to pick fruits from the waak tree and look for grass to make soup. I liked to sit on a tree branch and sing the songs from my village because singing took me back home. I would remember my sister teasing me when I had mud on my face or my mother smiling and waving at me as I took the goats out to graze. I'd smile to myself, as it seemed like the happiest time. The saddest too; my eyes would soon fill with tears.

In Pochala, I missed my home even more than I had before. In Panyido my thoughts had been distracted as I played soccer with friends or went swimming. Now, back in Sudan, I wanted to find my parents again. But fighting and flooding had sealed off the way back home. We had to wait for the flood to ebb. On the way to Ethiopia the first time, it had been the extreme dry season when we went through Pochala. Now with the heavy rain day and night, the ground was a swamp. Two months we waited for food, weak with hunger, ribs collapsed in. It seemed like a whole year.

People kept saying food was going to be dropped by plane, but when a plane finally came it was an Antonov that dropped twelve bombs on cattle that were grazing nearby. Many boys had been out on the airstrip repairing the worn-out parts and if that Antonov had hit its target a hundred or more could have died. We heard they'd also bombed two other towns the same day: thirty-two people were announced killed in Torit town market. The war seemed to be coming our way. I couldn't imagine my village, Juol. Did it even exist anymore? We were being driven down into the remotest corner of Sudan until we had nowhere else to go.

I often walked the two hours from the camp to town to see if food had come and to look for Benjamin or Lino. There were so many people wandering around. I'd see a boy with a limp and, thinking he was Benjamin, my heart would take off like a rabbit until he turned and I'd be disappointed again.

When the food finally arrived one morning, we thought the bundles were exercise books because the pallets were small and white as they swirled downward to the ground. I went to watch the bags of maize hit the ground with a thump, and that's how I met my cousin Athieng. She was there too, watching the plane drop the food from the sky, and I knew she was from my region when I heard her talking. I said hello. We talked and I told her about my village and my family. "You are my uncle's son," she said. She was a cousin, but I called her aunt because she was older. She gave me a letter to take to my group teacher so that he would allow me to go stay with her in the town.

The teacher didn't want me to go; they didn't like the boys to leave the groups. He asked me if I had known this aunt before in my village. I lied to the teacher. "Yes I know her and she is the wife of a commander." He allowed me then. "But only for two weeks," he said. "No more or no less. You must leave your bag behind and take only your blanket and mosquito net."

I sneaked my bag away anyhow because everything I owned was in it, and I moved to Aunt Athieng's house, happy to be rejoining my family, even if I had never met her before.

A Really Bad Boy

BENJAMIN

When the Ethiopian government troops drove everybody into the Gilo, whether or not you could swim you had to dive into that water. Even if you could swim, a lot of people stepped on you. Many people died. My leg wound was so bad, but the Lord God helped me.

After that we wandered through the swamps, sleeping in trees, and every night mosquitoes sucked out the little blood I had. Each morning I woke up weaker than the night before.

We survived on whatever we could get. We wandered around to local villages. If the Anuoak people saw us, sometimes they were friendly. They'd call us over and give us some food. But when boys stole from them they shot at them.

I tried to care for my leg but it was infected from the water we'd walked through. I went to the hospital in Pochala town and the doctor gave me a medicine but it did not cure me. The good medicines I needed were in the hospital.

One day I went back to the hospital and said, "I need a treatment for my wound."

They said, "No, you have already been treated."

I said, "All right. I don't need your treatment either." And I grabbed the antibiotics I wanted and ran away.

They shouted, "Look at this boy. He's a really, really bad boy. He doesn't listen to what the doctor says."

They tried to call me back to take away the medicine from me. But one of the doctors said, "Let him go. He is a young kid. He doesn't know what he is doing. He doesn't know how bad the medicines are. He'll find out when the medicine infects his wound."

But I knew what I was doing because I remembered the medicine from before. That is why I stole the medicine. I didn't want them to cut off my leg. I took care of my wound.

Fly from Pochala

BENSON

On my way to Aunt Athieng's house in Pochala, I saw a boy limping toward me. I prepared myself to be disappointed as usual, but as he drew nearer I began to believe that it really could be Benjamin this time. He was carrying a bag and didn't see me until we nearly met. It was him. I dropped my bag and put my arms around him. I was so glad to see him alive!

"They accepted me for transfer," he said. "I'm leaving by plane to Lokichokio hospital for my leg treatment."

I knew only the worse cases were eligible for flights to Kenya. His whole leg was swollen and the shinbone bowed out. The wound was yellow and leaked green fluid. I was fearful for his leg and his life, but happy to hear that he would receive proper help.

"Have you seen Lino?"

"No," he said. "But someone told me they'd seen him down by the river. I went looking many times, but I never found him."

We said our good-byes and I watched him limp off toward the hospital. We hadn't even tried to plan where we would meet again. He said he would be back, but of course he didn't know when. I told him to look for me at Aunt

Athieng's house, but I really didn't know where I would be either.

Aunt Athieng treated me like a prince. She had a two-year-old son and an older daughter, and a woman friend who was living with her had two girls and three boys of my age. They brought firewood and water from the river for cooking but were told to leave me alone because I was a guest. The boys and girls gave me odd looks, but Aunt Athieng said, "Never think my uncle's son will do anything for you. I will whack your asses if you bother him." I liked to escort the two girls to the river. With over fifty thousand refugees in Pochala and more flooding in from the fighting, the river was always very crowded. I always looked and asked around for Lino but never had any luck. Then I would walk back empty-handed while the girls carried the water as Aunt Athieng had instructed. The mother of the girls said, "He is a gentle boy. When he grows up and marries, lucky is the girl who has chosen him as a husband."

Before going to Aunt Athieng's, I had been feeling neglected and thinking only of home. Now girls cooked for me and I didn't have to work anymore. I was happy for that but still terribly lonely.

One day Aunt Athieng said she'd met Kuot, with whom I had stayed in Panyido, and he wanted to see me. I visited him and saw that his hands had scars on them. Kuot told me that they were skinned when he crossed the Gilo. "I went with the group that ran up the bank away from the attacks. A good swimmer was sent across with a long rope and tied it to a tree on the other side. The rope licked my hand skin off but that is nothing to me. How else could a one-legged man cross that hungry river without a rope?"

Aunt Athieng told me I would not be returning to the boys groups because her family name came up on the list of women who were booked for plane flights to reach Kapoeta, a safe place in the far south of Sudan. The plane would fly to Kenya, where there was an airport, and then we'd travel by truck back into Sudan. I was very excited to fly but I wondered if it would be frightening, like falling from the sky in a nightmare. Or if it hurt to go fast in the air.

Then, completely by chance, I ran into Lino near the river. He had survived the Gilo after all! I was so happy to find him alive. He was living with three soldiers and watched their guns while they fished. When I told Aunt Athieng that I'd found him, she sent me back to get him so that we could take him with us.

"I can't leave," Lino said.

"But Aunt Athieng is taking us out of here. She'll take us to Kapoeta and we can search for our family."

"The soldiers must fish to live and there is no one to watch their guns."

If an SPLA soldier lost his gun, he lost his life.

When I told Aunt Athieng Lino wasn't coming with us, she was very annoyed. I had been happy to leave Pochala for a part of Sudan where I could search for my family, but now I was leaving part of that family behind. It seemed that no matter what I did, this war was determined to fling us into the wind like moths.

A day later we went to the plane. Some were taken on board, including Aunt Athieng's two-year-old son with his older sister, but four of us were left waiting for the next plane that was due to arrive that evening. It began to rain heavily and we were told to go back home for the night and then come back in the morning. When we returned the next day, a Sudanese man who signed the flight tickets said, "You were supposed to leave yesterday. Today is other people's chance."

He would not sign our tickets and we could not get on the plane without tickets signed by him. We spent the whole day sitting in the sun with our belongings hoping he would change his mind and come back to sign our flight permits. That evening he sent a messenger who told us to go home and come back the next day because the planes coming from Kenya were canceled due to heavy rains and another storm on the way.

The next day he argued again with my aunt and said he'd sign our tickets when he wanted or we could wait for another month until he changed his mind. That would have been bad for me. My two-week stay with my aunt was over and I'd be taken back to the boys group. I wanted to leave and search for my family.

The first plane came and the captain allowed the people with signed permits to board. Aunt Athieng was getting more angry and worried about her two-year-old son being without her. A second plane came and Aunt Athieng talked with a Dinka man who spoke English well because his wife was a white woman from England. The man talked to the captain who then called for our tickets and signed them. We got on the plane very gratefully, thanking the captain and the Sudanese man for their kind effort to help us. However, a man followed us, trying to board the plane without a ticket. A whole family can be returned if they sneak in one person without permit. The Kenya authorities will even return all of the passengers if there is a sick person on board. When Aunt Athieng saw that man trying to sit with us, she shouted at him in rage to get out. He climbed back down like someone stepping on hot ashes.

The captain helped us plug in all of our seat belts and went to the cockpit to start the engine. Aunt Athieng unplugged her seat belt and then plugged it back in. "This is such an easy thing to do," she said. "That white captain was breathing like a fat bull on my face just to put on this seat belt."

I looked out of the window and saw people waving at us. I liked being inside the plane and seeing people wave to me the way I did when white people came and went.

The plane ran smoothly on the ground at first until it reached the end of the field. Then it roared and I covered my ears with my hands because it was so loud it hurt inside them. My stomach started tingling. I looked out the window. We were above the river. It looked like a road, the people like ants, and huts like stones. The plane was still climbing. When I looked down again the trees seemed like smooth, new growing grass. The plane went down and up again but it didn't feel that scary, more like the way we used to push each other on the swing. I'd always thought that people who rode planes fell unconscious throughout the flight until the plane landed on the ground, but we stayed awake. We tried to talk but we couldn't hear each other well and I had to shout so loud it tightened my intestines.

We landed in Lokichokio, three hundred miles south of Pochala, just across the Kenyan border. The ground there was extremely hot. The Kenyans checked and took our permits from us. They put us in old trucks and drove us up to Key Base in southern Sudan. There we got into Sudanese trucks to go on to Kapoeta, about a hundred miles away.

———————

After spending a day and a night traveling, we arrived in Kapoeta. Aunt Athieng gave me some money to go to the market and buy milk for her son. I returned to find many people sitting with her in the shade and chatting. I passed by them and went to sit inside the hut.

"Benson," she called. "Come outside."

I stood shyly in front of the group of people. She pointed to a man wearing soldier pants and boots. He had a little boy beside him. The man had lighter skin than me, wasn't tall and reminded me of my father. "This is your half brother, Yier."

My heart started beating. I had only seen Yier a few times in our village when he'd come home from the University in Wau. Because he was the eldest son in the family, all of us little ones had looked up to him, and followed him everywhere when he visited. I hardly knew him though, and was so nervous I didn't say anything.

"Hello, Benson. We didn't know what happened to you."

His soft voice was just like my father's. I looked up, remembering his face. He had a sad look and there seemed to be tears in his eyes.

"This is my son, Akuectoc." He put his arm around the

little boy. I realized I was this young boy's uncle. I smiled. I'd found my older brother and my own nephew. I'd found family.

"Yier is here in Kapoeta," Aunt Athieng said, "because his second wife was killed two weeks ago in a car accident outside of town."

I didn't know what to say. I just listened as the adults went on talking. I discovered Yier's wife had been pregnant when she was killed and that while Yier mourned for his wife, friends had been caring for his little boy, who was only three years old.

"I heard about the attacks on our village," he said. "But since I've been in the rebel movement, they haven't allowed me to go back to Juol. You're the first I've seen of our family. I don't know what happened to the rest. But I'll take you to Kidepo where I'm a security officer and I live with my family. From there we can search for everyone else. I think some of the boys escaped. I want to bring all of the boys together again."

This gave me real hope. I'd found a brother, an SPLA officer, who was able to search for the rest of the family. I'd be staying in Yier's home. He was an elder who cared about our family and could do something. That sense of loneliness finally left my heart. Things were going to be better. Maybe Akoon, Alepho and Nieu-nieu were in the same situation.

A few days later I said good-bye to Aunt Athieng, and an army truck took Yier, his son and me through the Didinga hills to Kidepo.

Escape Palataka

ALEPHO

Joseph's voice woke me. "We're leaving. Going back to Torit."

"We can't do that in the middle of the night. I haven't told Peter." It was difficult getting to the other groups. I hadn't yet been able to see him.

"We have to get out of here tonight."

We packed our few things quietly in the dark. I felt terrible leaving without letting Peter know. He was always alone and so weak and thin. Joseph was right that he could never make the walk back to Torit. He wouldn't survive. Still, I was deserting my brother and I hadn't even told him.

We snuck out of the building one by one, past the guards who tried to make sure the boys didn't run away. Anyone caught by the guards would be beaten as an example to the other boys.

Ten of us met outside the camp. I was the youngest. We traveled north in the direction of Torit, and came to the deep valley where the path split. Even though I had been in Palataka for a year, I still recalled that area. Back then I'd put in my mind that if I escaped someday I would have to make sure I knew the right way. "I remember these trees," I told them. "This is the way we came in. This is where the paths met. Then we went to Palataka."

Six of the boys said, "No. This other path goes to Torit."

We argued. "Shut up," they told me. "You're just a boy. What do you know about the path?"

I did remember. I remembered the trees. But we took the other way and walked from midnight until dawn.

"What the hell!" they shouted when we found ourselves going back to Palataka.

"That's what I told you."

They began to panic that we were going to get caught and beaten.

"Now," I said, "if I say something, will you listen to me?"

They got angry and said I didn't know anything; they had only wanted a shortcut.

"I don't know any shortcut," I yelled. "I don't even know this place, but I'm going to walk back into Palataka and tell them that nine boys just escaped."

They grabbed me. "If you say anything we'll kill you right now."

"Go ahead and kill me if that will make you happy. But I have been in Torit before."

Joseph pushed them away. "Forget it," he said. "We'll find a way."

We ran into a person from the Acholi tribe and he gave us directions. But Joseph realized this person wasn't directing us well. Joseph said, "Follow me." Two boys went one way and eight of us followed Joseph through long grass with sharp stalks. We had no shoes on and our feet were bleeding. Joseph showed me how to slide my feet as we walked, keeping them on top of the grass. By ten in the morning we reached a little stream between two hills. The water was clean and clear. I drank a lot, but I had no jerry can to carry more. Two of the other boys had jerry cans and I borrowed one saying I'd carry the heavy water. An hour later the boy said, "Give me back my jerry can."

"I have water in it," I said. "I will carry it for both of us and we can share the water."

"No, that is bullshit. I want my jerry can and I don't want your water in there."

So I drank and drank until my stomach was full and poured the rest on my head.

It was summer and here in the far south the sun got extremely hot. As we traveled we started getting very thirsty. When we passed papaya, banana and guava trees, the others picked fruit and ate it. I didn't eat any because once before I'd almost died from eating sweets and then walking with no water. I'd kept that in mind: *If you don't expect to get water, don't eat.* I watched the others having fun eating those fruits but by early afternoon all of them began to get dizzy.

"How come this place is so dark?" they asked. "I can't see anything."

We were in trouble now. Our thirst grew. The boy who had demanded his empty jerry can back from me wasn't saying anything anymore; he just looked sorry. Soon no one was talking. Thirst made me numb and my eyes began to see darkness too. If there was a piece of wood or rock, I would stumble on it.

We rested in the shade of a tree. When our vision cleared a bit, we saw a city on a mountain. "Oh, we've missed it," someone said. "Torit is left behind."

"I don't think it's left behind," Joseph said. "I think it's still ahead. We must cut through that plain."

"I'd rather die walking than cut through there," one boy said and he went his own way. We never saw him again.

We were all so confused. Then I sensed something familiar. "I smell water!"

The other boys listened to me this time and followed my direction. Everybody was too tired, thirsty and hungry to argue. Thirst makes you lazy. We knew that if we sat down to sleep we might not get up again.

Along the path, trees seemed to be moving and dancing and laughing. I was drawn to their shadow and rested a few minutes. My mind imagined different things. People came to me but I wasn't sure if they were real. "Let's go," they said. "Why are you lying on the ground? Come with us. You have almost reached the water. If you remain here, you will remain here forever."

I closed my eyes a while longer. Then I told myself I must get up to survive. When I was on my feet, I found nobody, just their footprints. Down the road I found the others resting too, and we moved on together. After another hour of struggling, we reached the river I'd smelled earlier. I left my blanket on the sand and threw myself into the water, relaxing for a while to cool my body before drinking. The current flowed across my skin, tickling me like a gentle breeze. I made my mouth like a cow and let the water go in across my tongue and down my throat, not minding the dirt. They say you can go without food for seven days, but when it is hot you can die of thirst in only one. At that moment I knew I'd never been closer to dying than I was under that tree. My body almost had not risen again; my mind barely knew I was there. Even though I knew with certainty

Peter could not have survived this, it didn't take away the heavy pain I felt for leaving him behind.

After we drank our fill from the river, oh, hunger overtook us then, but it was almost dark and there was nothing to eat. Only the chance that we might be eaten. Everywhere in the sand, footprints of hyenas and lions reminded us of who came to the riverbank to drink. We walked a little bit farther and found a safer place to sleep.

The next day we walked until late afternoon. To avoid a roadblock outside of Torit town, we left the main road and crossed a little bridge that led into an open air marketplace under tall African mango trees. Joseph, his cousin Santino and I were so hungry we tried to sell our only possessions, two bowls we'd brought from Palataka, for ten pounds. We walked around for a while, nearly faint with hunger, but no one bought them. So we cut the price back to seven pounds. They were pretty good aluminum bowls. A boy came by, wanting to buy them. He stared at us and said, "Oh my God, how did you make it here?"

His name was Anyar and he had escaped Palataka earlier. We couldn't even smile at him. When you are hungry you can barely think.

He bought us food. The three of us ate. It helped, although it also increased the hunger for me. Anyar told us he lived in a place called Kilieu, a small town, an outpost one hour's walk from Torit. There he'd started a small-scale business for himself.

After Anyar helped us sell the largest bowl for fifteen pounds and the small one for seven, we bought some beans. Santino and I collected firewood. It wasn't easy. The land mines were still out there from 1989. Even though they were rusty from rain, if you stepped on one it could still blow. Sometimes they exploded from wild animals.

We were eager to get to the post office to look for Yier. He was a grown man and a soldier. He was my brother. He'd know how to get Peter from Palataka and he'd help us get back home. We found the post office but they had no information on Yier. They told Joseph, "Keep checking back. Many people are looking for lost family members."

Anyar took us to meet his Uncle Madieu, who lived in Torit town at his first wife's house. Madieu was in the rebel army and had lost his left hand in combat. We brought our firewood and his first wife helped us cook the beans. They were such hard, tiny beans it took four hours to get them tender. She also cooked kesra, a paper-thin African bread. That was the best meal we'd had in a long time and afterward we were shouting and smiling.

Three days later, the beans were gone. We couldn't just stay in her home eating from the small amount her husband brought home, but we didn't have any way of earning money or finding food. Madieu had two wives and the second wife had a newborn baby. Madieu asked if I would watch the baby at his other house for food and a place to stay.

"What about Joseph and Santino?" I asked.

"They can stay here."

Madieu seemed like a good guy so I agreed to do that and he took me to Hambia, a town beside a military base. There I met a friend of Madieu's named Dhieu, and he became my friend too. He talked to me and told me many stories about what he'd encountered in the war and how many people he had killed. He was very proud saying such things.

One day I told him, "When I grow up, I want to be like you."

"Like me?" He smiled. "Nobody knows when this war is going to end so from this moment on when I call you son, you will accept it."

I was surprised. "No," I said, "I'm not your son. You can't call me son."

Dhieu got a serious expression. "Something came to me when I was sleeping, more real than a dream or a nightmare. My final day on this earth was shown to me by a person who came from nowhere and was just standing there. The person said, 'You have killed many people in the combat and it is not your fault that you made that mistake. But the sooner you can get a wife so that you can leave a son, the better you will survive.'"

Dhieu shook his head. "It isn't easy to get a wife in combat. There are no steady wives when the whole nation is messed up with war. A man who protects his wife, when he goes to fight, leaves her alone desperate. She goes to the next man and the next man. That is war."

I felt sad for Dhieu, but I wouldn't agree to be his son.

Madieu was not around most of the time and every day the wife went out and left the baby with me. She said she was going to make business. The baby had nothing to drink and cried all day. I was hungry too. I had a place to sleep, but no food. Sometimes she came back with men and slept with them in the house. One evening she called me into the house and undressed in front of me.

"Touch me here," she said.

I was scared.

"Come on."

"No! I can't do that." I cried and tried to move away.

"Come here. If you don't do it I'm going to beat you."

That made me angry. "Okay, beat me. If you try to tell me again, I'm going to tell your husband."

She became scared.

"Please don't tell my husband. He'll beat me up. He's not a good guy."

"I don't want to hear that," I told her. "It's not my business. I know what you're doing is not good to me. To me, you look like a mother. There's no way I can touch you. I don't understand."

She stopped bothering me. When Madieu came back, she was terrified that I would tell, but I kept quiet.

Then Madieu was ordered far away, and Joseph, Santino and I moved back again to Torit. Joseph devoted himself to finding food for us younger ones.

A few weeks later we returned to the post office and found out that Yier was in Kidepo, a town fifty miles south of Torit toward the Kenyan border. We worked hard to save money for food and a car ride, eager to get to Kidepo before he left. Joseph would go out early every morning to pick mangoes for us to sell in town. Then suddenly Joseph disappeared. First we searched everywhere in Torit. Then we went outside town and to the mango trees. Joseph was nowhere. We thought he'd left us. Maybe to find Yier. Santino and I kept searching and picking mangoes, but we were lost without Joseph.

I found Joseph eventually in the hospital. I had to go there because my eyes were bad again, infected and swollen so that I could hardly see. Joseph was so thin he couldn't even talk. He'd fallen from a mango tree and had almost died. Someone had taken him to the hospital. I felt so bad when he told me what had happened. I received medicine to put in my eyes. The next day they were feeling better but were as red as fire.

We went back to picking and selling the mangos as soon as we could, and when we had enough money we rushed to the roadblock around Torit. Any car or person going in or out was checked. Many people—women, children and men—had been waiting there for days.

The soldiers asked Joseph, "How old are you?"

"Eleven," he said.

"You're a kid. We can't give you a written document to travel to any other place."

We had to wait a whole week more. The money we set aside to buy food was nearly gone. Joseph was thin but very tall for his age. He decided to go back to Torit and say he was eighteen and ask for a traveling document. He wasn't sure it would help us get through, but it would get him to Kidepo safely and keep him from being taken into the rebel army on the way. We all hoped that he could find Yier. Yier would know what to do.

Right after Joseph left, a truck driver offered to take Santino and me through the roadblock and on to Kidepo. We didn't want to leave Joseph, but the people there said they would tell him when he got back and he could come later. We gave the driver the rest of our money and climbed onto the back of that flatbed truck. We were going to Kidepo! It was less than a hundred miles away. We were finally going to find Yier!

Boya Coconuts

BENSON

My *nephew, Akuectoc,* the little boy I had met in Kapoeta, was Yier's son by his first wife, Ayen. At Kidepo they all lived together in the three huts of his compound. Yier also looked after three other boys who were his in-laws. He was trying to save as many of us as he could.

I could see that he was sad about his second wife, who had died, but was happy to have us all together. A few evenings after I arrived, he called us to sit around him and, as is our tradition, began to talk as the eldest person. We were happy to have this guidance from an elder, one from our family we could trust to care about us.

"I heard about the attacks in the village," he said. "And I am so very happy that you are alive and we have met again. As a freedom fighter, I put your safety as first priority. War has destroyed a lot and I want you boys to stay strong and be the future of Sudan. It is important that you know the history of your country and this conflict.

"When you were just little boys in the village, too young to understand, I survived the 1985 slaughter of the black students in Wau. All of us at the university had been told that if we wanted to continue our education we must convert to be Muslims. Many students paraded in the city to speak for their rights as Sudanese, but special police forces intervened.

"The Arab students were separated from us and taken to their dorms. The black students were arrested and charged with causing turmoil and disobeying the Islamic laws. Some were lined up, made to kneel by the riverbank, and executed. Their heads were cut off with a machete and thrown in the river.

"We were led to the dorms and questioned. 'Do you know the leader of the rebels, John Garang?' 'Do you want to join them?' The students who resisted with loud voices were tied together, sprinkled with paraffin and burned alive.

"They locked the rest of us in the dorm. I was with many friends that I haven't seen again. We heard noises outside and saw they were preparing to burn down the whole dorm. We broke a window and ran, but a squad of troops was guarding the building. They fired; only three of us made it to the woods, leaving behind our moaning, injured friends. We reached the river, where another squad put a searchlight on us. We entered the cold water with silent steps and followed the current until the flame-lit sky and screams disappeared.

"The next day the government officials reported that either the black students had committed suicide or another student had committed arson. I joined the rebel movement and I fight for the freedom of all. I've survived during this guerrilla warfare by remembering my friends who were burned in the dorm. You are too young to get involved in this, but you boys are also the survivors of a killing. Stay strong. The SPLA will speak for you with a gun's barrel. You will be heard and the end will be peaceful for you."

I remembered the adults in the village talking about problems at the university, but they kept the details from us. I was saddened by Yier's stories, but it made me proud that Yier was doing well in the rebel movement and that he was a security captain already.

Soon afterward, Benjamin came by truck from Lokichokio with his wound half cured. I was so happy to see him alive and with his leg still on his body. Two weeks later, Emmanuel arrived too, having traveled from Buma with his teacher. Yier had now gathered seven of us boys in Kidepo.

We felt safe and happy to be together again, even though food was so scarce that we depended on coconut palms. Every morning we went to the coconut plantation to collect the fruit. We didn't climb the trees, only collected fruits from the ground because the local tribesmen, cattle rustlers with lots of rifles, were very dangerous. One morning on our daily chores at the plantation two men came running toward us very fast with their tongues sticking out. Within a moment we heard a gun firing. We all ran too, so fast the soles of our bare feet showed very close to our buttocks. The tribesman shot at all of us, but luckily no one got hurt. But the day that began ugly soon turned joyful.

Yier

ALEPHO

Santino and I arrived in Kidepo around noon. There were so many huts we didn't know which one belonged to Yier. We asked people if they knew Yier Deng. A lady told us to go to where they fix old cars. "You'll find him there."

We wandered around and asked another guy, "Do you know where Yier Deng is?"

A man in uniform pants, boots and a plain shirt was standing by the side of the road. The guy said, "That's him."

We didn't know whether to believe it. The man he pointed to might have just been a soldier who would give us trouble. I'd only seen Yier once in the village when I was very young and briefly two years ago in Thiet. Santino had never seen him at all.

We walked slowly toward him and I greeted him: "Hello, hello."

He didn't know who we were and started to walk away. We followed him. He stopped and talked to a guard in Arabic. Did my brother speak Arabic? Then he took off again but we followed. When he came to a gate, he stopped. "Why are you following me? Are you boys hungry?"

"You are Yier?"

"Yes."

"I am your brother."

I kept quiet looking at him.

He called into the house. "Hey, boys, come outside."

Many boys came out of the house. Yier asked them, "Do you recognize these little boys?"

I saw Emmanuel because his lip was a little red. Some of the others didn't look familiar, but one boy came forward who was a little taller than me and I felt that magnetic thing that only true relatives have, but I was afraid to believe it could be true.

Joyous Day in Kidepo

BENSON

Feeling lucky to be alive after being shot at in the coconut plantation, we were practicing our church songs from the hymnal in the afternoon when Yier came inside the hut.

"Boys," he called to us. "Come outside and see who these boys are."

The five of us went outside. Two boys were standing with Yier. "Do you recognize these little boys?"

At first I thought they were friends from the Panyido refugee camp in Ethiopia. Then my heart began pounding deeply and I knew at once this was my younger brother, Alepho, whom I'd left back home five years earlier. He was ten years old now and nearly as tall as me. He knew me too. We hugged each other in tears. Seeing my own brother again was the greatest moment of joy in my life.

Our cousin Santino was with him. They told us how they had escaped from Palataka camp together and made their way to Kidepo. Alepho told Yier how they'd been forced to leave Peter in Palataka and had been separated from Joseph on their way to Kidepo. But when Joseph arrived from Torit several days later, we laughed and talked for a week. Alepho gave me the sad news that our father had been killed a year after I left. It didn't surprise me. He also shared his fears for our mother, sisters and brothers. But the sad news could not overwhelm my joy that, after five years of not knowing whether any of my family members had survived the war, at last I was together with my brothers and cousins. After wandering for so long, I finally had a home and family. The war that had flung us to the wind had set us back down together.

Play Dead

ALEPHO

That Benson was alive after five years was like a miracle. But our happiness was short-lived. Only a few days later three soldiers came home with Yier. He went into his hut, came out carrying his blanket, said good-bye to his wife and left with the soldiers. She didn't know where they'd taken him and became so worried she grew sick.

For three months we did the best we could in Kidepo—at least we were with each other. Then one day, we heard heavy bombing coming from the north. It lasted three days non-stop. The government was attacking Kapoeta, fifty miles away. On the fourth day the survivors of the Kapoeta attack arrived hungry, thirsty and weak. There were so many. They came with broken legs, arms and even dead children on the backs of the women. It was unimaginable. I almost choked.

When we asked the survivors what happened, they couldn't even talk. They didn't want to stop in Kidepo, saying it wasn't safe, and headed to Torit because the SPLA controlled the town.

We all asked the chief what we should do. He made a short speech and said everybody in Kidepo had to evacuate right away. One group decided to go directly north toward Torit. The rest, about twenty thousand of us, thought that it was too dangerous to follow the main road and decided to take a path over the mountains to reach Torit. A few rebel soldiers would walk with us, but it was too huge a group for them to protect.

They had just begun distributing three cups of maize and two cups of beans for each person to eat on the way, and we were preparing to leave when a bomb fell nearby. I couldn't see anything. Everywhere was cloudy with dust.

A man shouted, "Lie down. That is how to survive."

I threw myself down, afraid that I would be killed.

When the cloud of dust cleared, dead people lay everywhere. People started to run in panic, not knowing where to go. We ran up into the Lotuko hills and into the arms of hell. Shooting started in front of us while bombs exploded behind us. We were in an ambush. I was helplessly confused. I stood motionless and couldn't remember a single prayer to save my life. I felt cold and began to shake. Everyone around me was lying down. There were so many that died. Everyone scattered into the grass as more bombs fell and explosions thundered. Those who had received their ration threw it all away and ran barehanded, carrying nothing, fleeing for their lives.

With shooting from every side, I chose to crouch in the grass with the women. Once the shooting stopped soldiers came toward us, checking, searching, looking for the living. There were so many people who had been killed, I made myself like a dead person, so they couldn't recognize me. One of the soldiers pushed me with his boot, turning me over. I didn't breathe. He would have killed me.

Once the soldiers left, I got up and ran. I ran, I ran, I ran. I didn't know where Benson or the others had gone. A few hours earlier we had all been together and now we were separated again. I didn't even know if they were alive. Shaking and trembling, I reached some survivors huddling in a circle. Fear and panic had built inside me like a small earthquake. The survivors counted themselves: there were so few of us left. Everywhere women were crying, children were crying, everyone crying, crying. In the midst of all that, a blinded child stumbled on a mine. People died like that. Blown to pieces.

The elder advised us that we were going to move on. "There will be no talking, no noise whatever. Do not shout, do not cry, do not to say, 'I'm hungry, I'm thirsty.'"

We settled our fear and tried to become like bulls mowing the grass. I was lucky; God had saved me. The people who had been killed were not soldiers but desperate women, good children, young boys like us. I saw all of that as a ten-year-old boy. When I left that place I was like a sleepwalker. Really, really confused. It was a desperate, unforgettable day.

Walk with Swollen Foot

BENSON

It would be difficult to understand how we could allow ourselves to be separated from each other again unless you have traveled in a crowd of twenty thousand exhausted, starving people fleeing a bombing. It is impossible to stay in a group. We could only hope we would all meet up again when we rested or reached our destination.

After our reunion and short spell of peace were shattered, I ended up alone without any of my family in the middle of a long line of people running for their lives. At the whistle of a rocket, then thunder, everything would turn to chaos. I spent that night with people I didn't know and it wasn't until the next day that I found Alepho, Benjamin, Emmanuel and Joseph. But we had nothing between us. Of the thousands of people on the move, only a few hundred had escaped with baggage and food.

The large group split and we made it to Lokupar, about thirty miles south of Kidepo, nearly on the border. We'd been told food would arrive from nearby Uganda. There was nothing to build houses from so we made shelters with grass bundles, but it rained there without stopping and the water soaked our bedding. The food did not arrive. We had to live on a fruit that looked like papaya but was bitter.

After two months, with no sign or hope of food from Uganda, all of us starved into sticks, we were advised to move on to Torit, nearly a hundred miles away over difficult terrain. We knew the walk would be exhausting with everyone weak from chronic hunger but we had no choice. Our only chance for something to eat along the way lay up on Imatong mountain at a mission rumored to have food and mango trees. But when we reached the mission, we found another group had consumed the last of the biscuits and stripped the trees of fruit. We left hurriedly to try to reach Torit before we dropped.

When we arrived the next day, I was so weak that darkness clouded my eyes. I tried to keep walking but I collapsed. I retched, but nothing came from my stomach. I could only lie there and shiver.

Alepho saw that I was in a desperate way and could not keep myself from starving to death. He had been to Torit twice before and knew the town. He found a small bit of porridge and brought it to me. I ate a little and began to sweat. I stayed on the roadside in a blanket for many hours, ashamed at being the first one to grow weak.

When my strength returned that afternoon, we walked through town looking for other friends. The town was very green with grasses, mango and papaya trees. The one-story houses had red brick walls decorated by white horizontal lines. We passed through the market but had no money to buy food. Down on the bank of the river, between long rows of mango trees, people had spread their mats in the shade and were selling things. We were weak with hunger and sat at the edge of a wide hole the size of a mud hut. A soldier came up to us. "See that hole. The Antonov bombed this market

and thirty-three people were killed during the blast. Ugh!"
He paused and shook his head. "That day nobody would have
considered going back again to look for food in this market.
The blast mixed bits of human flesh into the cooked food.
These are bad things for you to hear, but you must know this
is the consequence of war. A bomb made that hole and there
may be metal still stuck in the ground. Don't sit in that
hole." He walked away swatting at the flies bothering his eyes.

We left the edge of the hole and walked back to town. I was
exhausted and sick of Torit town. All we wanted was a place
to sleep for the night. However, food and a place to sleep
were not to be found in Torit. The elders told us that some
men and women, highly trained by the government to dis-
guise themselves among us, were planting land mines at
night in the crowded public places and by the doors of
homes and buildings. "Careful," they warned. "The victims
are always young people like you."

By the time the sun was in the west, Torit was wild. Government troops attacked with high-tech long-range wea-
ponry and air raids. Nowhere felt safe. A soldier in a jeep
with a microphone ordered evacuation. We'd risked our
lives to get to Torit but within a day of our arrival we were
being driven out—still without food. And without hope.

We fled, leaving the rebels to wait for the battle ahead.
Our bare feet remembered the misery of our previous flight
for survival. Without a moon to shine on our way, we
trudged through the dark, cold night. As it was the rainy
season, the ground was wet and muddy. No one slept until
daybreak, when the sun revealed a beautiful greenish jungle
and the flowers produced a dizzying aroma.

Many of the mud holes had been filled with logs used by

the SPLA to help their convoys across. The wood had embedded nails. We tried to be careful but as I plunged through a puddle of muddy water, my right ankle hit a sharp object. I cried out in pain. As I pulled my foot out of the puddle, my ankle left a trail of blood. I had to ignore the pain and keep walking because I didn't want to fall behind again. Artillery roared at our backs and I didn't want to lose touch with my family. But by the end of the day I was barely able to continue. I spent the night on the verandah of the rebel army's food and ammunitions store with some companions. The next morning when I awoke, my right foot was swollen to the size of my head. I couldn't walk.

A friend begged the captains of the three vehicles that carried the commanders' wives and children to let me ride with them. Their bodyguards, whips in hand, all refused to let me on. Finally, the last vehicle, an orange truck with forty women and children, lots of luggage, and no spare space, accepted me. I sat at the back, alone again, my bag on my lap, sweating with the pain in my foot.

After a four-hour rocky ride, we arrived in a town where I could ask around for my family. I found out that the group with Alepho, Benjamin, Joseph and Yier's wife had gone in a different direction toward Pageri. We were separated once again. Later I would find a way back to my family, but that night most of all I needed food and shelter from the rain. I went into a church building because it was a dry place to sleep in. It was crowded but I found a space on the floor between seats. I left my bag and a piece of plastic I used to spread on the ground and went outside to ask for some food to eat. Unsuccessful, I limped back to the building, too tired to search further, and found my bag and the plastic gone. Tired and hungry in wet rags, I curled my body between the seats.

In the morning, a crowd was still coming from the Torit area, where the fighting between the rebels and the government army was fierce. Looking for food, I hobbled from one group to another asking for a handful of wheat grains. Anything to cook and refuel myself. Everybody I asked for a little bit of food said, "Don't ask here. Go to your tribe."

Since no one showed sympathy, I decided on another plan and sat down near where the grain bags were distributed. The ground was clean from rain and no one had yet stepped on the grains. I picked up those scattered grains and had just enough in my hand to fill a small spoon when a man nearby said, "You pick on the ground? What is wrong with you?"

Not waiting for my answer, he kicked my hand, scattering my grain all over again. My fingers felt dislocated and I grabbed at them with my other hand. A grain he'd kicked flew right into the eyelid of his friend and his eye started watering. I was limping away, trying to get out of that place, when the other man with a grain in his eye broke a stick from a nearby tree. As he came after me, I heard women shouting, "Run, son, run!"

I looked over my shoulder at him coming toward me with quick long strides, waving the stick. I wanted to run, but my foot refused. When he reached me he gave a good whip blow to my shoulder, breaking the stick with a sickening noise. He shouted, "Go back where you came from, stupid greedy one!"

By now I didn't know where I came from, much less where I was going. Nobody asked me what was wrong with my foot. Nobody! They surrounded the food like mongoose waiting for termites to leave their mound. Never in my lifetime had I come across such ignorant people. The pain left my thin body shivering and sweating. I sat down in the shade regretting every move I had made, thinking only of my parents and the homeland I'd lost five years earlier. Back in Juol, anyone who knew my father's name would treat me with respect. On my own, people insulted me, kicked my hand and whipped me. I was nobody.

A young lady passed by to see if she could recognize anyone from the new arrivals and saw me weeping from the thoughts raving in my head. She stopped and talked to me. Her heart was glowing, but in my misery I could not bring myself to speak to anyone, male or female. She stared at me in puzzlement and then asked, "Will you come with me to my home? I'll take care of you until your wound is gone."

"No," I said. That was all I said. She might have been talking to a tree.

"You must come so I can care for you."

I gave no response nor was I listening to what she said. My body was there but my mind had wandered beyond.

She stretched out her hand.

"Don't touch me! Leave me alone!"

Her offer added to my pain. I could tell that she was a very kind person, even though she was from the same folks who treated me like an animal. I knew she felt sorry about me when I saw she was choked with tears as she looked back, wondering if I might change my mind. Still, I hated everyone: for stealing my bag, refusing me food and beating me.

When night came and it began to drizzle, even though I had no jacket, blanket or sheet to keep me dry or warm, I refused to ask anybody for anything. *Let me die of hunger. They can be stuck burying me.*

Good Samaritan

ALEPHO

I hadn't eaten in three days and had become separated from my friends one by one on the walk. When we stopped to sleep, I went into the bushes to look for food. I saw a couple of mangoes up in a tree but I was too weak to try to climb up to them. My arms wouldn't pull my body up; my legs barely let me stand.

I went back to the group and lay down. There was no way I could get food. My mind could not think of anything except that I was going to die this time.

A man nearby with long legs and dark boots looked at me. He had an honest face and his look told me that he realized I must be starving. His wife was cooking a small amount of grain. When his wife brought the food to him, there was only one spoon. He said, "Bring another spoon."

"This is too small," his wife said. "There is no way you can share it with that boy."

My mind was not working well while they were arguing. Their angry words seemed like a dream. I was unconscious until I heard the man say, "If that kid dies, you will be responsible because it won't change my life to share this little thing."

I opened my eyes. The wife threw her things down and walked away.

The man said, "Share this with me."

After only a few bites, I felt good. I just looked at him. What could I say? I couldn't even say thank-you. I was alive again. He'd saved my life.

Hunger makes you different. It changes you. Like the cow that sees grain on the ground and walks in without being invited and eats it. It makes you like an animal.

War had ruined a lot of things. I had become convinced that people were not good; people were bad. Sometimes I try to remember the man who shared his small meal. That incident made me think differently about people.

The Thief

BENSON

The churches had become shelters for desperate people. I found one near the ration distribution station that was less crowded and sat next to two women. One was Sudanese and the other Ethiopian and pregnant. They were both wives of an army lorry driver. I found an empty maize sack in a corner with a few grains still in it. I wanted to eat the grains but there was nothing to cook them in.

Outside I found fire sticks and came upon an artillery bombshell lying in the grass against the church wall. I boiled water in it, then washed it with more hot water and used it to prepare my first meal in three days. Cooked, the grain was enough to fill one of my hands. I chewed them lying on my back staring at the ceiling of the church. It was getting darker and colder so I went outside to find a fire to warm myself up before sleeping on the dirty, itchy maize sack.

When I was warm and dry, I headed back in to try my sleep. The pregnant Ethiopian lady saw me and pointed her finger. "There is the thief!"

"Who are you calling a thief?" I asked.

"You stole my oil and now are coming back for more. Stupid you! This is your bad luck! If you don't give it back to me right now, I will kill you!"

I was so surprised that for a minute I didn't know what to tell her. I thought of my own lost bag.

"I am a victim of a thief too," I told her. "My bag was stolen and I have been cold without a blanket or sheet."

From the expressions on the faces of the other people around the church, I could see that because of how I looked they also thought I was a thief. Then a boy several years older than me said, "A thief would not come back to where he steals." I was so thankful for his words in my defense.

"You are wrong," the woman argued. "I have been watching him all this evening. I felt something was not right. At the moment my oil was gone I doubted nobody else. He is a thief. He is lying and a foolish thief to come back here."

I listened to them argue over me without the energy to say more than, "I have to sit down for my foot is hurting from standing a long time."

"You must stand!" the woman shouted. "I do not care whether your foot hurts. All I care about is where is my oil. Then I will let you go."

I remained standing, as she had commanded me to. "I don't know anything about oil," I said. "I had nothing to do with your oil!"

"Shut up! I will punch you in your dirty mouth! All I need is the direction to where you hid my oil."

My foot was burning. I felt nauseous and ready to collapse. I sat down on the muddy ground, bitterly confused by all the unsolvable problems.

"Yea!" she shouted. "So this is how thieves pretend? I will teach you a lesson for stealing from me."

She kicked out at me and I toppled backward like a twig. The kick did not hurt but it broke the surface of the wound on my leg, which began to bleed. Pain spread all over my body, covering my skin with sweat. I held my foot with both hands and moaned.

The Sudanese lady leaned over me with a torch exposing the blood on my hands and the ground. "Look at his foot. You hurt him."

"Yeah! Well, he is a thief stealing people's properties."

She did not know how I hated being called a thief. It hurt as much as my foot!

The Sudanese said to the Ethiopian woman. "You have a baby in your stomach now. How would you feel if your child got into such a condition? At this time of war, it is not good to mistreat anybody. Especially the young people who are without parents. Can't you just forget that tiny tin of oil and forgive him?"

The Ethiopian lady stepped back. "I have not forgiven him yet. Tomorrow I will take him to the army police."

"Will you sleep here?" the Sudanese lady asked, inviting me.

I wanted to leave all of them, but where would I go? "I have no place except the shelter of this church building. My family went to Pageri on foot. I was dropped here by a vehicle because I had a wound that did not allow me to walk."

"Where do you get food?"

"Somebody left behind an empty sack with a few grains inside. I cooked my meal just a half hour ago in a bombshell I found at the back of the church building."

"*Bombshell!*" Where is it?"

"It is inside the building."

"You could kill yourself. These things are poisonous. You sit here and wait for me."

When she returned, she boiled water and washed and cleaned my wound. She gave me some food and asked her brother to let me use one of his bedsheets for the night. I slept well that night, for my foot felt much better after it had been cleaned.

In the morning the Ethiopian lady was still after me about the oil. She took me to the army police station. I had never been to a court before but I knew that if they said I was guilty I would be jailed, beaten, and made to work everyday. I feared that I could not defend myself because the woman could easily defeat me with her words. We waited for a half hour but it seemed like all day. No one spoke to us. Eventually they sent us away with instructions to come back in the evening.

On our walk back to the church, she asked me about my family and how I came to be there. I told her my story. At the end of my explanation, to my surprise, she apologized for misunderstanding me. When she threw her arm across my shoulder to show how sorry she felt, she touched the whip wound on my back. I jerked away.

"What is wrong?"

"A man whipped me." She rolled her eyes like maybe it was another injury from a theft. I turned my back to let her see the wound. "I was trying to pick grain from the ground."

"We'll go look for the man that whipped you and take him to the police."

I was beginning to see that this woman was good at taking people to the police station. "I don't want to do that," I said.

"We can find him," she said seriously.

I looked down. "He might have mistaken me for a thief the same way you did."

Her voice quivered with shame, and she said sorry countless more times.

When we returned to the church, she treated me with as much respect as a family member. She said I could wait for her husband, who was a driver, to come and he might give me a ride to Pageri.

I ended up staying with her for a week. Every morning she gave me money and sent me to buy meat for the family lunch. When her husband returned, he offered to take me to Pageri. Although she urged me to stay with her, I told her that I was going to leave, to try to rejoin my brothers.

Holding the bombshell in case I couldn't find any family members in Pageri and needed it again for cooking, I climbed onto the truck and waved good-bye as she stood in the middle of the road watching the truck blowing clouds of dust.

Radio News

BENSON

I arrived in Pageri with my face painted orange from dust on the road. When the lorry stopped at an army station, everyone went different directions and I found myself alone. It was quiet and calm. Against the beautiful open sky I could see the blue and foggy hills near the city of Juba close to the Ugandan border. Pageri was ringed by green trees with white bark. A few thatched huts stretched their necks above the tall yellow grass.

Around the army station, the earth was clean and bare. Inside the wire fence compound there were two small huts and a big iron-roofed red-brick building. Smoke wafted out of the chimney of the big building and up into the evening sky. A green jeep sat under a tree with two long-barrel machine guns. A fat soldier, hunchbacked like an RPG bomb, sat on a wooden ammunition box smoking a cigarette. When he belched loudly, a puff of smoke came out. I wondered if I could go near the fence to ask him where to go but there was a line made by sprayed ash on the ground that read Stop. Do Not Cross! The soldier looked tired and I was afraid he might not help. I was also frightened by the way the jeep stared. Its eyes didn't even blink. I'd heard that when the jeeps went into battle they saw people with their eyes and chased them while shooting. I took a few steps to the side, but the jeep never moved its glaring stare from me.

Just then I heard laughing and chatting and two men came out of the grass. One of them was tall, with light skin like an Arab and a beard covering his chin. He was wearing a bright red shirt with white dots and blue trousers. The other man was short with a mustache. His white shirt had pictures of giraffe, elephant, hippo, rhino and lion and read BIG FIVE, AFRICA. MADE IN UGANDA 1992. He held a radio with a brown cover to his chest. I recognized that short man. His name was Thiik; he was a distant cousin. I was so relieved to see someone I knew, thinking it might save me from having another bad first night in town trying to find my family.

I interrupted their merry laughing. "Hello, Thiik."

They both turned and looked at me holding the bomb-shell under my left armpit.

Thiik smiled. "Hey! Is that you, Benson?"

He even remembered my name!

The tall man said, "Is this the missing boy from Yier's family?"

"Yes, he is the boy who disappeared. His four friends were searching for him just this morning."

"Welcome," said the tall man. "I am Riiny, half brother to Thiik. It's good that you came, everyone was worried about your whereabouts."

"Your friends live a forty-minute walk from here," Thiik said. "Come to my house first."

Thiik's wife, Abuk, was cooking a nice warm dinner.

"Congratulations!" she said when she saw me. "You came at last. We were worried about you."

I began to feel that Pageri would not be such a bad place, even though I hadn't yet found my brothers. Abuk served me a warm, delicious meat soup with okra and lulu oil. After dinner Thiik switched on the radio. "Let's listen to the *jallaba* news in Khartoum."

We called the Arabs *jallaba*, and they called us *abeed*.

Drumbeats and noisy singing came from the radio. A man shouted in Arabic, and then the crowd sang in unison repeating his words. "Allah Wubhaar! Allah Wubhaar!" I didn't know what Wubhaar was or what misery it could bring.

"That's President Bashir," Thiik said, translating for me. "He's shouting to seven thousand new recruits ready to leave Khartoum to come and fight against the south."

Riiny waved his hand. "Oh, let them come to paradise. They'll face hell. The southern problem cannot be solved in the six months they say."

I didn't like hearing this news that so many government troops were coming south. Riiny had fought in the SPLA for many years so he knew how to fight, but still I didn't believe our rebels could defend us against a government who came armed with Antonovs, tanks, and Kalashnikovs. Even though I didn't know exactly what a thousand was and I didn't know how many troops made up the SPLA forces, seven thousand sounded like giant multitudes to me.

"Four months ago," said Thiik, "we scattered four thousand of them at English Valley. One of the soldiers we captured was a student, hardly more than a boy. The government had told him he'd be home in two months as soon as the rebellion in the south was crushed. They'd also told him that we rebels were barefoot and so starved we lived off the roots of plants with ten of us sharing one rifle.

"The government soldiers were all just students who don't know that *jallaba* gambles with their lives. Now *jallaba* government is happy because they've captured Torit town again, but it took two months of heavy fighting in the English valley with SPLA bullets spilling the *jallaba* blood." Thiik laughed. "They were cowards! The *jallaba* troops couldn't do anything until they hired Iraqi troops."

My ears were open to all the news Thiik and Riiny were giving but it was shrouding me in fear. Tomorrow I'd join my brothers, but it was obvious that we couldn't stay here long without the war finding us again. I wondered what kind of land was this country called Sudan where men were dropping bombs from the sky to kill their own countrymen. Where the men on the land wheeled weapons and shouted up into the sky at the plane that dropped bombs on them. Where rebel soldiers wore uniforms stained with blood and bullet holes, pulled off the corpses of dead government troops.

On the radio the president shouted, "The *abeed* stinks and goes naked! Dinka are the disobedient rebel tribe and criminal to the Arabs. Go! Go! Go to the south and find them in grass and bush rotting with hunger. Crush the Dinkas! Let them run for days and nights. Next year, all of Sudan will be smelly with the Dinka children born and rotting in jailhouses. Bring the Dinkas to jail. If they disobey, the barrels of tanks and Antonov can escort them here."

Thiik and Abuk made me a comfortable bed in the corner of their house but my mind ran like a cheetah with all the news of multitudes of troops coming to the south. We'd been scattered like leaves growing browner and thinner, never to put roots into the soil again. Where could we go next?

I just wanted to go home. I wanted to find my mother and brothers and sisters still in Sudan. I wanted the wars to come to an end. But all the radio said was that the war against the Dinka was just beginning.

———

At first light I hobbled outside just as Benjamin and Emmanuel came down the dark grassy road joking excitedly. It hadn't been long, but I was so happy to see them again.

"Where is your bag?" Benjamin asked.

"It was stolen."

"We're going to Ashwa. The well in Pageri is going dry and Ashwa has a river. The UN is bringing rations."

Everyone without a swollen foot transported all they needed. My brothers and squad of cousins took care of me, equipping me again, and Alepho carried my few things with him. Ayen was still missing Yier and sick with that feeling, so I kept up with her slow walking.

In Ashwa we joined the gathering crowds fleeing the fighting in Torit and Kapoeta. The camp grew larger and crowded with grass houses. We built a big one for us and a small one for Ayen and her son and baby.

One day white people came in many small cars from Uganda to see the camp. We gathered in the open field where the food distribution always took place to welcome them and followed them around.

A woman asked me, "Do you speak English?"

"Small English."

She showed a map. "We are from America. Do you know where America is?"

Emmanuel told her. "Yes, America is where the sun sets."

"Good, good boy," she said, which sounded like goot, goot, and means bitter and itchy in Dinka dialect.

She carried a small picture and the back was blue with white stars like I'd seen on the oil tins called USA. "This is our new president, Bill Clinton. He is a good president. He sent us to see you."

When they left we all followed Emmanuel around and laughed, "Goot, goot boy." We had a fine day trying our best English with the Americans.

Soon after, huge trucks called Transit Good came from Uganda with more grain and we were thankful to the American visitors with their good president, Bill Clinton. At the distribution field, I found a pack of cigarettes in the bags of corn and took it home. When others smoked near me, I liked the smell but I didn't want to admit that I wanted to try smoking. People said, "If a smoker comes to your house and you serve food, water and tobacco, the smoker will choose the tobacco first even if he is thirsty or hungry." I smoked that whole pack in a week trying to find out why people who smoke had to suffer so much when they couldn't find cigarettes. Emmanuel laughed at me, "Hee, hee, where will you get money to buy tobaccos?" But I decided smokers were foolish anyway. There was nothing delicious or tasty, just puffing and coughing.

In Ashwa we went to visit an uncle who was a watchman for an old library and an army ammunition store. He told us that although some soldiers had broken into the library and taken most of the books there were still a few left, but that the headmaster who had the keys had gone to Uganda.

That night we found two long poles, tied them together

and climbed the library wall. Between the wall and the roof there was a space where we squeezed inside. Books of all kinds were scattered on the floor. We lit a torch and saw that termites had tortured some but we filled boxes with the books.

Books were rare and valuable. We sold them to other children who wanted to read. When people asked where we got them, we said, "Our uncle went to Uganda and bought them."

Ayen received word that Yier might be returning soon from Juba. Life became more comfortable than it had been in a long while until Alepho shook me awake one night. "Get up! Get up!" Drums began beating fiercely to awaken the sleeping people. As we ran outside an Antonov roared overhead and we rushed to find holes. We counted twelve bombs beating thunderously on the ground. People came out of their hiding places and expected to find terrible casualties under the bomb's thick smoke. We found the twelve huge holes in a line outside Ashwa. The Antonov had seen the mission church building with its white cross on top but the bombs had been carried away by wind.

When we went to church the next Sunday, the preacher said, "God has shown us his wondrous power in protecting the Church from being destroyed." After the mass we collected stones to close up three bomb holes in the center of the road to make it safe for the next food convoy. In one crater we found a puff adder left dead and headless. It was the only killing of that bombing.

Yacht

ALEPHO

Benson and Emmanuel would gather us together and read from the books because they had been to school in Panyido. I didn't understand the English but they would translate it into Dinka and that made the book interesting to me. It wasn't easy, but I would put my hand under my chin and listen to them. I wanted to learn the language.

Reading made us feel good. As we learned a few things, we saw that in order to understand the world, we needed to be educated. We needed to know about the world around us. I still didn't know how to write my name or read it aloud if it was written on paper. When I was back in Juol and Yier was at the university in Wau, he came home once on holiday. He wrote the names of all the children in the village, maybe a hundred, on a piece of paper. Then he called all the names. I couldn't believe it. I thought he'd learned to be a wizard. I wanted to learn to do that too.

So they started schools under the trees. The teacher had only one book for the class, a primary two book with the alphabet and pictures. I always remembered the letters Y and Z the best. Y had a picture of a sailboat and the word "yacht" below. Z had a zebra. I learned to read those few words and showed off to the other boys. "You're a zebra. You're a yacht." We'd laugh and joke like that. We had to have humor. It is human nature. No matter how bad the situation is, if you can't find any humor then life is not worth it.

I hadn't learned anything in Palataka when the teachers hit our fingers, but now I liked school. The teacher had another book called *Hello Children* that had big pictures and big writing. It started out "Tom and Mary are going to school." I can see every page of that book in my memory.

From the library, I brought out a hundred books. One of them was *Hello Children.* I kept that one.

The Fire Goes Out

BENSON

We found out that Yier would be coming home and given one
month of freedom before going back to the front line. Ayen
was still sick and so was her baby because she couldn't
breast-feed him due to her illness. Since there were no animals that produced milk the baby ate watery grain porridge.
His sickness improved, but porridge every day was making
him thinner and weaker. There was no clinic or hospital.
Ayen was a medical nurse before the war and she came back
one night with medicine. As it was dark, she told me to light
a grass bundle and hold up the fire while she injected the
medicine near the baby's shoulder. The baby's arm was the
thinnest arm I had ever seen and the size of the needle compared to it made my stomach lurch. Before she could give
the shot, the fire devoured the grass I was holding and
crawled near my hand, trying to lick my fingers off. I
couldn't hold it up and had to drop it on the ground.

"What is wrong with you?" Ayen shouted at me. "Can't
you hold anything right?"

"There is no more grass bundle."

"Then go get more from the roof of the house."

I brought another bundle. She finished the injection and
washed the baby and covered him with a warm towel. The

baby shook with the cold and started making a quacking noise on Ayen's lap.

"Benson, light up a fire. The baby is cold."

In the firelight I could see the baby's eyes rolling and thick, foamy saliva on his mouth. Then the poor little baby couldn't stand it anymore. He ran out of breath. We stood motionless, wondering whether his mother's injection with a medicine we didn't know or his long sickness was the killer. Ayen cried for a whole week invoking my name, saying I didn't even mind about her baby's safety and I didn't hold the fire up right.

When Yier returned, he moved us boys to where all the commanders lived. We'd see them waggling their asses around with their bodyguards trailing behind wrestling with machine guns and jiggling bullet belts on their shoulders. You never knew the commanders' real names. You only heard of Colorless Lizard, Commander Buffalo, the Rhino or Merciless Crocodile.

One named Honorable Chief was our neighbor. It was rumored that he was a sworn foe of Merciless Crocodile, and if they ever met face-to-face they'd get into a fight. Every night Honorable Chief's troops filled the trenches surrounding our houses and we had to stay inside for the whole night until the soldiers left in the morning, not going outside to urinate for fear of being shot.

Yier was very worried about us being in the middle of all this and moved us back to the displacement camp. A few nights later a thunderous gun battle kept us awake and we knew those two commanders had started warring against each other. In the morning we heard that Honorable Chief had been ambushed by Merciless Crocodile. The sound of their big guns came everyday. John Garang, the leader of the SPLA army, came and he was angry because half of the troops fighting the government had to be withdrawn to stop the fighting between his commanders. He talked all day while we sat in the sun. "Some people are climbing the tree," he told the gathering, "when other people are cutting it down."

The end of 1992 came and the green leaves withered away as the dry season settled in. We were worried about the fighting but the soldiers reassured us, "Let the *jallaba* and the rebelling commanders come. They will face the music."

The war moved into the hills and an army lorry with its countless bullet holes and tiny windows stained with blood brought masses of wounded soldiers into the camp.

We continued our business, trying not to worry about the fighting all around. One afternoon, Emmanuel came to me in the market. "We're leaving to go to Kenya," he said excitedly.

I wasn't excited. I didn't feel like leaving because I was making money selling cassava and yams to the soldiers and nearly had enough for some sandals. "Stop your usual lie," I told him.

"It's true. Two commanders are taking their children in a lorry and Yier asked them to include us."

I had three pieces of yams left to sell, but Emmanuel told me to save them for our journey. I didn't want to go and leave my business, but I thought of going to school and learning English and Kswahili, of being able to say, *haraka*,

haraka or *hakuna matata*, like the Kenyan drivers who came to southern Sudan. We'd heard much about a new camp, Kakuma, just over the border past Lokichokio. It was supposed to have schools and food and even a clinic. The government troops couldn't reach us across the border. Maybe Kenya offered more hope for peace and safety than a pair of sandals.

Commander's Sons

BENSON

Yier was a loyal SPLA warrior. That was why the commander respected his request to take us to Kakuma camp in Kenya. Alepho, Emmanuel, Benjamin and I stood in a line near the compound feeling proud to be with the commander's sons.

"Let the boys climb on board," the commander told his guards.

We rushed up with our bags into the gray lorry that still carried the dry blood and bullet holes to tell us it was one of the survivors too. They called it a Mercedes. The driver slammed his boot on the ground and saluted.

The commander said, "Drive the boys safely."

"Yes, chief." The driver saluted again and jumped to the wheel.

There were seventy-five of us boys and fifteen escort soldiers. We waved good-bye to Yier and sang, feeling important being escorted through the town. When people came out of their houses and looked at us, we thought they were thinking we might be coming from the front line.

Pageri town disappeared out of our sight through the dust behind us and the road became rougher. A soldier told us to stop singing or we would key up the driver, who was known to all the commanders as a drunken hero who nonetheless had never had an accident and that was why every commander chose him. He'd gained his fame when driving a weapon vehicle in battle. They been ambushed, all the troops were gunned down, and only he remained with his truck looking at the enemy approaching from every corner. They said he drank gasoline and drove through the hissing bullets. He was the only survivor and rescued the weapons from being captured. The commanders had a high regard for his bravery and let him drink, smoke and drive anytime he wanted.

We stopped singing as the soldiers requested, but soon we would have stopped anyway because the driver was going so fast the wind swept our tears into our ears. When he went uphill, everything was silent except the engine that was so loud our eardrums hurt. We emerged on one flat hilltop where soldiers stood beside poles placed across the road to stop passing vehicles. But not our drunken driver. The soldiers leaped out of the way as he ran through, breaking the posts. Still not slowing down, the lorry flew off the road and hit a tree. We were hardly noticeable under the dust and tree leaves that had fallen on us. The engine stopped and the soldiers came out of the grass after almost being ground into the dust. "Lual! Lual!" they shouted. "Drive the boys safely." They had recognized him and realized they could do nothing to stop him.

With the lorry jumping up and down once again in the deep holes on the road, I noticed that the mouth of the boy sitting in front of Benjamin was trembling. Suddenly it exploded open like a hose and Benjamin was wet with vomit of cassava pieces and red peanut skins. Benjamin grabbed his shirt and pushed it close to the boy. "Clean it! Clean it now!" The boy's mouth still shivered. He looked guilty.

"Stop that!" yelled the soldier behind Benjamin. "Vomit can't kill you. You will go wash it later."

It got darker and the driver drove more smoothly than we had expected until we arrived in Magwe at midnight. The whole town smelled like burning feathers and we were warned not to walk anywhere until it was day again because there were three thousand land mines. We obeyed and slept without the thought of a latrine.

An early morning explosion in the trees woke us. "It is probably a dog or hyena stepping on a land mine," explained the soldiers.

We followed a soldier, putting our feet where his boots stepped, to get to a market. We wanted to buy groundnuts from the local Acholi tribe to carry for our journey. There were dark slimy mounds everywhere by the roadside, inside the trenches, and on the grass. I realized that was what the whole town smelled of. We asked, "What are those mounds?"

"Dead bodies sprinkled with paraffin and burned. Too many soldiers killed and no one to bury them because everybody was busy fighting."

I couldn't count how many people had fallen by the roadside.

When we returned the lorry was gone. A commander told us that we had to walk to a place called Imarok because our lorry had taken some wounded soldiers back to Pageri. He ordered us to leave and said the lorry would catch up to us on the way the next evening.

Imarok also had seen heavy fighting and there had been no time to bury or burn the dead. Countless skeletons and

skulls still remained. By the scarification on their foreheads
we could tell they were southerners and even which tribe
they came from. I thought of Yier and all the soldiers we'd
met and prayed they wouldn't be in a battle like this one. We
came to a very long skeleton among the others. I'd never
seen anyone that tall, maybe eight feet. Everyone gathered
around it. "Wow!" one boy said. "That was a tall son of a
bitch!"

We spent the night in an old building with a grass-
covered roof that made it invisible to the Antonov. A commander arrived in the afternoon in a different vehicle
called a Nissan that was filled with many soldiers. We were
happy to see it because it was a bigger lorry than the Mercedes. He ordered the soldiers to dismount and stood
watching with his hands on his hips as seventy-five of us got
on. He asked the soldiers if they would like to walk or ride.
"We'd like to ride, Chief. The way is far and dangerous to
walk."

"Get on then. These boys don't appreciate how the truck
was captured. You've earned the ride."

"But it is full, sir, and there are small boys."

The commander pointed at the soldier. "Get on. That's
my order. I'll be responsible if there is any problem."

They came running and jumping on us with sharp boots
and rattling chains of bullet belts dangling from their machine guns.

"You knocked my head with your gun barrel, sir," we
complained. But the soldiers said we were a lucky flock
coming out of the commander's compound. They told us to
be grateful: we were riding in their vehicle only because they
respected our commander.

The lorry started down the road. I tried to stand up because I couldn't breathe with the soldiers pushing and banging me from one person to another. One very young soldier, his hair dotted with ringworm, pushed me out of my place and sat in front of me. A huge fat Nubian standing in front of him smashed his buttocks on the young soldier's face with every bump in the holes. The young soldier opened his gun catch and shoved it onto the soldier's huge buttocks. The big guy must have felt the pain. He turned and asked, "What are you doing with your gun like that?" The young soldier replied, "Only your mother shall mourn if you push on me with your buttocks again!"

The big Nubian saw the gun catch was open and pushed the entire crowd forward with his bulk. Alepho and Benjamin cried out. The soldiers at the front, being squashed, yelled back, "Who is pushing people like that?"

I was behind it all, next to the young soldier, but Benjamin was further up, buried under all this wrestling. I heard his voice change completely and he began squeaking instead of crying. I worried about his wounded leg. A boot might step on it and break it! I wished I had big muscles like the Nubian to push them away and rescue him. Alepho began crying loudly too. He was squeezed and I couldn't even see him. Benjamin went silent. He was suffocating in the darkness but there was nothing I could do. My heart started to beat fast and I couldn't breathe. I screamed. A soldier sitting at the edge realized what was happening below people's feet and fired his gun into the air.

The driver put his head out. "What is going on, soldier?"

"A boy is buried below!"

The driver stopped. The soldiers pulled Benjamin out.

He was nearly unconscious and dark with sweat like he'd been swimming in the mud with pigs.

"These children are being tortured!" said the soldier who had shot the gun.

The driver said to our hero, "You can jump down and leave more room for the boys if you want to make their situation better."

The other soldiers all laughed at that. But I was grateful to him for firing his gun. He was the only good-hearted guy among the rest who laughed while Benjamin was being crushed. No one else cared about us small boys. I wanted a gun like that young soldier so I could shove it onto their fat asses and make them stop laughing.

Man Sits on Bag

ALEPHO

After they pulled Benjamin from under the pile of passengers and we climbed back up into the truck, a man was sitting on my bag. I told him, "You are sitting on my bag, sir, can I have my bag?" He ignored me. "Please," I said. "I have some books in there. May I have my bag?"

"Shut up," he said.

There was nothing I could do. He was a grown man. A little while later some of the passengers were complaining about a bad smell. The man had shit on my bag. The whole truck smelled so bad. Tears flowed out of my eyes. I didn't know why he did that to me. Maybe because I didn't have adult family, because I was just a kid.

A few minutes later the Nissan hit a big ditch and threw two men off the truck. One of them was the man who had shit on my bag. Everybody began banging on the door, "Hey, men have fallen off," but the Nissan didn't stop for half a mile.

When the men caught up, I saw that the man who had sat on my bag had broken his front tooth in the fall. I covered my bag with a plastic sheet but I was still crying, thinking of my beautiful blanket, my books and how people didn't care about anyone else. It didn't matter if you were a child or an adult. Nobody cared. That's what war was doing to people. They only cared for themselves.

Sometimes when adults saw that we had a little thing, they'd rob us boys of what we had. "I'm fighting for this country," they'd say. "You're not fighting for anything. Give me the blanket. If you don't give it to me, I'm going to take it by force."

"Why should I give it to you? What about me?"

"I don't care. I'm the one fighting. You're not fighting."

Many people were out of their minds from the war.

When the man got back up on the truck, he was so angry he started kicking me for no reason. A soldier became upset about that and wanted to fight the man with the broken tooth right then and there. Everyone stopped them, saying, "Don't fight; you'll kill yourself with the truck running."

"That guy is stupid," the soldier said. "He shit on the kid's bag and now he wants to beat him. What's the reason? Shame on you. I'm glad you broke your tooth. God doesn't like you to do stuff like that. If you try to hurt him more, then you are going to kill yourself: you are not going to kill this kid."

Hijacked

BENSON

W*e reached a river* where someone had overturned a beehive and the swarming bees were keeping people from going ahead. The commander stopped the Nissan. All seventy-five of us boys decided to abandon the vehicle to the soldiers. They had almost killed Benjamin, and we had our fill of all of them.

The soldiers laughed after us. "You'd better walk because you can't stand the army riding style."

We still hoped that the Mercedes would return for us as promised. If it didn't, we preferred to walk all the way to Kakuma. We'd crossed most of Sudan so many times; we could do this. But the walking became difficult, especially for Benjamin. His wound was bleeding where the pink skin had been scraped off by the soldiers' boots and he hobbled. We made it as far as Kilieu, a small town, where we ran into three thousand boys who were on their way from Palataka. We looked among the boys as much as we could but did not see Peter. When the commander saw us, he said, "You must join up with these boys."

"No," the elder boys told them. "We are the commander's children and the Mercedes will be returning for us."

"I don't want you in a vehicle," the new commander said. "You must walk like these boys."

In the morning he announced to everyone, "You will be walking from Kilieu to Kenya. It will take three weeks. You will be escorted by soldiers because the tribes on the way become enemies if they see anyone carrying a bag or wearing clothes."

The boys from Palataka began their walk. We separated ourselves and refused to go with them because we had been told the truck would come for us. The commander's bodyguards came at us with sticks. Five soldiers started on the boy who was our speaker and beat him until he spit blood. We scattered, leaving some of our belongings behind, then set out on our own for Imatong mountain.

The next morning we left Imatong and searched for the path of the boys from Palataka so that we could find the way to Kenya. It grew very hot and we were so exhausted that our line broke up into groups of only two or three boys walking together, far apart from the others. Sometimes I walked alone. Ammunition shells were scattered across the ground and I could feel the sorrow in the trees as they stood still, all dried, their leaves banished by the wind.

We came to a town liberated by the rebels and met up with the three thousand Palataka boys again. We were awakened in the early morning by a whistle and the commander's order to walk on. This time, we knew that it was dangerous to refuse. Instead, we hid and let the Palataka boys go on with their commander. We agreed among ourselves to tell the soldiers in town that we were not well and had to stay until a vehicle came for us. We waited for another week but there was no sign of it. We knew walking through those hostile hills meant suicide because the tribes there were enemies of the SPLA soldiers and we were SPLA children. Finally a squad of soldiers equipped with machine guns and ammunition was selected to escort us on the walk to Chukudum, a town on the way to Kakuma.

We walked all that day, exhausted and thirsty, because the soldiers walked faster than us, but with hope in our hearts to finally reach Kenya, a safe place with schools. We came to a village that night and the friendly people offered us food and water. We couldn't believe it when the soldiers told the tribal women, "No, we are not thirsty." It seemed like a punishment to us. "We're sorry," one soldier told us. "But these are cunning people and we might get poisoned."

Alepho was strong on that walk. He carried the heaviest load the whole way. Everybody admired him. Benjamin was brave, never complaining, but I could see that his leg was worse. The wound bled easily and the bone bowed out from the knee to the ankle.

We reached Chukudum but did not catch up with the Palataka boys. Cooking potato leaves as soup, we spent a week there until the Nissan lorry we'd abandoned to the soldiers at Kilieu arrived. It was now loaded with bombs and ammunition, but they said that we could ride on top of the grenade and bomb boxes.

The lorry drove throughout the night until a golden sky appeared behind the mountain horizon and a blazing orange ball emerged. Even though we were still far away, I was excited knowing that somewhere out there lay Kakuma refugee camp and that I would get there soon because I was on a vehicle.

The sun grew hotter. We had reached an area where the Taposa lived. Sheep, goats and cattle with ringing bells around their necks walked among the trees and crossed the road, raising dust clouds. Taposa girls' skin skirts flapped against their legs, bangles jingled from their ankles, and they flashed gleaming smiles at us. A few houses came into view and more people walking through streams of mooing cattle.

The lorry climbed high into the hills and entered a valley. It stopped at an SPLA camp with grass huts and uniformed soldiers all around. They ordered us to get down. The stony ground burned my bare feet. Everything was dry and so different from the lush green southeastern equatorial region where we'd been. The hills were gray and the riverbed that ran through the valley was dry. The Taposa had dug a water hole and were watering their cattle.

"This way," said a soldier who led us to some shade where a man wearing civilian clothes stood waiting. "This is your teacher. He will divide you in groups."

"Follow me," instructed the teacher and he led us up into the hills. My feet were suffering with the sun's heat but I couldn't leave the road because the splinters of dry grass pierced my soles. After a twenty-minute walk, we came to another valley with trees on the edge of a dry river. We heard murmuring voices and tree chopping, and smelled the smoke of cooking fires, but we didn't see a single house.

"This is Natinga," the teacher announced. "You will be in group three. Go find yourself some shade and rest, and then begin building your houses."

I looked at Alepho in surprise. "What is this? Natinga?" I went to the teacher. "Sir. We are going to Kakuma."

He ignored me and left us in the bush in the middle of nowhere.

Some boys started marking the ground, saying that was where they wanted their huts to be. They didn't understand that we'd been tricked. Lied to. Hijacked by the soldiers and taken here instead. There was no school, no houses, nothing.

Flies bothered my wounds as I breathed the heated air smelling of rotted foliage and dead leaves. The three thousand boys from Palataka had been at Natinga for two weeks already. We found friends among them, including our cousin Akuectocdiit, who was several years older than us. We learned that Natinga was a rebel army camp started by some SPLA soldiers who had survived when their truck overturned. The local Taposa people called the place Loros. It had been their cattle watering place. The name Natinga came from the SPLA men: *nga tinga?* in Dinka dialect means, Who can see me here in this hill? They gave it this name because it was so far up into the hills and well hidden with only grass roofs and small buildings that it could not be seen by the Antonov bombers.

We complained again to the teachers that we wanted to go on to Kakuma. They said, "This is the place; you're not going farther. That is the order from the commanders. Kakuma is crowded. People in the camp are fighting and going crazy."

I doubted this. Kenya was another country and I didn't think things like that would be happening there. In Ethiopia those bad things hadn't happened in the camp; we had been living in a good way. They just didn't want us to go to Kakuma. But all I wanted was school. In Natinga we would have to depend on the soldiers. We would be live under trees and it would be years before we had a good school. All I'd dreamed of, going to Kenya and learning to speak English and Kswahili, reading words in books or doing figures, was lost.

Crazy Work

BENJAMIN

Life became very wild in Natinga. There was no food and no water in the camp. They said we had to go out and find our own. But there were the three thousand boys there and it was summertime. No fruits were ripe and no wild green vegetables were ready to be eaten. We tried. If we found one green leaf or one fruit we would take it to eat as our dinner. Forget about breakfast.

They made us do crazy work in Natinga. What I mean by crazy work is that we boys were forced to build a road up a hill. Every morning we climbed up the mountain for the road building. When people came and saw what we were doing they were really surprised and asked, "How can kids do such a job?"

There were no big people, mature people or construction workers. No one. That work was dangerous and made me really sore. My leg got worse. It was difficult to walk. I asked God why he put me in such a situation. First I'd thought I'd die in the war. Now I was sure I'd die in Natinga.

Natinga

BENSON

The teachers divided us into groups and we began building our weird, crooked little huts from branches to shelter ourselves. Classes began under the trees, but they only lasted two weeks until they changed the subject to building a road way up the mountain. They told us the top would be a good place for a school. We were awakened at 3:00 A.M. every morning to climb up the mountain carrying our water and food. The mountain was high and it was cold; most of us had bare feet. The soldiers supervised us. They made sure we stayed with our groups and told us, "Work here. Clear all the stones." We dug out rocks that weighed thousands of pounds and pushed them off cliffs with big poles as levers. They'd roll down, breaking trees, sometimes hitting other rocks that split with a crack. When the work was over, the soldiers fired their guns up into the sky so we could follow the direction of the sound to make it back to Natinga. We'd return in the early evening to get our food and water. The work on the mountain was torture. There was no school. Natinga was nothing but hell's work camp.

Fifteen boys attempted an escape and were caught. The soldiers built a thorn-fenced pen in the middle of the compound as a jail. The boys sat inside. There was no roof, no shade, no protection from the rain. The prisoners were guarded constantly and only taken out by the soldiers to be lashed twenty times twice a day, once in the morning and once in the evening.

The punishment was for one month and on the day of their release all of the boys in Natinga were gathered together and the soldiers talked about the dangers of escaping. The boys being released received thirty lashes with a tree branch before going back into their groups. It was actually sixty because they were forced to lie down before being whipped by one person on each side. For each count they both hit together.

Alepho got a fever and didn't feel like eating much. He'd fall asleep early and talk to himself. When I awakened him and asked why he talked in his sleep, he couldn't remember. After a few days when the fever got worse and his eyes grew yellow, I really began to worry. He was barely eating anything. I asked one of the soldiers to look at him. "Yellow fever," he said. My worst fear.

Each day after work we went to the Taposa water hole to get water for drinking, cooking and showering. We shared the water flowing out of the rocks with the soldiers and the Taposa, their cattle and goats. That really irritated the Taposa. The line was always long and this task of getting water could take hours. As small boys we were always pushed to the back of the line.

We needed water desperately. Hungry and thirsty, we often left in silence with our empty water containers. My mind raced as tears rolled down my grimy cheeks. They kept us at Natinga but they didn't care about us. I had no water for my sick brother. He'd go nights without food, water or a shower. I was twelve, but he was still a young boy and terribly sick with yellow fever.

A person with yellow fever is easy to care for in a Dinka village. They must not eat meat, salt or oil in any food. The food must be served in a clean container safe from such things and sour milk is the best kind of food. But now I had to care for Alepho, but the things that he needed were not affordable. Emmanuel, Benjamin and I were all going around with empty pockets. In order to get a cup of milk, I sold any scrap of cloth that I could find, even though our clothes were all dirty rags.

I went into the forest to look for plants with fruits and found the tamarind trees but they had no fruit as it was the driest season of the year. I collected the leaves anyway, boiled them, sieved out the water, and mixed it with flour to make the sour gruel Alepho needed. I collected those leaves everyday. Soon he refused to eat the sour gruel. I began feeling very sad because there was no other way I could help my brother, and there was no way to get him better as long as we were trapped in the camp.

Our cousin, Akuectocdiit, as he was the oldest was our leader. Any idea that we brought up, if he didn't like it, he would strongly oppose it. He called a meeting where we discussed the difficulties of living in Natinga and what we should do about it. Emmanuel said, "Can't we try a way to escape?" Before Emmanuel could even finish the word "escape," Akuectocdiit interrupted, "What? You talk about escape! When you have seen a lot of people in jail! I don't want any of us to go to the jail. What is the point of escaping? Forget it. The reason you want to escape to Kakuma is to go to school. They say they are building a school here."

"We are building a road up the mountain," Emmanuel said. "There is no school."

"Yes, we are building the road so we have the school. When we finish the road there will be a good school. They will bring the books. They will bring the food."

Joseph and Emmanuel kept quiet. I kept quiet too. I didn't believe that road was being built for a school, but I could see not everybody liked the idea of escaping.

Soon after that, Emmanuel and Benjamin made a plan that the four of us could escape together.

"Alepho is not well enough," I said. "He can't walk that long and dangerous distance when he is sick."

I told them that I wouldn't leave Alepho. I refused to go and wished them good luck on their journey.

Escape

BENJAMIN

It was midnight and everybody was sleeping when Emmanuel and I came together. We talked and made the decision to leave that night. It was dark: no lights, no fires, and no moon. We went a short way and ran into soldiers who were a security patrol to protect the boys. When they saw us they called out to us to make sure that we were safe and not escaping. We didn't stop, we just said, "We'll be back soon." They thought we were just going to relieve ourselves.

We walked up the mountain in the pitch dark, following the road. We didn't know where else to go; there were local people all around and if we went the wrong way we might be killed. We'd been going for nearly three hours when we suddenly came upon a security gate. Two soldiers surprised us from behind. "Don't move. Don't do anything. Keep your arms up."

We stopped and did as we were told. They came to us and checked our clothing. "Where are you guys going?"

"Lokichokio, on the border of Sudan and Kenya."

"No, you're not. We know you guys live in Natinga and you have to go back now."

They called on the radio. The soldiers in Natinga said, "Yeah, those boys are from here."

They walked us back and took us straight to the jail.

Sad Talking

BENSON

In Lokichokio, Kenyan doctors had removed a splinter as long as his hand from Benjamin's leg, which had been embedded there for two years. His leg was finally beginning to heal, when he and Emmanuel were put in the thorn-fenced jail. Every morning and afternoon they received twenty lashes with a cane. Benjamin's leg became seriously infected again and he grew emaciated.

Once they got out, Emmanuel wanted to escape so much that he kept telling us that even if he was jailed many times, he would keep trying. The second time he succeeded by pretending to be the son of a lady passenger in an army truck.

Besides caring for Alepho, I had to work in my squadron. We were living in an army system and had to do what the head boys told us or we were in trouble. Twice a week I pounded grain and went to the Taposa borehole to get water for drinking and cooking. Other days I needed a few hours to collect firewood, which was becoming scarcer and forced me into more dangerous areas. We had to wake up so early to go up the mountain to build the road that I hardly had time to properly take care of my sick brother.

I asked the group teacher to let me off some of the work in order to look after Alepho. He did allow this. He was a good man and also concerned about my brother. He sometimes asked his friends for money and gave it to me to buy sour milk for Alepho, whose fever was getting more serious. He would get up at night and walk around until he hit an object and realized that he was not in his bed and go back. All night he groaned and grumbled. Sometimes he talked like he was talking to our own mother. That talking made me cry and worry a lot. That was sad talking.

By day he could walk a little bit around the compound but I had to take him outside to the bathroom. He could hold his spoon, but I had to beg him to eat because he had come to hate the porridge I served every day. It made him vomit. However, it is good when a person with yellow fever vomits. I told him, "Please, just one bite and I will stop it." When he took that bite I would say, "Please, be brave like a man and take this one more, it won't hurt you." Or I told him, "You know, as your brother, I would like you to get over your sickness and be well like others, but you are making it hard for both of us by not eating." I encouraged him to eat in any way I could. He was so skinny you could count his ribs from a distance and his dry cracked skin had turned gray. His eyes and tongue were yellowish, and his legs, feet and stomach swelled. The brother I had just found again seemed about to die.

When the convoys brought grains at the end of the month, the older boys climbed into the vehicle to help throw the bags down. They liked this work because they swept up the grains scattered in the vehicle from the torn bags for themselves. I decided to do this too. At first the bigger boys chased me down saying that I was not strong enough to throw down a bag of maize by myself, but I proved to them that I could.

By the next month I was working beside them unchallenged. I poked holes in some of the bags so that more grains tumbled out onto the ground. By the end I sometimes collected nearly three bowls of grains and had to take off my shirt and tie the ends to make a sack to carry them home. I walked only in my shorts across the group area, not caring about my bare chest and feet. In my hut I cleaned the grains by spreading the sack on the ground and picking out the pebbles and chaff.

Taposa girls came to the camp to sell us sour goat milk. I made a friendship with one of the girls, buying her milk with my collected grains. I told my friends to buy her milk too and she soon brought a friend also. We'd sit in my hut and talk while the other boys in my group bought all of their milk. When we were talking together, the girls laughed so loudly that my hut became noisy like a weaverbird nest in an acacia tree. The girls made fun of us trying to pronounce words in their dialect. They were happy girls and their spirit reminded me of the way Dinka girls were in our village.

As older boys heard the girls' laughter, they also came to buy milk. After the milk was gone, the boys played with and teased the girls, gently slapping and poking them. The girls wore hide skirts and their breasts were naked, which almost made our eyes poke out of our heads.

The older boys liked to play tits-catch, pinching and grabbing the girls' breasts. But the girls slapped away their hands and shouted "Hiihh!" Soon they became tired of the boys doing this, swept the dust off their goatskin skirts and said to me, "My friend, we are leaving. We will come see you again."

"You chased away my guests with your bad actions!" I told those boys.

They laughed at me. "Girls need reactions from a boy. You should mingle with them like a boy. Staying quiet around girls, like you are their kind, will get you nowhere except to be considered an idiot."

The next day the five Taposa girls came back. More than ten of us crowded into my friend's bigger hut. We talked and laughed until our stomachs were worn out of energy. The four girls broke up our conversation and went outside, but one stayed and talked with the seven of us. One of the older boys whispered into my ear in Arabic, "Taposa girls like a man brave enough to lift up her skirt in front of other men and slap her on her bare buttock. Do that now, and that girl will always think about you."

This was a scary thing. My heart beat so noisily I could hear it saying, "Do it! Don't do it! Do it! Don't do it!"

Everyone supported this wicked idea that I should do, because the girl liked me and this was my chance for her to like me more.

The girl saw that nobody wanted to talk with her anymore and said good-bye. As she bent down to go through the door, I suddenly threw her skin skirt onto her back for all the boys to see her bare buttocks. Then I jerked back to my seat quickly and sat still because I was not brave enough to touch her. She turned with a wild swiftness and slapped down her skirt. The room went quiet and every one of us was looking at her as her eyes searched each of our pupils.

"You! It is you!"

She pointed at me because my neck had stiffened with fretful fear and I was the only one sweating. Her hand was shivering. My throat was so tight with regret that I remained still and said nothing. She bent and went out backward. My friends burst out loudly laughing and praised me, "You did bravely!"

I said nothing. I was annoyed at myself for listening to them and doing such a shameful thing. I wanted to apologize to the girl but she would listen no more. Our friendship withered with the lift of a skirt.

About that time, news came to Natinga. We gathered together to listen to the leaders introduce a new kind of education. "You will have army training and carry your guns with you to school and in classes and wherever you go."

Most of the boys sang songs of joy, but this decision was sad news, particularly for me. I kept my mouth shut. Now I knew for certain why they had brought us here to Natinga and why they were keeping us here. They wanted more boys for their army. Soon we would be on the front lines, where they didn't care whether you lived or died. They said, "Thousands die and a hundred are born a day. Who cares about your life at your age?" Our lives seemed of no consequence to them.

I'd met a man from my region in the army. He knew my father. He was there with his wife and a small child. After seeing how serious Alepho's sickness was, he took him to stay in his house. He and his wife took good care of him. Her cooking was better than mine and Alepho began to eat a little more. But still he wasn't getting cured.

Later the man taking care of Alepho received news that all of the very sick boys were being transferred to Kakuma refugee camp in Kenya, all in one go, just this one time.

The commander had ordered that the sick boys should go alone; no healthy boy could go with them to care for them. The man collected money from all of his friends in the army and because he was a close friend and a bodyguard to one of the commanders, he made it possible for Alepho to be transferred out.

I worried about Alepho traveling on his own, but I knew it was his only chance. And even if I had to go to the front lines, I didn't want Alepho to be there. He was too young. He deserved to be in a refugee camp like other children.

Soon the day came for Alepho to leave. I knew he had a chance of recovering if he went to Kenya, but my heart ached as we lifted him into the back of the lorry wearing only the shorts I'd given him. I hoped Emmanuel had survived and was at Kakuma camp already so that he could take care of Alepho when he arrived. Once again I was filled with a terrible fear that I would never see my brother again.

I said my good-bye to him and stood on the road watching. I didn't know for certain where Alepho was going and he was too sick to know. People he met might not know exactly what a person with yellow fever needed not to eat. No one cared about a sick boy with no family.

As I watched the lorry leaving, I realized I had to make a plan to escape Natinga to reach Alepho in Kenya. I might not succeed, but I had to try. Sudan stank of blood. If I wanted to see my brother again I had to get away.

Part Three

Lost Boys

Kakuma

ALEPHO

Benson stood on the road looking very worried and then he disappeared into the dust as the lorry rumbled away.

Adults and children were crowded all around me. The adults mostly stood and the children sat on their bags and blankets. When the truck hit a ditch and bumped us all into the air, they sometimes landed on me. My legs were so thin, like dry twigs, I feared they would be broken before we reached our destination. I hugged my knees up to my body but soon grew tired doing this and just took my chances with the falling people. The first hours were the most dangerous. Mountain gangs of Dinka and Taposa had mobilized in the hills and lived by robbing people.

Once we were free of the gangs and dropped down from the hills into the desert, red dust swirled up from the rear tires and covered our skin. With no shade, the sun heated the back of the truck like a stone oven. I became very thirsty. I looked outside at the desert ahead of us. It seemed to stretch on forever. Looking out made me worry more about Benson if he tried to escape on foot. Gangs, desert, soldiers and wild animals would confront him. But what choice did he have? When the local Taposa people came into Natinga to sell the soldiers some wild animals they had killed, they warned us that the government army was close by, just thirty miles to the north in Kapoeta. "Madakuri lac lac," they said, meaning the government army is huge. "If the government finds out about this place," they said, "they will come here. Where you boys going to go?"

We heard that the boys who escaped Natinga and weren't caught by the soldiers or the local people then risked their lives to cross this desert to Lokichokio. We didn't know if it was true, but the soldiers told us many had perished along the way. I was riding in the back of a lorry and even so the heat and thirst of this desert were nearly intolerable. I hadn't seen anyone walking. I was suffering in a truck. How could anyone cross on foot?

After a full day's drive, the sun nearly down, the lorry arrived in Lokichokio, just across the Sudan border in Kenya. As it rolled to a stop, the guys said, "This vehicle is going on to the SPLA station."

I knew I didn't want to go there, so I climbed out and one of the guys threw my bag to me. As the truck took off again, I stood in the middle of the gravel road wondering what to do. "That's the immigration center," a man said. "That's where you need to go."

I walked toward a nearby building. My legs wouldn't have taken me any farther. From an outside faucet I washed the red dust off my hands and face, satisfied my thirst, and headed to the immigration center where every refugee who comes from Sudan, Congo, Eritrea or Ethiopia must go and register. I hadn't eaten all day. But I was so weak and tired and overcome by sickness that I couldn't feel the hunger. I took my colorful blanket from my bag, spread it on the floor with all of the other waiting people, and lay down to sleep for the night.

In the morning, I went outside to the shelter and waited. Without food I was growing weaker. If I didn't get food or treatment soon, I feared I wouldn't have the strength to get up again. It was easy for all the people rushing around for their own survival to ignore a boy who appeared to be sleeping in the corner.

In the afternoon, they announced the start of the registration. I stood in line. The sun was really hot. I waited a half hour and then came to a man who spoke Kswahili and English. A man translated and I was registered. They gave me six pieces of biscuit.

I returned to the shelter to eat. Many kids were playing and they called to me to join in. I just looked at them. I couldn't move, I couldn't even call back; I didn't have enough energy.

"Stonehead!" they yelled. "Stonehead. Stonehead. Stonehead."

I couldn't see myself, but I'd seen enough other emaciated boys to know my head looked like a big stone on my little body. Even my knees, feet and elbows looked huge on my twig-thin limbs.

That evening, when I took out my beautiful blanket to sleep, a Kenyan man tried to take it from me. "No!" I yelled and held onto it with all my strength. It was the only thing I owned besides the shorts I was wearing that Benson had given me. But the man kept pulling on it. When I began to cry, he gave up and walked away.

The next day, enough refugees to fill a couple of vehicles

had accumulated and they loaded all of us onto trucks. So I began the last leg of a journey to Kakuma refugee camp that we'd begun so long ago. This had been our shared dream, but Benson, Benjamin, Lino, Joseph and Emmanuel were not here to experience it with me.

It was night when we arrived. The whole area was clouded by dust and the lights of the camp glowed through like a kerosene lamp. The vehicle stopped. The other people on the truck didn't speak my language. When we unloaded, they went off quickly into different directions as though they knew the place. I was by myself and confused.

A man came up to me. "What group are you in?"

I didn't know what a group was. "I am coming to the camp."

"This isn't the camp. This is the UNHCR compound. Where are you from?"

"Bahr al Ghazal in southern Sudan."

"This is the way the groups work. There are six groups from Bahr al Ghazal. You can pick one. Fifteen, thirty-seven . . ."

"Thirty-seven," I interrupted. I don't know why I chose it; it just came to my head.

After a ten-minute ride down a dirt road, the car dropped me in Group 37. There were no lights but the moon was full. Lots of people were talking.

"Are you a new arrival?" they asked.

"Yes."

They asked me my name and about my family. "Oh, your Uncle Ajak is here," they said.

I knew his name. He was part of our clan but I had never met him before. They took me to where he lived. There were three houses, but two of them were burned. No one was there. I could barely stand any longer. I went in, found no one, spread my blanket and went to sleep.

In the morning, when I sat up, the room seemed to move around me. I was too weak to stand. When a boy came into the room I squinted and tried to focus on his face. Could it be my little brother? He was so tall.

The boy was looking at me too. "Peter?" I said.

He looked unsure as to why I was calling him by name. Then he jumped forward and grabbed me. "Oh my God, what happened to you?" He shook me by the shoulders.

I was happy, but I said weakly, "I don't feel that good, don't shake me like that."

He didn't hear me. "My God, is that you?" He grabbed my shoulders tighter. "That's not you." He let go and walked away. Then he came back. "It doesn't look like you. What happened?"

I should have been the one surprised. I was sure he'd not survived that chigger-filled camp at Palataka two years earlier. Except for one eye that looked milky and didn't follow the other one, he looked good. He was now taller and much stronger than me. I wanted to leap up and hug him but I could barely even sit up. "Sit down," I said. "Let me explain."

"I still don't believe it. That's not you. I was not bigger than you."

"I'm sick, like you were sick."

There was so much I wanted to tell him and so much I wanted to know from him, but it took too much effort to speak. Peter must have recognized that. "I've got fifteen shillings," he said. "I'll get you some food."

He returned from the store a while later with small cartons of milk. I couldn't swallow it; it tasted horrible to me. I had not eaten any meat or milk since I left Juol and my parents over three years before. Peter cooked yellow corn, which is supposed to be good for a weak person, but I couldn't eat that either.

I wanted to ask him how he escaped Palataka and where he had been all this time, but I could do nothing, not even listen. My energy was gone. I slept the rest of that day.

The next morning Uncle Ajak said, "We're going to the clinic."

With Peter and Uncle Ajak's help, I walked out of the hut. The wind was blowing. "It blows every hour of the day," Uncle Ajak said. Red dust filled the air, covering the buildings and scattered acacia trees. Kenya did not look like southern Sudan. Sudan was covered in green grasses; it was never dusty like this. The wind and dust were uncomfortable but at least I knew I was safe.

We made it to Kakuma Clinic 2. I explained to the doctor where my body hurt. He examined me and looked in my eyes. I don't know what he saw. I hadn't looked in a mirror since Torit, more than a year earlier.

"Your eyes are nearly green," the doctor said.

He gave me a medicine called Septrin and three sets of pills. I went home and stayed in the hut. Sometime soon afterward, I saw Emmanuel and Lino. They came and went but I wasn't sure if I was dreaming or if they were really there. Once I started eating some food, I realized they were real. We'd not heard word from Lino since Benson had seen him on the riverbank in Pochala living with the soldiers. Knowing that Emmanuel had successfully escaped

Natinga and crossed that desert reduced my fears for Benson a little.

"He's sitting up," Peter called to Uncle Ajak after a full week of all of them coaxing me to eat and making certain I took the medicine.

Peter stared as though he was seeing me for the first time. "Look at you. You're like a little baby. What happened to you?"

I closed my eyes. How could I explain the crazy months since Joseph and I left him in Palataka? Now that my mind was a little clearer, that same sickening ache I'd felt leaving Peter in Palataka swept through my body and I thought of Joseph, Benson and Benjamin still stuck in Natinga. Joseph had saved my life so many times. Now here I was in a safe place, too weak to walk, when he might be on the front lines already. And Benjamin, his leg so bad in that dirty jail. To Benson, I owed my life. He could have escaped with the others but stayed behind to nurse me and now he was stuck.

"I was sick," was all I could tell him. "What happened to you? How did you get here?"

Peter told me his story. He had become very sick in Palataka and was sent to the main hospital in Torit. It took some months for him to recover enough to join with many of the boys who had fled from Ethiopia, who had to flee again from a huge group of government soldiers. Peter and thousands of other boys waited in a camp before they made the difficult crossing to Lokichokio in Kenya. From there, thanks to the UN, they had all been settled at Kakuma. I asked about his eye, but he just said, "A guy beat me up for no reason. I can't see out of it." His story sounded simple put this way. But I knew it had been a terrible time for all of those boys fleeing the battles with no food or water, a nearly impossible situation when thousands are together.

Peter smiled at me. "Stand up," he said.

I struggled to my feet with him pulling me up most of the way. I knew why he wanted me to stand. He was two years younger than me and the last time we'd seen each other he was still a tiny boy when I had already begun growing. I stretched to my fullest height, shaking like a newborn giraffe. He was taller than me. And bigger everywhere. It made him feel proud. After years of fearing we'd left him for dead back in Palataka, I was happy that he looked so well.

New Kind of Education

BENSON

Just after Alepho left Natinga, the commanders gathered us together. They said the rebel movement might have been weakened but they were still alive and kicking, and although tall and thin, they were not fragile. The movement may have subsided but it smoldered like a firestorm awaiting the winds to add more force. The next SPLA victory would devour the jungle in raging flame.

They ordered us to stop building the road up the mountain and introduced a new kind of education. First we would be trained and then given guns to protect ourselves. Most of the boys were happy at the idea of training and carrying their own guns because it would give them the power to defend themselves. We had been helpless for so long.

I liked the colorful uniforms I saw on the soldiers who jiggled along with an AK-47 assault rifle at their side. But I knew that once you had a gun, you could not go anywhere of your own will. The rebels controlled you like a dog. I'd seen it was that way with Yier. He'd disappeared from Wau school and joined the Southern Sudan Rebels, where he fought as a warrior for years. None of our family knew where he was until I met him in Kapoeta town. The SPLA high commanders ordered him around to any dangerous battle, whatever they wanted, and he had to obey them and fight for his survival.

If I had a gun slung over my shoulder but then decided to flee for the refugee camp, what would I do with it? Lose your gun and you lose your life: that was the rebel way. I was thinking while the other boys were singing. I couldn't understand why they were so happy and I started planning how to get away before being recruited into carrying a gun.

But not all of the other boys were singing. Because some continued to try to escape, the commanders called another meeting. They told us that abandoning our country and running to other people's land like Kenya was hazardous. "Why do you want to escape to Kenya?" they asked. "That is other people's country. It is dangerous. Nobody is forcing you into exile. You don't need to be worried while you are staying with your own people."

I talked with Joseph and Akuectocdiit again. "There is no school and we have stopped building the road up the mountain. Why can't we try to escape?"

Akuectocdiit still insisted that a school would be built and argued that fleeing was too dangerous. "It's a two-day walk with no water to Lokichokio. If the soldiers don't catch you, or the Taposa catch you and trade you to the government army for a scrap of food, you'll perish in that desert like the other boys have."

A month after Alepho left, Benjamin was released from jail. He was warned not to walk around a lot because they suspected he might follow Emmanuel, so he stayed in unless he was sent to get water or firewood for cooking. Even then his wounded leg kept him from going far.

I didn't talk to him about escape because the two of us

couldn't go alone. To escape on foot you needed at least five people, enough to scare animals on the way. No group would let Benjamin go with them with his leg so bad. Even I knew he couldn't survive the walk.

So although I had no particular plan for my own escape, I began to prepare in case an opportunity came up. First I washed my ragged clothes and put them into a plastic bag. Then I softened some maize [grain] in water and pounded it into flour to make food for the journey.

Every night I was restless with thoughts about getting away. Everyone was scared of going to jail, of the beatings and labor that were used to punish the escapees. Soon no one spoke of escape. I couldn't even talk to my cousins. I couldn't tell my best friend because he was the group head boy with the power to throw anyone who attempted escape into jail. I could trust no one, so I prepared alone and waited patiently for my chance.

Settling in Kakuma

ALEPHO

*K*akuma camp *was created in 1992,* when all the Sudanese boys were driven out of Ethiopia. By the time I arrived a year later, they said there were nearly twelve thousand boys. We were divided into four zones; each zone had five groups with four to five hundred boys in each group. The rest of the camp, many tens of thousands, were families or just women and children, mostly Sudanese but also Ethiopians and Eritreans.

It was the driest place I'd ever been. When the wind blew, which seemed like all the time, very fine dust was lifted from the dry riverbed and landed in our cooking pots. Half of what we ate was sand. Red dust sat on the Makuti roofs of the houses and when the wind direction changed, it went through the palm fronds into the houses and covered our beds with dust.

A month after my arrival, when I was strong enough to walk around, Uncle Ajak took me to the school. People were learning under trees. The teachers were black Sudanese, southerners like us. Everybody wanted to go to school and learn English. The headmaster accepted me and I was registered in the classes. There were seven subjects: English, mathematics, Kswahili, science, art and crafts, geography and Christian religion. I entered at the end of the term, so it was only one month until finals.

For the first week I had no books and the kids in level 1 said, "You're going to be the last in the exam. We're going forward to level 2 and you're going to be left here in level 1. Why don't you just wait for the next year so you can start at the beginning of level one?"

I didn't say anything. They began making fun of me, calling me "big head" because I was the skinniest in the class. "Woooo woooo," they shouted together. "Big head will be the last person in the class."

When I received my books, I went home and started reading. The exam was less than a month away. I didn't do anything except study. I was always reading, practicing spelling, asking everyone to read to me and explain the word meanings to me.

On exam day the teacher passed out a piece of paper and half a pencil to each of us. "Put your name in the upper right corner," he instructed us. "I'll write the questions and multiple choice answers on the board. You write the number of the question and the letter of the correct answer beside it." He pointed his ruler at the class. "Work alone. If I see you showing something to someone else, even giving a pencil, I'll put a mark on your paper and take some points away from the total of your exam."

Some of the kids finished in fifteen minutes, as soon as the teacher finished writing. I kept going over it the entire hour and didn't give my paper to the teacher until he asked for it. When the results came back, I got a 98 percent on the English, 100 percent on the math, 90 percent on Kswahili and 90 percent on the science.

At that time, I didn't know how to draw. But when I had left Natinga, Benson put a picture he'd drawn of a car in my bag. I remembered that and ran home the day of the art exam and brought it back with my name on it. The teacher gave me a 99.5 percent. I got 85 percent in geography and Christian religion even though I knew nothing about religion at that time. Overall I ranked second out of 150 students.

I never stopped thinking of Benson, Benjamin and Joseph. They posted a list of new arrivals and I checked it all the time. Every time a truck came, I waited to find out who was on it. I hoped to see someone from Natinga who could give me news. Sometimes I went to the compound looking for information, but it was an hour's walk and I didn't learn anything more. Now that I was well and could think clearly, they were on my mind every minute. But I couldn't imagine how Benjamin, even if he could escape that awful jail, could make the trip across the desert between here and Natinga with his bad leg. I could only hope they wouldn't send him to fight. I worried that Joseph might have been taken with the older boys to fight. Benson was clever and smart and strong. I knew he could escape and make it here. I had to believe that; thinking of anything else was unbearable. As I awaited the arrival of each truck, the thing I feared most was meeting someone from Natinga who would tell me my friends had disappeared long ago.

Your Worst Enemy

BENSON

One quiet summer Natinga night, a few months after Alepho had gone, I heard whispering voices at the back of my hut and peeked out of the window. Two boys were pushing a blanket into a bag. I recognized one of them. The tall, thin silhouette was Alier, who was a few years older than me. The other boy's back was to me but I heard him say, "I'm going out to get water. Meet me down by the stream. Don't let anyone see you."

My heart beat fast. They were escaping. This was my chance.

I rushed outside. "Alier," I whispered. "What are you doing here?"

"Sssh! Don't talk. Go back to sleep!"

"I'm coming too."

"No. You're too young."

"I've waited for this opportunity," I said. "If you talk more I'll report you to security." I wouldn't have done it and he probably realized it, but I knew they wouldn't take me unless I forced them.

He gave me an angry look. "Okay. But you have to be quiet."

I went inside to fold my blanket and get my yellow one-gallon jerry can, thankful I'd filled it that afternoon. When I came back out, he was gone. I remembered them whispering about meeting down at the stream so I carefully walked in that direction until I heard voices and came upon eleven guys sitting at the darkest part of the dry riverbed.

They all looked up. "Where do you think you're going?" a boy said.

I gripped my things.

"Look around. Do you see anyone of your age?"

I knew a couple of them—Aguek, Anyoun, Moror and Anyong—but the others were older than Alier. Some had been in the army or had escaped before and been captured and jailed. At twelve, I was the youngest and smallest by a few years, but my mind had determined that getting to Kenya was the right thing. "I can do it," I said.

"Don't you know it's risky? Three days and no water. You'll be slow in walking and that will give us a hard time on our journey."

I insisted.

"Don't argue with him," said Aguek, a tall boy with a hunch on his back. "Let him follow, he'll taste it for himself. But if you don't walk fast, make sure you understand that nobody will wait for you."

They'd made the point clear. I would be food for the ravenous hyena if I strolled too slowly. But I wasn't the weak bone they imagined. I wasn't daunted at having to walk or run any distance they set.

I kept quiet and stayed near the front of the line as we started off into the cool night. The moon was low in the east as we marched in one line along a dusty road that went all the way to the border of Kenya. We knew that the commanders would send soldiers the next day after finding us missing, and we needed to get as far from Natinga as we could before daybreak. We watched for mountain gangs: meeting them would be worse than the soldiers. Hyenas screamed in the bushes but we didn't care about them because our number was enough to scare them. When we reached a place where we suspected others had been caught, we abandoned the road. The thing that frightened us most was being caught by the Taposa tribesmen who grazed their cattle in the area. They were friendly with the government and had a reputation for capturing escaping rebel boys and taking them to the government troops in Kapoeta, where they were paid with sweet sesame butter cookies. The Taposa men loved those cookies and you were as good as dead if the government troops got you.

As we came down out of the mountains to the flat desert, the sun's rays lit up the eastern horizon. It grew very hot, even so early in the morning, and we found some bush to hide and sleep in. We did our best to be quiet, get some rest, and not be seen.

By noon we'd hardly slept and the little water we'd carried from Natinga was already finished. Late afternoon, finally exhausted, we dozed off only to be awakened by chanting songs from Taposa men herding their cattle. Unable to see them, we waited in silence. When a few of the grazing cattle came toward our hiding bush, some of the guys panicked and whispered, "Run!"

"No," Aguek said.

He was right. If we had fled it would have frightened the cattle and alerted the tribesmen. We couldn't outrun those grown men with their spears. Our eyes were the only things that moved. My heartbeat didn't slow down until the cattle passed by.

At dusk, Aguek and I wanted to leave before we wasted away without water, but most of the guys wanted to stay until it was very dark. The others ignored us. "You are too young," they said, "to know what to do." They even threatened to beat me up if they were caught, saying that it would be my fault because they hadn't wanted a young boy to make things complicated for them.

So we stayed until it was quite dark and then started through the thorny scrub. I was continuously warned that if I didn't walk faster, I was going to be left behind. Most of the boys wore long trousers and rubber sandals on their feet. I went barefoot in my shorts. The sharp tiny teeth of the thorny bush hooked deep into my skin. I had no time to carefully remove the thorns or I would have been left for the hyenas as I had been warned. I pulled at them as I went until my legs became slippery with blood. Still, I kept near the front of the line behind Alier, forcing myself forward by thinking how much I longed to see Alepho. Inside me the feelings of how happy I would be to reach the camp allowed me to forget the pain of each step. I hoped there would be a clinic to treat my wounds and that any scars would forever be a sign of my successful escape.

We walked for several hours trying to find the road. A few hours after midnight we found it and rested there a few minutes. Just as we started down the road again, something jumped out and roared at us. The group scattered in different directions and left me standing there alone. A leopard's eyes flashed right at me before he slunk off. The guys in the bush whispered out to me. When I joined them they scolded, insisting that I brought nothing but trouble to them. I just kept quiet.

That was the first and last time we saw the road that night. We made our way back into big dark bushes and ended up going nowhere because of the thick thorns. We eventually found a dry stream. Now we were so thirsty that we imagined the smell of water. Five of our friends followed the direction of the stream, but they saw no wet place and came back. We slept our second night in a small clearing. After walking a full night and day, we were so tired and thirsty that nobody cared about the danger possibly lurking in those unknown dirty dark bushes.

At daybreak, I was the first one up and I woke the rest. We walked all morning, our mouths and throats so dry it hurt to breathe. We weren't sure of our direction until we heard planes in the far distance. "They're going to the airfield in Lokichokio," said Alier. Using the last of our energy, we struggled up a hill and saw the road in the far distance. By noon we were so hot, thirsty and weak that no one could go further.

We collapsed on the ground, unable to even speak to each other, but the fear in our eyes spoke for us. We could never make it to Lokichokio, maybe not even to the road. Without water, there were no steps left in our weary limbs.

Then one of the guys suggested our urine. The idea came from the experience of soldiers who had been in brutal situations after being dispersed by battle. Now, on the day when I felt closest to death, we recalled how they survived.

As disgusting as it sounded, the situation allowed no alternative.

Everyone tried. I could only produce enough to have filled an empty chicken eggshell. My jerry can still looked empty with so little in the bottom. At first I took only half of it into my mouth. The taste was unbearable, bitterly stinging on my tongue. It increased the pain in my throat, leaving it burning up with dryness so rapidly that I needed to repeat it again. The last of it wetted my mouth just enough to allow me to speak for a minute. I could move my tongue, swallow and breathe freely enough to keep walking, which was all I was fighting for.

And so we continued our journey down the other side of the hill. Along the way, Moror asked, "May I use your jerry can to cool my urine?"

It was a strange request. "No," I replied. We both were quiet then and kept walking. He looked sad but didn't say anything. I didn't want my jerry can to be used by somebody else for his urine. There was no way to wash it and I didn't want to mix my urine with his if I was fortunate enough to produce more.

We reached the road, but Anyoun, who was as light-skinned as an Arab, short, fat and older than the rest of us, gave up walking there, stumbled to the shade at the side and crumpled down. "Please, anyone who is lucky to get the water first, try to remember me."

"Don't give up," we urged him.

"I don't think I will be alive past three o'clock. Please remember, please. Help me with a drop of cool water in my mouth or my ear if I'm found breathless. Then I can live again."

That was scary talk. We looked at him and didn't have anything more to say.

Anyong broke the silence. "Don't stop here. Let's find better shade so that we can wait until the heat subsides."

Four guys followed Anyong a short way down the road to sit under a hegelig tree, but Anyoun and the others stayed there by the side of the road. To me, waiting until the heat of the sun faded was an odd idea. We'd been traveling in summer heat without water for more than thirty-six hours. I was feeling dizzy, my mouth was dry and I couldn't talk: it seemed risky to wait longer in the desert heat. I just wanted to keep walking. I could see smoke and dust over the trees from the planes taking off at Lokichokio. It might only be a two-hour walk away. Waiting until the sun began to set added three more hours without water. My urine had saved my life, but now even that was exhausted; I hadn't produced any more.

Alier had been keeping the same speed as me although he was taller but just as skinny to the bone. He said, "Let's just rest here in this shade for a minute."

Rather than go on alone, I agreed and sat beside Alier, who used his bag as a pillow. He was soon asleep. My eyes closed too. I began to feel like I was fainting or floating and tried to open my eyes again. They wouldn't wink or move. They were sealed. I wanted to stand up but my bones were too heavy and nothing would move. I'd seen this happen to others when we crossed the Ajakageer desert going to Ethiopia in 1987 and twenty-four people died resting in the shade. A breath of fear blew on my face. My body reacted. I swung my legs under me, forced my eyes open and stood up. What felt like a sudden sweat covered my face. My heart beat rapidly.

"Alier, Alier, wake up." I shouted. He didn't move. Just so calm, like the shade we were sitting in. "Alier, Alier, wake up!" I hit him on the shoulder. Still no response.

Across the road, Aguek, who was resting with the three others, sat up at the sound of my voice. He looked at me and then around every corner of the bush, as if he thought I had been awakening Alier out of fear of danger.

I tried to awaken Alier again, knowing this was the way people died, but I had no success. For me, I'd rather die walking than wasting too much time going from one shade to another. I picked up my bag and headed back onto the road. Aguek was awake and watched me prepare to leave but said nothing.

I looked directly up the straight road. It was spinning and I could see limpid water like a lake ahead. I glanced back to Alier; he was still not moving. My tongue was too dry to say something like, "Come on, join me and let's go."

I hoped others would follow, but regardless I was determined to take my chances going alone rather than lying under a tree and never opening my eyes again. But once I had decided to die walking, I found myself alone, with desert all around and no place to hide if danger came. My heart pounded against my belly with each step. The sun grew hotter. Walking barefoot at the equator line in the blazing African summer sun is like walking on a path of fire. My feet burned so painfully that I had to leave the road. I tried the grass, but it was as sharp as a thorn. I moved to the dry leaves and dust on the roadside. My fear of soldiers, mountain gangs and hyenas was forgotten and I hoped only that someone would come by with water before I was roasted alive.

In the mirage on the road in front of me dark lines appeared that looked like a vehicle emerging out of a lake. I looked behind and saw the exact same image. It was only the heat playing tricks on my eyes. I still checked to see if the other guys had woken up and were catching up with me, but they'd long ago vanished from my sight.

Aguek had warned me earlier that a road leading off to the left over a small hill went to a base where SPLA soldiers were stationed. They were the same soldiers who had arrested Aguek on his earlier escape. When I neared the divide in the road and looked up the branch that led to the base, I saw a man in the far distance coming toward me. Ahead, the buildings of Lokichokio were already visible. I was now so close to Loki that I could hear the murmur of people, chickens crowing and grazing cattle mooing for their calves. But to add to the fears that I might die in the broiling sun, the man coming from the base seemed to be walking faster than I could.

I realized then why the others had sat down and waited for the sun to cool. They knew that if they were still alive by night, they could pass the base without anyone seeing them. Perhaps they even wanted me to try the way for them.

The approaching man walked even faster. I recognized him as a bodyguard to one of the commanders who came to Natinga. There was nothing I could do. He caught up with me and my breathing seemed to almost stop as he passed me by whistling, "Liw, liw, liw, low." He never said a thing. He walked on so quickly that he was soon out of my sight.

It was almost three when I arrived at the edge of Loki and I knew that at least I would not die from thirst. I felt happy inside. I would have sung if I had been able to. All I needed was to find water.

Two policemen sat smoking at the police post up in front of me, their guns leaning against their shoulders. One was huge and fat. I recalled some advice Aguek had given me along the way. Entering another country like Kenya, I should not carry any army material like a gun, bullets or uniform because they would think I was a soldier trying to intrude. Soldiers were not allowed into refugee camps; anyone caught carrying military materials could be put into jail for seven years.

I had no such materials, except a scrap of an army uniform I'd picked off the ground in Natinga and sewn on my own shirt as a patch. If a policeman spoke to me he might see the army uniform piece on my shirt. I sat down on a rock and took off my shirt. A Turkana boy standing nearby grazing his cattle smiled at the sight of me removing my shirt. Tearing off the uniform piece left a gaping hole. I buried the scrap under the rock and took my other shirt out of my pack and doubled them up as they both had holes.

I walked past the two policemen. They didn't say anything to me, but one pointed at me and the huge one laughed until he coughed from his smoking.

The sounds of the cars, planes, and generators of Lokichokio grew louder. Dust hung like smoke over the hills and horizon. I didn't know where to go and I didn't want to ask the police. I let God guide my journey and came to many green tents arranged in circles under some acacia trees. I thought it might be the UN compound, where I could find out what to do and ask for water. Just inside the gate two men wearing green overalls the color of the tents were smoking and washing plates. A bearded man looked up as I approached the gate. He stopped washing the plates and had a surprised look on his face. He said something to his friend in a strange language and walked toward me where I stood outside the fence. I put my bag down in the shade under the tree and took out my bowl to ask for water. Both men came to the fence, stared, and spoke more in their language, probably Kswahili, which I couldn't understand. They were Kenyans or Haraka Haraka as we said in Natinga, when they came in the grain trucks. They always said "twende, haraka, haraka" when they drove away.

One of the men shook his head and went back to his washing job. The bearded man stared. I had no strength to run. I was like a rock, unable to move. My lips were dry, like they'd been smeared with ashes and I couldn't talk. I'd come across countless difficulties, like going on an empty stomach for longer than I'd expected, but the worst thing of all my life was this thirst. Dinka people have a saying: Never mind the person who refuses you food, he is only a glutton. Take a good look at the person who denies you a drink; he is your worst enemy. Was he going to save my life with water or turn me over to the army?

The man reached through the fence and took my bowl from me without waiting for me to open my mouth to ask. When he returned with it full of cold water, I drank half and poured the rest over my head and my boiling body. I gave the bowl back to him. My English was not good but I said, "Water more." He took the bowl, filled it again and brought it to me. I drank it all. I gave him the bowl for the third time.

"No," he said. "You drank too much. Where you coming from?"

As I said, "Sudan," my body felt like there were flames

under my skin. I stumbled to the shade, not even thanking the man who had given me all that free water. I spread the blanket and tried to rest, but the blanket was burning and my body was burning. I couldn't relax. A painful heat kept me switching from sitting to lying. I walked back and forth, from the shade to the sun. Whatever I did it was all the same pain. My skin felt like it was melting, as though I'd been locked into an iron cage oven and set on the fire. I'd never had so much pain in my life as that pain from drinking water after such dehydration.

The man came out and asked me for my bowl. I quickly gave the bowl, thinking he was going to give me more water that I could pour over my burning body. But this time he gave me rice cooked with meat. I put a small amount in my mouth. My tongue felt thick and the food tasted strange, like chewing mud with a scrap of clothing. A tall Turkana boy with a stick came and stood on one leg before me. I thought he wanted my food so I gave him my bowl. I wanted the bowl emptied in order to ask for more water. He ate the food but he still stood on one leg with his stick and stared at my bag. I was consumed by pain and totally exhausted. I didn't even know what he wanted. I rested on the blanket while the ground spun around me. The good man with the beard, who had given me free water and free food, was still keeping an eye on me. He came back out and told the boy, "Go away from here." The boy left with my bowl.

"Water more," I told the man.

He brought me a new bowl and said, "You must get out of here. Go to UN compound. Go and find the Sudanese. This is not the UN compound. It is another organization and I just work as an employee. I don't have the power to accommodate you. Don't stay here. The Turkana will take your bag, even kill you for it."

I folded my blanket and headed toward where he pointed his fingers. As I walked I felt sudden cold with the sun going down. When people suffer, their senses are overwhelmed and they forget the world around them. I was a way down the road when I wished I had the strength to go back and thank that man who had saved my life, but instead I just walked on.

I came to houses of a type that I'd never seen before, made of flat sticks with carton covers on top. Children ran out of the stick houses and put their hands on their hips and stared at me with suspicion. When I got near them they ran and poked their heads out from their mother's skirts looking after me. I saw a water tap surrounded by muttering women and children. I needed water, but didn't know what language to ask with. A girl with long braids came toward me and said hello. I heard that familiar word and said "water." She said yes and took my bowl and brought me some water. I sat down and drank and hoped the fire wouldn't start again under my skin. Everybody around was looking and pointing at me like a stranger dropped out of the clouds.

The girl with the braids asked, "Where you coming from?"

"Sudan," I replied.

She said something I couldn't understand except the word "kilometers." I didn't know what she was talking about. I just shook my head and said yes because it would be rude to get quiet with these people who had been so nice giving me free water.

"UN compound. Where?" I asked.

She pointed in a direction and tried to explain it but her English was too quick for me to understand all that she was saying.

I waved good-bye and walked toward where she pointed. On the way, I asked another man if he knew the compound. The man said, "Go to SRRA. SRRA stands for Sudan Relief Rehabilitation Association. At SRRA, you go ask the Sudanese and they might show you where to find the compound."

When I reached the SRRA, I was feeling too sick and weak to walk to the compound. All I wanted was to lie down and cover myself with the blanket. I found a Sudanese man there with a lot of people. He asked, "Where are you coming from?"

"Sudan."

"Who is with you?"

"Eleven more boys are left back in the bush. Some of them already might be dead because of their thirst. They need help. They need water."

"Oh yeah," he said. "Let them die. They're stupid. Why did they have to escape? That's how they'll learn."

When he said that, I guessed he was a commander in the SPLA army by the way he spoke so cruelly and heartlessly. I didn't want to talk any more. I wasn't finding help and I didn't have the energy or strength to walk back and bring water to the boys in the bushes. I prayed they would survive on their own strength.

Thirty minutes later the man came back. "Get up," he said. "Don't you want to go to Kakuma? I know that is why you escaped from Sudan. There is the truck going to Kakuma now. If you miss it, you'll spend a week here with no food to eat and no place to sleep. The soldiers might even take you back to Sudan."

Even though I was shivering and exhausted with sickness, going to Kakuma was my only choice. No one was going to help the older boys back on the road and I couldn't do it alone. If I could make it, I knew they could. This was my chance. Surviving here for a week seemed impossible. No one cared about a sick boy, except to turn him over to the police.

I climbed into the truck with a lot of Turkana women wearing heavy necklaces that smelled of the oil smeared on them. The truck started off and with every bump, the bangles on their arms and ankles jingled. I covered myself with the blanket. The truck moved from one stop to another around Loki, picking up a lot of people. As the truck ran, my body seemed to be moving in the opposite direction, like a circle and I was feeling dizzy and ready to vomit.

The road to Kakuma took about three hours and it was after midnight when they dropped us inside a fenced area. "Sleep here," they said. "Tomorrow you'll go to UN office. Those who have their registration will go to their group. Those who don't will be registered."

Everything was quiet; the only noise came from the generator at the UN compound. All night I had a terrible chest pain and in the morning when I woke up I coughed up a lot of thick green saliva. They brought biscuits in cans for two people to share. The man with whom I was supposed to share put our can in his pack. A woman with many children saw this and gave me her two extra cans. A green vehicle came to take us to the International Rescue Committee for registration.

I was so sick and weak and felt like I was waiting there for nothing until suddenly I recognized a voice and laugh. An old friend from the camp in Ethiopia, Nicodimus, walked by with another boy who had a familiar walk. I called out, "Nicodimus!"

He looked at me with a strange expression like, "Who's this?"

"Oh my God," he called to the other boy, "this is Benson."

The other boy came close. It was Lino. The three of us hugged and greeted one another.

"Alepho?"

"Group 37," said Lino. Relief flooded over me like cool water and we had a joyous greeting again. Lino picked up my bag. I'd survived and made it to Kakuma. I was with my friend and my cousin. And most importantly, Alepho was alive and well.

Lino and Nicodimus took me to their house and cooked wheat flour in water as a soup. I tried to eat it but it tasted different. Spicy to my tongue. "What *is* this?" I asked.

They showed me little shiny cubes. "Beef flavor."

I took a few more bites.

"How did you come here?" Lino asked.

"I came by vehicle." I was feeling too sick to tell them about the whole journey. "Can we meet Alepho?"

"We'll go. He's with your other brothers and cousins."

We walked to Group 37 and went to Uncle Ajak's house. No one was there.

"It's morning," said Lino. "They're all in school."

Nicodimus and Lino and I talked for a few hours until Peter arrived. I didn't recognize him. I hadn't seen him since he was a little boy back in our village. Emmanuel came soon after and wanted to hear all the details of how I'd escaped Natinga. As I was finishing telling him, Alepho walked in. He was clearly over the fever and looked stronger than I had even hoped. I was so relieved and happy to find him healthy, and he was surprised to see me; he hadn't heard I'd made it to Kakuma. "We will not be separated again," we pledged to each other and spent the rest of that day talking and enjoying being together. Now the only ones not there from our family were Joseph and Benjamin. I knew Joseph could get away before they put him in the army, but I also knew he probably wouldn't leave his younger cousins. But after my own near death, I couldn't imagine how Benjamin was going to escape Natinga and make that journey.

The next day, the boys who had waited in the shade on the road arrived in Kakuma. I was relieved to see them.

"You are one of the toughest guys we have ever met," they said. "How did you make it? You strode along alone and left everybody behind. Were you not scared?"

"I *was* scared," I said. "That's why I left. I was not strong like you to wait until the sun is cool. That's when I noticed only ten of the eleven boys were there. Aguek was not with them. "Did you all make it?"

"Not really," Alier said, "After you left, about thirty Turkana men with AK-47s came down the road. Aguek was awake and he saw them. He shook the other guys, 'Get up, get up, people are coming.' We woke up too slowly. Aguek got scared and ran away. Two gunmen followed him into the bush."

Alier stopped talking. I waited for him to tell me what happened.

Anyoun looked at him and added, "Well, you know how a gun sounds when somebody is hit. Then the Turkana guys came around us and took all of our bags but we didn't mind because we were thinking we'd be killed too like Aguek. Then Anyoun asked them for water. I thought he was crazy, but they provided water to us from their gourds. They said they were hunting for Taposa men who had stolen their cattle.

"That night we were too scared to go into the bush to find Aguek's body. Aguek was usually the wisest of us, but he didn't remember that surviving is the only thing that matters. When he ran he was holding a bag and tobacco. A person should know that if you lose something, you're going to get something else, but never your life again."

A few weeks later we heard from another group of boys who had escaped Natinga and made it to Kakuma that the head commander had called all of the boys together after our escape. "Do you remember the twelve boys that escaped?" he asked. "Bad news. All eleven of them were killed. And do you remember the younger one among them? The Turkana men who killed the other eleven took him away."

I thought of Benjamin stuck there with his leg rotting. With this news, he might think I was captured and the others dead. He might lose hope but there was nothing we could do.

My Mom Is There

BENJAMIN

One afternoon I was told to fetch water for cooking. My hands filled with jerry cans, I headed to the Taposa borehole by way of the military base. The SPLA commander John Garang was there with all of his trucks and cars loaded with soldiers to escort him and their families. They looked like they were preparing to leave. There was only one road out of Natinga, and it headed toward Kenya.

With my hands cramping from carrying the jerry cans, I stopped and watched. I wanted to be with my cousins: I had no family left in the camp. But my leg wasn't getting better; I couldn't make that walk. The soldiers weren't paying any attention to me. My palms became sweaty. My heart began beating. I wanted to be on that convoy out of Natinga.

My time in jail came back to me like a nightmare in the day. Beaten every morning. Sitting all day in the sun. Every evening a beating again.

Three guys ran out from nowhere and jumped up under the canvas sheeting into the back of a truck. *I should be on those trucks.* I dropped the jerry cans and jumped into the back of the same truck. I'd made my decision just in time; within minutes the convoy of military trucks and cars was moving. We drove to Key Base several hours away on the road to

Kenya. The truck stopped and we sat quietly in the dark listening to the voices and noises outside, not knowing if this was the final destination and hoping we wouldn't be discovered before the trucks moved on or the soldiers left the area so we could sneak off. The other boys were older and it didn't matter to them if they rode any farther on the truck. Lokichokio was now in easy walking distance for them, but with my leg as it was, I couldn't keep up with them and wouldn't make it alone.

Our waiting was soon over. Two soldiers threw up the canvas sheeting. "Where you guys going?"

The three boys didn't answer; they just sat there.

I remembered the excuse that Emmanuel had used when he escaped: "My mom is there. In some other car ahead."

I was so little compared to the other guys they couldn't tell that wasn't true.

They said to the older boys, "We don't want you to go to the refugee camp. We need you to stay in the country and fight," and grabbed them by their legs and hands, dropped them to the ground and closed the canvas.

The trucks and cars rolled on to Lokichokio. There I caught a truck to Kakuma and arrived late at night. They kept us in a little compound until the next morning when a car took us to the camp. The driver was from Kenya and he told me to look for my family in Zone 4.

I asked around the community and they directed me to my Uncle Ajak's house. Everybody was there. Uncle Ajak, Alepho, Lino, Peter, and Emmanuel. Everyone was there except Benson, who was playing soccer. I waited and waited until he came in.

"Son of Ajaktem," Benson exclaimed when he came in. He grabbed my hand. "You are here. How did you come?"

I explained how I'd sneaked onto the army lorry and pretended to be the son of a lady.

"Well done! You're sweating. Are you sick?"

"It's hot in this camp."

Benson laughed. "You'll become accustomed."

I didn't care. I was safe and I was with everyone I loved.

Everybody Except
Cats and Chickens

BENSON

We were all so happy to see Benjamin. Except for Joseph, now we were all together. We set about doing our best to adjust to Kakuma refugee camp. Few trees grew there and the dust was often so thick that vehicles ran with their headlights on during the day. There was no wild food or water for cultivation, so we depended on the food that came to the camp from the outside. Because of that, as time passed, the Turkana people, locals outside of the camp, began to think of us as some kind of rich people. They attacked by night, taking the food and blankets given to us by UNHCR. The camp security was not aware of this looting until two boys were shot.

The second year, camp officials began work on a very large enclosure with a barbed-wire fence. We wondered what this was and then an announcement came that the center was being constructed to count all the refugees in the camp. "Everybody, youth or adult, must go in the center to be counted. It's your responsibility to bring all of your family members, all of your children, even the newborns, into the center. Everybody except cats and chickens. The head

262

count will begin when no one is lingering outside of the fence or elsewhere in the camp. Don't miss your chance to get your ration token."

Questions and rumors flew about this fence and the headcount. Whose idea was it? What was the harm of delivering the food to the groups as it had been before?

We were concerned over how strongly the fence was being built. Even a swallow couldn't fly between the poles and wires without catching its wings on the wire's teeth.

Some people said, "Never mind. You are a refugee. Just go inside the center and be counted like cattle."

Others reminded us of the Kenyan saying, Money can move the mountain. They claimed that the greedy Kenyan compound officials were getting paid by the National Islamic Front (NIF), Sudan's national party in power, to move a mountain and the refugees were the mountain that needed to be moved. It was assumed that was why they'd built the fence.

One night, refugee men demolished the nearly finished fence, leaving it scattered in torn ugly pieces. The Kenyan officials laughed. "That was a good deed! No food will be given to any refugee until the fence comes back to stand firmly and untouched."

The fence builders went slower the second time. Meanwhile babies wanting food wailed all over the camp. The local Kenyans heard that the refugees were being punished and tripled the price of their goods. We who had no money survived by boiling kale leaves that we grew near the water tap. I wanted to flee Kenya to another country that might help. But there was no way. You needed money to bribe your way out of the country.

Once the fence was completed again, although we still had fears that our lives might have been sold, we swarmed in like locusts. The headcount went faster than we thought and ended peacefully. The fears in our intestines subsided. But there was never anything good about the headcount system.

Jobs were not available in the camp. Our only task, once every sixteen days, was to take our ration tokens to the distribution center. Each day of the sixteen-day cycle was for a specific ration group; individuals, couples, up to a large families. After pushing through the crowd all day against the sharp-toothed fence with blood on our elbows, we received half a tea glass of oil, lentils and a spoon of salt and three kilos of dried corn. That was when you were lucky enough to get into the center and receive your ration. The trouble came when you missed your day. If you discovered that your name had been ticked off by mistake on the list even though your card hadn't been punched, then you had to wait until the last two days, when complaints were dealt with.

There was always a crowd who wanted to get their rations before the center closed each day. If we weren't lucky enough to get it, sometimes we crowded the UNHCR compound gate and shouted so that the officers would pay attention to us. The police would push the crowd back until their uniforms were dark from sweat. If the head of the food distribution center, Mr. Hyena, came and told us to leave the gate, we just had to leave, forgetting our ration, and feeling sorry for our bad luck because the police would be ordered to use their whips.

Mr. Hyena called every refugee that he registered a hyena because we didn't have a home and lived by getting food from others. So we called him a hyena too.

Because of Mr. Hyena's rules if your card was stolen or lost or you missed your ration, you had to wait until the next distribution after the sixteen-day period. Then you'd better be awake at 2:00 A.M. to enter the distribution center for the 9:00 A.M. ration. But even at two in the morning, you'd find people who had given up sleeping entirely and were in the center for the whole night to get those three kilograms of corn grains. Missing those three kilograms meant sharing with a friend, and your bodies felt again the pain of hunger.

Meanwhile, the people who carried out these regulations looked like they had never suffered hunger, eating food without pause day and night. But we had to stay strong and were always chided by the message announced clearly on the loudspeakers, "Why did you leave your country to come to Kenya?"

But we were human beings, not donkeys, and couldn't chew the damn hard dry corn grains every day. It made our teeth strong, we needed no dentist, but our stomachs and our intestines became infected. Many people died of stomach problems. The corn needed grinding so we collected our ration together and sold some to pay to grind the remaining grain. Sometimes we stood three days in a line in the local town waiting for the grinding machine. Other times when people went to the market to sell some of their grain in order to get money to grind the rest, gangs robbed them of it all. If you were robbed, you went back to the camp weeping for the fact that war in your land had driven you to this arid part of northern Kenya, where the starved local inhabitants were as ravenous as wolves. We knew we didn't belong there and didn't deserve to own a thing, even grains of corn.

When the camp officials heard that refugees sold their grains in town, they took advantage and started rumors that the refugees were being fed so much that they were selling the food; as a result we received a large grain ration amount reduction and no more oil or lentils. At other times, when the ration was cut way back, we were told things like the food was stuck at Mombassa port because a bridge had collapsed on the way.

Many things in the camp were difficult to manage. The food ration arrived every sixteen days, but firewood distribution was once in two months. If you didn't cook the food well, your stomach rumbled and cramped and bothered you all day and you were constantly running to the bush. It took hours to cook the food, using lots of fuel and leaving us with nothing to cook by. We risked stealing dry sticks from the scarce trees outside the camp, but the local Turkana men waited in ambush to search our pockets for money if they caught us taking firewood from their environment. Women and girls who went far from the camp were ambushed and raped as punishment for stealing the wood. But they didn't stop because their children were crying from hunger.

Living as refugees meant always hearing news that was sad or threatening. Our stomachs jumped up and danced with problems we couldn't solve.

As years went by, due to these difficulties, many boys changed their ways to become pickpockets and thieves. Gangs lived in the Zone 3 markets, where they drank beer made from sugar and fought when they got drunk. We nicknamed that market Hong Kong 2 after the martial arts movies we'd seen in the camp video show about gangs and corruption and the Vietnam War.

In our groups, we stayed happy by killing time playing games like dominoes or ludo and dancing on the weekend. In the evening we gathered to eat together. If one person wasn't yet home, we'd wait until he showed up, sometimes until midnight. We had to wait in order to share the food equally together from one plate. Then we told stories and made jokes for each other. We managed our lives well in this way until 1996, when a famine hit the whole of northern Kenya. The refugees and local Turkana people were both seriously affected, but most of the Turkana starved, especially at places like Lokichokio on the Sudanese border. The Turkana living closer to Kakuma were the luckiest ones, but even they were dying. Women and children were the biggest victims of this famine because their young men only knew how to go and steal cows at the borders between Uganda and Sudan, leaving behind the starving villagers. Most children, nursing women, and very old people were saved by us and the small food restaurants that were built by the refugees.

One day my friend and I were in the marketplace selling some beans we'd bought for three shillings to sell for five, when a local Turkana girl with a tin of charcoals came and sat near us. I knew she wanted to tell us her troubles, but she only said "Brothers" and fell unconscious. We were astonished, not knowing what to do.

Suddenly she took a breath and opened her eyes. I realized that she was starving and I told my friend to buy her something to eat. My friend rushed to a small restaurant and brought hot gruel back with him. When she ate the gruel, she was sweating a lot. I asked why she let herself starve. She told a sad story of how her father left them without food some months before and didn't come back. Her mother had starved to death a week before and her brother migrated to a refugee friend's home. She was left forlornly in the *manyatta*, their traditional shelter, and struggled against starvation by making charcoal to sell. However, she had walked through the camp for three days and no one even asked for any charcoal. Because of the famine that had so affected the Turkana people, there was not much food for the refugees to cook, so nobody cared to buy charcoal.

We gave her two cups of our beans and she thanked us gladly by kissing our hands.

Even though there was much hardship in Kakuma, the education was good. At first we studied under trees and then the UN helped us build schools. We also had a lovely Sunday school, where a group of young girls and boys seven to twelve years old entertained the congregation at church celebrations or when we welcomed an important guest like the bishop.

The children danced, narrated poems, and composed a lot of simple but reasonably good songs to entertain the audience. My favorite song was the one below. To sing it, the teacher stood in front of the children who were organized into groups representing continents or countries. The teacher began the song by asking the question. "Who are you?"

One group of children would answer, "We are the Africans."

"And you?"

"We are the Asians."

"And you?"
"We are the Americans."
"And you?"
"We are the Australians."
"And you?"
"We are the Europeans."
"And you?"
"We are the Arabians."
"Forget those names. We are all the children of God."

Being a Refugee

ALEPHO

Until the famine in 1996, life in Kakuma was fairly good compared to what we'd been through before. There was enough food and water to survive and our education was organized. When the UN had seen that we were interested in learning, they came up with the idea of building schools in the camp. One by one we built them, until after a few years we'd completed nineteen. Each one was named for a town in southern Sudan and had eight levels of education. I went to Juba primary school.

Those first years, I thought Kakuma was going to be the nicest place I'd been since leaving home. But the famine changed that. The camp officials told us the UN had said there was not enough money to feed us for years. They reduced everything, school facilities, food, medical care, shelter, all those human needs. Food, water, supplies for the clinic, everything required waiting in line for hours. Grown men would cut in front of lines. The refugees began to fight each other. The war had given everybody so much anger inside that if one person got hurt in a fight, then friends or family joined in and the fighting spread, even over small things. I fought many times at the faucet trying to get water.

This made me think that perhaps there was no safe place in this world and there would always be fighting. Everybody was depressed and angry. Sometimes captains or lieutenants of the SPLA who were tired of fighting came to Kakuma camp to rest. They came with news of Sudan and news of the war. But all that time there was never any news of my family. I didn't know what had happened to Joseph and I could only hope that Yier was still alive even though as a soldier in the rebels, I knew it might not be so. It had been nearly ten years since I left my home and I didn't know anything about my mother, brothers or sisters.

The soldiers who came to camp always said, "You know, I think there will be peace." But although people always hoped and prayed for peace, peace never came and we lost hope.

There was no future to a life in the camp. We were going to school, learning English, science, mathematics, history and home science. We learned about ovens that cooked food without fire, water taps inside the home and spatulas. They taught us how to clean a house: daily cleaning, weekly cleaning, the process of cleaning a toilet. I'd never seen a toilet or flushed one. The teacher said, "Draw these in your exercise book." We drew forks, knives and pans. We learned everything reading a book and looking at the pictures. We bought seeds and used our spare water to grow okra and sell it. When we'd saved five shillings, we'd go to the Somali area and watch movies on a TV with Arnold Schwarzenegger and Richard Norton. We saw another world. We were getting our education in Kakuma, but what was the point of it? There were no jobs in the camp. We couldn't go back to Sudan. The Kenyans didn't want us in their country and wouldn't allow a Sudanese to work. There was no place in the world for us. We lost hope in the future.

In late 1996 I saw Joseph, just standing there. I couldn't believe it: he appeared in Kakuma in the middle of the day. He didn't have anything, just his bare hands. He came and lived with us. It took a while for him to get a ration card, so we shared what food we had. I only had one bedsheet I'd bought with 180 shillings, a lot of money that had taken a long time to save. When he arrived with nothing, I gave him the bedsheet. He wasn't well. From Natinga he'd been taken into the army and fought for four years. He'd seen so many deaths in that war. You can tell if a person has come from the war: they are haunted from all the killing they have seen.

It was nearly a year before Joseph's mind freed a little bit and he talked about what he had been through. I liked to sit and listen to him. I'd ask him how he had survived all of those things. It was terribly difficult for him to explain it, to be able to put it in words.

But Joseph was amazing. Just like he'd saved Peter and me as little boys on the walk and in Palataka, he'd saved himself in the war. He saw that many times it was the younger boys who all died in the battles. When he was ordered to go fight, sometimes something appeared to him and warned him that if he went with that group, he was going to die. He'd say to his commander, "No, I'm not going this time." The lieutenant would say, "This is an order, you must go." He'd say, "No. If you want to shoot me, okay, shoot me, but I'm not going." They'd punish him with knee jumps, staying in dirty water, making him roll until he was exhausted and then beat him up. He went to fight many times, but he said that those times when he refused to go, all of the boys died.

After Joseph arrived things got harder and harder in Kakuma. Lack of fuel was one of the major problems people faced and we risked our lives getting it outside the camp or went hungry.

One Saturday in 1997 I went into the Turkanas' forest to collect some firewood because there wasn't any fuel to cook my grain. I knew that sometimes women who went into the forest were attacked by the local people. Some were even shot and killed. I usually bought charcoal from the locals who came into the camp. But that week I had no money to buy fuel and I had gone two days without eating. I had no choice.

Since we often walked together, my two friends, Deng and Bul, accompanied me. We went farther from the camp than usual and collected a bunch of sticks. We tied the sticks firmly together and headed toward home. We went a few steps and met a gunman. He ordered us to lie down on our bellies. The most terrifying thing was that his hand was on the trigger. He moved around us, watching us sternly with deep red eyes.

"You guys are victimizing our trees," he said.

We watched those fearsome eyes.

"I won't waste time talking with you. Money and clothes are all I want."

We kept quiet for a moment. Then I collected my courage and said softly, "Sir, we don't have those."

"You don't have those." He chuckled. "You are telling me creative stories."

Like an angry lion, he grabbed each of us and the air was filled with the sound of heavy slapping. "You guys, all I need is money."

We said in unison, "No money, sir."

He tortured us as his heart desired. After a long beating, he'd finally realized we were as poor as church mice, spit at us as outcasts and left. Without wasting a fraction of a second, we fled as fast as our bare feet could carry us.

Being a refugee is something that many people cannot understand. Refugee life was like being devoured by wild animals. We lived five of us in one house. The little ration we received we collected together and cooked as a meal once a day. Though we had an appetite there wasn't enough to eat as young growing boys with tender bones and body. Nutritional diseases were rampant in the camp. Children died from marasmas, kwashiorkor, anemia and beriberi. Rickets was the worst with the young boys; almost every boy was bowlegged. It was hard for boys to go to school with empty stomachs. An empty stomach cannot carry a healthy mind.

Black days came every two weeks. We could not stretch out our ration for sixteen days and when there was nothing left to eat in the three days before receiving rations again we went hungry. Worst of all, on ration day when we were so weak from lack of food, the line formed at dawn. We stood all day and the police beat people to make them remain in the sun. All we could do was read to keep busy or gather together and tell stories to forget the hunger.

Color of Hunger

BENJAMIN

Since I'd left home, my life hadn't been safe; I'd always thought I was going to die. At last in Kakuma I believed I would survive. The clinic had given me medicines and bandages and since the stick had been removed in Lokichokio and I was out of that dirty jail in Natinga, my leg healed.

Although we never had enough food in Kakuma and it was hot, windy and dusty, and people were sick without help, we still had some fun. All week we went to school and studied and cooked our food. It took hours to prepare, finding the firewood, getting the water and when it was done around ten in the evening, we'd eat together at once. Friday evening, Saturday and Sunday we mixed with the other groups, played soccer and enjoyed fresh air outside with our friends.

The Kenyan police were not friendly. Sometimes, when I went to collect rations, the ration center police came and beat us there in the line. They beat us whether we were a little boy or a big guy. If we made ourselves strong and asked, "Why do you beat me?" they would jail us immediately. If you were taken to the jail, as a rule you would be beaten first. Your arms, your legs, your joints, would be beaten until you became paralyzed. Then they would lock you up. It was best to let yourself be beaten like a donkey in line until the time you received your ration and then go back home and rest.

Things got worse when the UN cut back the rations and I soon learned how it goes in a refugee camp. There is food and there is education. The education is fine, but the food is not enough. You have to choose between education and food. If you don't want an education you can make a business for your survival. If you want education you have to take the little bit of food that is given by UNHCR and eat only once a day. It is your choice whether you eat in the morning and sleep in the afternoon or just stay hungry for the whole day and eat later. My cousins and I managed this. We went to school and ate once a day in the evening. But reading was really difficult because when you read there was a certain cloud because of hunger. It's black when you look at the words in the book. The black covers the words and you can't see because of that color in your eyes from the hunger.

Hopeless, Hopeful

BENSON

After six years I found that I hated Kakuma more than any-where else because of how people thought about us. The word "refugee" was very strong on the Kenyans' tongues. It meant "useless" to them. When things were difficult and we complained, they said, "Don't forget that you are a refugee. This is Kenya. Why did you leave your country?" This made me and the other refugees want to leave.

I had thought people always felt sorry for miserable homeless people, but the Kenyan officers felt proud when they saw us being homeless in their country. In the mean-time they were depending on us, using refugee items and food for themselves. There was a saying in Kenya, "If a refugee is in your country and you do not get rich, you will never, ever get rich in your lifetime."

The Kenyan officers had us build a social center where they could go to rest. Sometimes they would make some boys clean the place so their people could use it as shelter from the hot sun. When it was ready, all of the officer women and men came and sat in the shade and drank a lot of sodas. The hungry boys who worked on the place all day had only their saliva to swallow.

When you went to the hospital, there was always an inadequate supply of medicine. Very powerful medicines were being donated from all over the world but when they came to the camp they disappeared from the hospital. Friends of mine working in the hospital saw the medicine come and then go. When we were sick and went to the hospital, we were told the medicines were not available, but if we went to the market, the medicines were there, and they were very expensive and we couldn't afford them.

We survived in Kakuma because we learned to share. We shared food, chores and games. If a friend wanted to build his house, we collected other friends and did it all together.

Sometimes there were good men who came to work in Kakuma. One old man of fifty-eight years was kind to us boys. He even sent some boys to boarding school with the money he made working there in the camp. When he was caught doing that, he was dismissed.

A good priest named Benson came to Kakuma and baptized me. He brought medicine to treat people and he'd visit the sick in the hospital. If someone was seriously ill he'd even pay to transfer that person to Nairobi. But when it was found out he was doing that, he was transferred to another place.

Any visitor who came to the camp could only go around the community accompanied by three officers. When they came to visit our house, one officer would arrive first and instruct us, "There is a visitor, so please keep quiet and we will explain everything to him." They didn't want us to speak. If the visitor asked about something, they were ready with an answer that made themselves look good.

A lot of people were trying to get out of Kakuma; going to Uganda, South Africa, or anywhere in the world. But the police were very aggressive and you had to pay one thousand shillings to go to another location. Where could we get the money? I spent weeks growing handfuls of okra to sell for five shillings. A lot of people were stuck in the camp.

I did so much thinking when I was in Kenya. At first I was thinking about going to any country that would receive me so that I could compete for my own survival. I didn't want rations that people always insulted me for. What they called us was very bad. That was why I hated Kakuma. It convinced me that there was no country where I could be free. I felt hopeless.

Imagine someone starving, dreaming that he has plenty of food beside him. But when he wakes to have his delicious food, there is nothing. He realizes that he was dreaming and goes back to sleep with no hope in his heart. He fears that he is going to die early in the morning because he has spent three days without food or water. But by the will of God, early in the morning, the guy gets lucky. He finds food in wild trees. He thanks the Almighty and starts to feed on one of those wild trees.

That was how I felt in 1998 when the process for the Lost Boys to go to America began. It gave back hope.

But I was worried about two things. The first thing was passing the INS interview that some of my friends, who, I thought, were more intelligent than me, had failed. But I soon learned that the INS interview didn't demand being clever or intelligent. It needed me to relax and listen carefully to the interviewer's questions and then answer the questions simply, as well as I could.

Some of the INS questions were:

When did your father marry your mother?
How many cows did your father pay to marry your
    mother?
How many times was your mother married or how many
    husbands did she have?

These questions were silly. How could you know them when you were not yet born?

Now that there is war in your country, which side do you
    support?

This question was difficult. If you said you supported the north or south, they would ask more questions. This would take time and there was a crowd waiting for the interview. The best thing to say was, "I'm not supporting any part but I hope they come together, they are both my people."

What are you going to be or do in USA?
Why do you want to go to USA?
Why do you want to leave Kakuma when you are getting
    free education and free food?

I realized this last question did not come from the INS but from the Kenyans who were working in the refugee camp. When we were ready to depart for the US, the Kenyans sometimes picked out someone's name to start the interview process again. They did this to delay us because they didn't want us to go to the USA: they said their people would lose their jobs working at the camp.

My biggest worry was my file. Files were often "missing," but every Lost Boy knew that they were taken and sold. If you had no file, you had no hope.

In Process

ALEPHO

All those years we were in the camp, we knew the best thing you could do for your life was to finish high school. If you graduated, the UN paid 3,500 shillings (about $50) to teach in the camp. It wasn't bad pay, but you had to give up the ration card and live only on your salary.

After the process to go to America began, many boys quit school. They said, "Why do you want to go to school? You can go to America." They tried to make business to earn money in order to chitchat with the girls. The girls in the community said, "I've come to the camp safely and I don't ever want to be in Sudan again. I want a guy who will graduate from high school or have a business and can provide me with some money. If you don't have any money, forget about talking to me. That's the bottom line."

Some of the guys who had girlfriends told them they would never see them again, since they were going to America, but they would remain in their heart. The girls said, "Oh, America! That's the best place to be. Go there and get money and send me the form to get me out of here. We can forget about the dust in this camp and live happily in America." They lived only in imaginary worlds and didn't know that when the guy was in America, he could only send for his parents, children or wife.

Some of the older Lost Boys had already left the boys' groups to go to the community and get married. Anyone who was married when the Lost Boys process started in 1998 was not eligible.

Once the process started and the boys gathered together, they stopped discussing the past like they used to. No more: "Oh, I have seen a lot of tragedy. I have seen a person who got shot in the head. I was there and I had to play dead." Now it was all about America. The boys in high school discussed economy and politics.

When I first heard about the possibility of going to America, I was very excited. I said, "Forget what happened in Sudan. America is the best place and I'm going to be there the rest of my life."

I also told myself, "Okay, everybody speaks English in America. If I go there and I don't know English, then that will be really embarrassing. I need to learn so that I can communicate with everybody."

Many days in Kakuma camp I hadn't been able to study because when I was hungry I couldn't think and if I couldn't think I couldn't read or do anything else. But the process of going to America gave me a new dedication that motivated me to study even when I was hungry.

The missionaries had opened a new library in the camp. I went there every day and read. I had a dictionary with quite a few words in it and I would look up all the words I didn't know. I studied American cities and states, their economies and what they provided and looked through all the pictures.

There was a magazine called *Downtown* that came from Nairobi. It had many things about America: American gadgets, American TV shows, and beautiful girls. Sometimes I spent all day there in the library. I wasn't a happy person in the camp, but this made me feel happy. I forgot about the hunger and became successful in school. I was at the top of the class.

Girls knew me because of that. That didn't make me less shy with them. I talked to them like friends; about school or life in general, but if they discussed something like a relationship, I said something like, "Ah, well, I think today I have to go to the library or I have to go to the church or get water or play soccer or read and study." The one thing I didn't like to do was stand up and speak to a large number of people. I would get so nervous and sweaty that I couldn't say anything. When I became the monitor in the class as a reward for being number one and spoke a few times, I could see the surprise in everyone's eyes.

Two years slipped by until the next interview came up. The INS interviewers seemed to know right away if you told the truth. If refugees didn't want to talk about what they'd seen or experienced or they tried to invent it, the interviewers would say, "Okay, you're lying. You don't pass." And the next thing you'd get was a letter that said "negative."

I kept working hard and mostly I pretended there was no process for America. This process had seemed to come out of nowhere. How long was it going to take to process so many thousands of boys? I knew they couldn't do it all at once. And once they did, how were they going to take so many people out of the camp? So many things could go wrong that the process might disappear just as quickly as it arrived. Also, if I didn't pass all of my interviews, all hope would be gone.

Inside my heart and mind I kept the hope alive. I felt that my life would be transformed, and the best way I could prepare for it was to get ready to communicate with the people in America. After I did the best I could and passed my interviews, I had to wait for my name to appear on the board.

Part Four

Preparing for America

Is John Travolta Dead?

ALEPHO

In 2000 our orientation began. The teachers were Africans who went to America and came back so that we could learn about America from an African perspective. They said that living expenses were highest in California. That didn't discourage me. I wanted to go there because that was where all of the movies were made—I didn't believe all those things in the movies could be real and I wanted to find out for myself. I'd only seen a few movies—videos—and they left me curious and confused. In the *Terminator*, was all of that real? John Travolta was killed at the end of *Broken Arrow*. Was he really dead? I wanted to find out about that.

The teachers explained how the agency assigned to us would help us to resettle for the first few months. They'd show us how to apply for a job—how to describe ourselves so that we would be hired. They told us we must be very friendly in America, more than people were in the camp, because Americans were used to being friendly. Some people never smiled at all in the camp. If you smiled at them, they looked back at you like they were angry. But they weren't angry at you, they were angry at themselves for some reason. I was one of those people who never smiled. So I knew that when I got to America, even if I had not been a happy person in Africa, I had to try to be a happy person there.

Some Americans heard that a large number of boys who had been fleeing for years from the war in southern Sudan were now going to America. Those Americans were excited and said, "Oh, I want to go see those boys," and they came to the camp with video cameras. When they wanted to take my picture, I said, "No, no, don't." I didn't say that with my mouth, but the expression on my face said no. I didn't want anybody to touch me or take my picture. The other boys said, "If you don't want your picture taken, why are you going to America? That's where the cameras come from." It was stupid of me.

After orientation we waited months again. Every day people left from our group and more than ever we wondered if we would ever leave. We were all so nervous. Benjamin's process was a mess and he hadn't had cultural orientation yet, but even so it looked like it would work out and he would leave after us. Emmanuel and Peter's files were both missing, along with more than a thousand others. The officials said they were working on that. It was known that the Lost Boys were a priority, so we had a little hope for them because of that. But Emmanuel and Peter were still worried. Peter needed treatment for his one good eye; it was often infected. His brothers and cousins were leaving. My heart ached for him and I told him every day, "Don't worry, when we get there and get settled, we will send for you." But I didn't know if that was possible. I just knew that if we stayed in the camp with him, none of us could help anyone, not even ourselves.

I kept studying and took my final exam, the KNCE,

Kenyan National Certificate of Education, which I passed in January 2001.

So I only had to wait for notice of the flight. I went to the library and read more about America because cultural orientation had ended two months earlier. It was easy to forget, and the day they had showed everyone how to use the flush toilet, I hadn't been there so I had to read about that in a book.

Finally our names came up saying that in seven days we would be going to America. One more week. I was still nervous that something could go wrong.

My friends said, "When you get to America remember me. They say there are so many beautiful girls in America. You're gonna be rich. Go find a beautiful girl; don't forget that. There's a beautiful girl with a lot of money looking for a handsome guy like you."

I asked, "How would I do that? I'm a little shy about girls over here, I can't go do that there."

They said, "It's so easy. All you do is just smile to the girl and say 'I like you and I want to be your friend.'"

I didn't think it would be so straightforward. It wasn't even that simple in the camp.

I visited friends in the other groups, announcing to everyone, "I am going to America!" A lot of people didn't even know I was in the process.

The third day I went to the community group where they held a huge meeting for the boys who were leaving. "We've never acted like your elders," they said, "but at this meeting we're going to be like your elders. We stayed away from you because we knew that you had been through a lot of things and we didn't want to come in and tell you what to do in the camp when you had survived so much already. Now that you are going on another journey to a new world there are a few important things we're going to tell you. While we don't know much about America, we know certain things are always available in the world. Don't do drugs, don't drink, and don't flirt with ladies too much. You can get lost in the drinking and you can get lost flirting with girls. All of you are young men, so we are not saying don't have a relationship. Have a relationship in a good, appropriate way. The most important thing is that you keep up your goals in school. We won't give you any more advice. We are so happy and thankful that the American government has come to take you out. Some of you will come back and try to help us out here in this desperate situation. You'll shape our lives in the future. We are too old and we will stay and do our best with the babies and kids. You, the young men, have the chance to go to such a place as America."

I wasn't listening to everything they were saying. I didn't always take advice from elders. I heard what they had to say and made my own decision to do what I thought best. Some adults didn't like me for that. They said that I was a disobedient boy. I knew what they were saying now was right, but I was too excited and nervous to concentrate. I was thinking more about America and what it looked like. I'd never been on a plane. What would that be like?

In the last two days before departure, with the little money I saved, I went to the Ethiopian shops in the camp and bought a bag to carry my things—toothpaste, soap and one nice shirt and pants. I divided my old clothes among my close friends. People came and talked for hours and hours, even people I didn't know I had done something good for at one time. That day I realized when people live together sometimes you don't know what kind of person they think you are until you go away.

All my friends said the same thing. "We know that you don't talk to girls a lot, but as you grow up, there will be chances that you will have a lot of problems with girls and not in a bad way, but in a good way. And you, my friend, don't get lost in the middle of those beautiful American girls with the long hair tails."

The last day I got up and took a shower. For five years I had not showered with the soap that had the perfume smell. I only showered with the normal soap that they made in the camp for refugees to wash their clothes. That soap didn't smell good and it left my skin all white. When I came out after my shower, everybody said, "You smell like America already."

I replied by speaking in my nose like white people do. "Yes, I am already an American."

Twenty people came with me to the compound. At the gate, I told them, "Thank you for accompanying me, I feel like a really great, like an important person. I will miss you guys. I might see you in the future or I might never see you. I'm not going to promise you anything about America. Whatever the misconceptions are that I've heard, I will experience them for myself. If it is like people say and the machines do all the work and people stuff money in mattresses and just sit and eat all day, I will give you that feedback. But if I go and I am quiet, you will know that life is the same the world over. Don't blame me for that."

Joseph's flight was the first one in the morning. Benson, Lino and I waited in the compound all day. It was good I had recently studied the use of the toilet because I needed to use it and was able to do it myself.

Other boys needed to use it also, but they had forgotten how. They came running out with the water all over the floor. "Oh shit! The thing is broken!"

"You just broke it, man," I said.

"Shut up. I didn't do it. That's a crazy machine."

"You'll get more crazy machines in America."

At 12:30 we went in buses to Kakuma town airport and watched the plane land in a big cloud of dust. Just as we'd done for lunch, we walked toward the plane in a line. They told us that for the whole journey to the US we would travel in a queue.

When I had been waiting in the compound, I was excited. As I climbed the ladder into the back of the plane, chose to sit where I wanted and fastened my seat belt, I wasn't sure what I was feeling. People were on board with a video camera, doing interviews, and filming some of the other boys. Lino sat behind me, and Benson was nearby. I took a little bag out of the pocket in the seat in front of me and looked at it. "What is this for?"

"For when you get nauseated," Lino said, "and puke on the plane."

As the plane took off down the dirt strip, I was numb. I watched Kakuma camp vanish and thought about the friends I was going to miss. I thought of all the activities we'd done in the camp: eating together, making jokes, playing ludo or soccer, taking a walk to the riverbed when the sun was down and it wasn't hot anymore, watching other kids there playing, sitting, talking about different subjects, discussing things we'd learned in school.

Kenya slid by below. I looked north, toward Sudan. Twelve years since I'd had any news of my family or village, yet I sensed that my mother was still alive. I could feel her. Would peace ever come to my Dinkaland? Would I return and find my village still there with our houses around that tall, tall palm tree and my mother outside making a basket or preparing the next meal?

I wondered what America would be like. As a kid I'd heard stories that made me wonder if I could ever return to Africa. Some said the reason people don't come back from America is that those girls who fly the planes have never seen a black man before and they cut off their legs so that they can't escape. At the time I heard that, I didn't know slavery existed. Once I read books in the camp about the slave trade, I knew that those old stories weren't true.

The plane's propellers droned like a hive. When the plane pulled downward, I felt something pushing in my stomach. When it fell quickly, I grabbed the armrest. I think that's what made Lino vomit. I heard him behind me and turned around, I didn't know he'd been puking all along. I laughed at him. The little food he'd had in the compound was gone now.

From Nairobi International Airport, buses took us to a place called Goal Accommodation, where we waited for three days. On August 8, 2001, we boarded a flight to Brussels. This was a much larger plane than the one from Kakuma. There was a little television in the seat in front of me and I asked a white guy sitting next to me several times if he would show me how to operate it, but he didn't seem to understand or just didn't want to help. He looked tired.

When I went to the bathroom, I made sure the door

locked behind me, but then it wouldn't open when I was ready to leave. I worked on the handle, turning it every which way. Voices began giving me instructions from the outside and I was sure the whole plane was aware of my predicament. By the time I was able to turn the handle to the right position and open the door, I was covered in sweat. As I walked back down the aisle to my seat, all the white people were just sitting there like they hadn't even noticed my desperate situation.

Dinner came after a few hours and I mostly ate the rice. After dinner I was just beginning to relax when the stewardess came down the aisle calling, "Dessert, dessert."

I jumped to my feet. Was something wrong with the plane? We'd had instructions on how to put the air bag on our face and breathe, but I couldn't find mine. She was still calling, "Dessert, dessert," but no one was jumping up. Maybe they didn't understand English. I grabbed my backpack. Now the white guy talked to me. "What are you doing?"

Ignoring him, I headed for the exit in the back, wondering where I was going to go from this plane. I remained there, awaiting the next instruction. After a while, people nearby asked, "Are you lost?" As the stewardess came closer, still repeating "Dessert? Dessert?" she added, "ice cream." I went back to my seat. There were going to be a lot of new things for me to learn, including ice cream. I'd never had that before.

Flying Sabena

BENSON

As I sat in the Nairobi airport, my mind struggled with the fear of flying in Sabena, the Belgian airbus. I had heard of some cases of plane misery—that people sometimes got in trouble in the air. Whether it was safe was a huge puzzle to me. That feeling of anxiety and mistrust of the unknown made me recall the day I crossed the River Nile in a small wooden canoe without knowing how to swim.

As the Sabena airbus lifted from the runway, pushing me back against the seat like a big wind, I found it was much quieter than the flight from Kakuma and very comfortable.

Once the plane settled like a boat on smooth water, I noticed the small TV screen in front of each seat. Many white people began having a good time finding and watching the movies they liked. I liked movies too and couldn't believe my good fortune: my own movie machine right in front of me. The stewardess said we were supposed to get all channels on the small device by our right hand rest, but I couldn't work out how to turn on my little TV. I looked to the screen of the man on my right side, trying to share with him, but he kept changing the movie. If my eyes searched for another screen in the row in front of me or to the left, the same always occurred. I retreated and tried to read the instructions. I finally turned on my own TV after hitting every single button, but I still couldn't change the channel. The man in front of me was watching a movie, *Spy Kids,* that I wanted to see. I finally found that picture and the sound too and enjoyed watching my very own movie.

When the flight attendants came around, they had a difficult time explaining the food selections to us. We wouldn't choose until we heard a familiar name, like chicken or beef. There was plenty of food, mostly what they called salad. The white people were busy clearing their plates, but it was not a good time for me to be admiring the food. A few minutes earlier the plane had pulled itself downward and my stomach remained tingling with nausea and giving me an alarm.

"We are now back to a world of eating green leaves again," said my friend, Santino, who was sitting next to me. "Why do American people eat flowers?"

I didn't know much about Americans, but I'd eaten abundantly of leaves on my way to Ethiopia in 1987. I told Santino, "This is probably not a good time for me to be eating those leaves. I'm not starving anyway."

When the flight attendant collected the dishes from us, they were as green as they had been served.

"Hey!" said Santino. "Do you believe there is really a toilet inside this plane?"

"Maybe." Santino had been asking me many questions that I couldn't answer by that time. I wanted to use a toilet too and I could see that people were going to the back of the plane and then returning to their seats. I unfastened my seat belt and went to check out if the toilet was truly there. We'd been instructed in cultural orientation to be careful when opening doors on the plane. One of the boys on an earlier flight when looking for the toilet had tried to open the exit door instead and they cautioned that this could cause the plane to crash.

I went to the back of the plane and at first I couldn't see the word "toilet" or "restrooms." I saw signs for "men" and "women," but the other written word was "lavatory." I waited for about fifteen minutes to see if anyone would come out or go in. A man waited behind me for a few minutes and then he went in and came out with a lot of water flushing loudly after him. I took my chance of going in next, but I wanted to make sure there was that flush they'd shown to us in orientation before I used the lavatory. It was not easy to find and I almost left without using the toilet before I finally found it under the seat on the left. I'd been searching the top.

When I returned to my seat I told Santino, "There is a toilet there but it is called a lavatory on this plane."

"Was that the right toilet you got? Why is it called lavatory?"

"I saw a white man go in there. Maybe 'lavatory' is the nickname or the owner of the plane's name." I explained to Santino how to find the flush.

He went to use it and when he came back, he said, "I can't believe it! It is truly there."

"Yes, I told you it was there."

"Wow! Man. Americans are way up in everything. Where does it go? The urine and waste that goes in it from all these people. I guess they blow it out into the clouds like a smoke. Wow! That is why I hear from the radio that there is air pollution around the world. But, man, this is a good idea. I almost urinated in my trousers."

We laughed and watched the TV. I remained nervous about the safety of the vehicle and didn't get a wink of nap throughout the entire flight. I noticed that most of my friends had open eyes too and must have been sharing these same odd feelings.

New York

ALEPHO

On the plane from Brussels to New York I awoke dripping in sweat like I'd been playing soccer. I'd dozed off and dreamed I was back in the truck going to Torit. That had been the first time that I'd ever been in a vehicle and now, even awake in the plane, I could still smell the smoke that had made some of the boys vomit. In my dream, after the truck passed Torit and got stuck in the mud, all of the soldiers jumped out just like they had in real life. I'd been curious and stuck my head out and seen many damaged trucks and human bones lying all around. But in my dream, when I looked out, all of those skulls smiled to me and said, "Son, you will fight this war. We all paid for it. Everybody will pay for it. To pay for it you must start the process."

"The process," I said to the skulls. "What is the process?"

They said all together, "The process is to find peace in your heart."

"How can I do that? I already don't have peace in my heart."

"That's the question you need to ask yourself," the skulls replied. "How can you find peace yourself? If you answer that question, everybody will answer that question."

That question lingered in my mind as the plane's engines

roared into reverse. I was in the middle section and could only catch a glance out the window of the tall New York buildings. *Find peace in my heart.* That wasn't something I'd been searching for. Revenge had been there so long. It would have to move aside first and I wasn't willing to let go so easily or quickly.

In the huge New York international airport, Benson, Lino and I, and two other boys, Bol and Nhial, who were on the same flight to San Diego, found our gate and sat down. My eyes popped from one area of the terminal to another looking at people. They seemed very white. I held up my arm and looked at my color and said, "Oh man," wondering for a moment if whatever made them white was going to make me white too.

"They eat a different kind of food," said Bol. "That's how they get white. See the sodas. Red, yellow, brown."

I didn't believe that. I moved my chair over separately from the others, closer to the soda machine, to watch the people. "You're going to get lost," Benson warned. "Don't go anywhere."

A short white man with a mass of hair and a backpack walked by pulling another bag on wheels. He looked very intelligent to me. I thought he was a businessman or something. He pulled up a chair and sat down near me. After a bit he asked, "Do you speak English?"

"Yes."

"Where are you going?"

"San Diego."

"I'm going there too. My name is Payson."

"I'm Alepho."

Where are you coming from?"

"Africa."

He nodded. "Where in Africa?"

"Sudan."

"I had a friend a long time ago from Sudan. He was a good guy. How is the situation there?"

This was my first conversation in America speaking real English and I had just met this man, my first American; I didn't want to tell him how horrible it was in Sudan. "It's fine," I said.

"Would you and your friends like a drink?"

"A drink?"

"A soda. Would you like a soda?"

The other four guys said that they would. Payson handed me a five-dollar bill and I went to the food counter and ordered and paid. The man gave me empty cups.

"I want soda," I said.

"You get it yourself."

Payson showed me how to first put the ice in the cup, then the soda, the top and a straw. I gave each of the guys their drinks. I'd had only a couple of colas before in the camp, but they had been warm in the bottle. These were very cold. Nhial took a sip, made a face, and set it down. That made me angry. He should have said he didn't want the soda. I had just met this American man and we had already wasted his money and offended him.

"I'm sorry," I said to Payson.

He laughed. "It seems like an appropriate response to soda for the first time."

I was still angry and embarrassed, but Payson didn't seem

upset. I drank all of mine very slowly. When they called our flight, Payson handed me a piece of paper with his name and phone number. "Give me a collect call."

I didn't know how to use a phone or what a collect call was. I entered the plane first and as he passed by my seat, he waved, "See you there!"

City of Destiny

BENSON

We *rushed through the sky*, but time was not rushing. It was still. I would soon be settling in the United States, my new and better home, but I knew it would take me a while to live like a real American. It had been fourteen years ago that I'd left my home, my village and my parents, who had adapted to jungle life in the best way they could. Now here I was, on the other side of the world.

I once enjoyed the jungle smell of fresh air and melodious songs from all kinds of birds. I remember the gentle cold breeze at night and often stayed awake because of the night screaming of ferocious carnivores. I knew it was important to be careful when walking in the jungle, to watch for the spitting cobras and other deadly venomous creatures. Now, going to a city, I thought it would all be different and yet the same. I would have to learn to respect road signs and cross streets without getting attacked by crazy car drivers. The Dinka people say, "Children are protected from fire till they grow fully mature," meaning that we keep learning to the end of our lives. But I could see that it was not going to be so simple in my case. In this new place, a child of five would know many things that would be a puzzle to me.

Life in the city would have its own style. I'd been told I could get a job and make money for myself of which I would be proud. But I'd heard there were many strong young men and women who loitered at every corner of the city, wearing rags, asking the passersby if they have dollars or quarters in their pockets. I wondered why and the best answer I could come across was that they must be idle. Where I came from at the refugee camp, everybody wanted to go to a place where he or she could work for themselves. In that camp they had been job sick. Maybe in America they were sick of jobs.

I heard many things about the USA. I heard that I would be able to lead a better life and whatever it was going to take for me to do that, I was going to do it. They said that the USA was the most developed country in the world. They call it the New World because of all of the technology used to create many amazing things. Things that even take men to the moon. It made me think of the movie *Star Wars*. America would be a miscellany of confusion and magnificent experience to stumble upon. This made me want to be in my new country to see such wonders.

I also heard rumors that you didn't need to study for years and years. That in just six months you could learn from a computer what takes four years in African colleges. But I didn't pay much attention to that as my only aim was to find a good place that would change the life I had led for fourteen years.

I heard some bad things too. That there were people in America who killed people for no reason and if you were killed or happened to die by accident, and you had no parent or relatives, there would be no burial for you. They would burn your body if there was no one to pay for cemetery ground.

I wasn't going to worry too much about that either because I'd heard so many more good things. Good health care, good food, good security, a good life with good people to live with and good education. America was the land of many gorgeous goods.

Outside the airplane window, the earth seemed to go on forever. I was looking forward to my future whatever it brought.

The pilot announced, "We will soon reach the city of our destination, San Diego."

Tall buildings and a snaking bridge came into view. The plane's engine roared as the wheels hit the runway. The pilot's words stuck in my mind. San Diego, city of our destiny. I would find my destiny there too.

Epilogue

The day Benjamin saw the burning towers on the New York skyline from his plane, he was one of the last to arrive of the first group of thirty-eight hundred Lost Boys approved for resettlement in America. Halted for security reasons after 9/11, the resettlement program didn't resume in Africa until 2004. By then peace talks were underway in Sudan, and other refugee groups had taken priority. Thousands of Lost Boys remain in Kakuma refugee camp, including the half brothers of Benson and Alepho: Peter and Emmanuel.

The Lost Boys in the United States are scattered in approximately thirty cities, from Seattle to Jacksonville, averaging a hundred or so in each location. The fortitude that enabled their survival helps them meet the challenges of starting a new life in a strange, competitive culture, but their struggle is not over. They endured and witnessed as small children things that permanently scar mature soldiers. With death by starvation, thirst, wild animals or enemy forces constantly at their heels, they lived in a state of continuous fear that few of us ever experience. They are among the most badly war-traumatized children ever examined.

Are there any Lost Girls? When the villages were attacked, many of the girls were raped, killed or taken as slaves to the north. Less than two thousand made the journey across Sudan. However, once they reached Kakuma, they did not live in distinct groups like the boys, but moved in with families in the general community. Less than a hundred now live in the United States. Of those still languishing in the camp, some married and others became domestic slaves. They are generally considered one of the most vulnerable groups in the world.

The desire for education that lured the Lost Boys and Girls, first to Ethiopia and then to Kenya, still burns bright in America even as they discover that education is not free, that college takes more than a few months, and that mattresses are not stuffed with money. Managing work, school and household duties without familial support is a struggle. In some cities, groups provide varying levels of assistance. The International Rescue Committee, a nationwide resettlement agency, founded the National Lost Boys Education Fund. The only one of its kind, it offers grants to Lost Boys or Girls in America who are furthering their education. More information is available at www.TheIRC.org/Lost BoysEd.

Creating this book has been a journey that I was privileged to share. We were blessed when Joni Evans, vice president of William Morris, took a leap of faith in not one but four unproven writers and agreed to represent us. She placed us with a wonderful editor, Clive Priddle, who gave us so much more than excellent writing guidance; he became a caring friend.

Bringing these stories to print required a courageous undertaking by Benson, Alepho and Benjamin. They demonstrated tremendous bravery in putting on paper experiences so painful that many veterans hide similar memories from their closest friends and family for their entire lives. They say that their reasons for sharing these experiences out-weighed the difficulty of telling them. They realize they are the voices for those still suffering in silence from the world's longest war. Although difficult to extract, relaying these events has been a valuable part of the healing process. And as Benjamin said, "I have no photos as a child. These are my memories for my children and my grandchildren so that they will not forget me."

In a world where we witness war on television as imper-sonally as an action movie, personal accounts are necessary reminders that for someone, somewhere, war is all too real. It has tragic and lasting consequences on people's lives, particularly children's.

Judy A. Bernstein

Afterword to the
10th Anniversary Edition
ALEPHONSION DENG

I'm often asked, "What have you done while in America?"

"A few things," I answer.

I've worked in a grocery store, at a hospital, and on a major movie set. I've been the target of a hate crime, and I've starred in a play called *Since Africa* and cowrote and acted in another called *Across Worlds*. I've written a book, volumes of poetry, essays, and tirades that I often destroyed mere hours after creating them. And I've spoken to thousands of people about my life.

Writing and speaking have had an impact I never could have imagined. Anita Henderlight read our book the first week it came out and then moved to southern Sudan to start a school that has since educated over fifteen hundred girls. Students read our book and raised money for Water for South Sudan and H2O for Life. Hundreds of wells have been drilled in villages that desperately need them, including my own. Education and water are essential building blocks for a new nation.

But the most important thing for me has been trying to learn: Who is my enemy?

A few months after arriving in San Diego, California, my first job was in a large grocery store. I recognized some fruits and vegetables—mangos, yams, and a few others—but I'd never seen meat put into little trays and wrapped in plastic. As for the other 95 percent of the items, I had no idea what they were or what they were for. My job was to put the customers' items in a bag, smile, and keep the food separate from the soap. But soap came in bars, bottles, and boxes, like most food items. Soaps had names like Tide and Cheer, yet Cheerios came in a similar box. Most customers were kind during my learning curve, but others were understandably impatient with my blunders. I wasn't the only one struggling. The manager had been kind enough to hire four of us Lost Boys. A customer asked one of my Lost Boy coworkers where to find Kleenex. He led her outside the store, thinking she'd said "clinics." Another accidentally bagged an armor car delivery of $25,000 in with a customer's items, and she went home with it. Fortunately she was an honest woman and called the store when she found the item she hadn't purchased.

My job stress and anxiety peaked when a young woman came in and asked, "Where are you from?"

"Africa," I answered.

"Yes, I know," she said. "What country?"

"Sudan."

She looked at my name badge that read Alephonsion. "Can I call you Al?" she asked.

"You can call me anything," I answered.

As she left, she came close to me and said, "Al, you're hot."

Heat surged through me. I smelled my armpits. They

seemed okay; I'd showered that morning as I did every day. I asked the cashier, "Linda, am I hot?"

She gave me a strange look. "Well, yes." She'd confirmed my worst fears. I fled to the restroom to wash under my arms and I began taking two and three showers a day. Whenever anyone came near me, I broke out into a sweat. The manager allowed me to move to graveyard shifts, where I stocked shelves, ripped cardboard boxes, and was less stressed by the occasional customer who wandered in at 2 A.M.

Four months after my arrival in the United States, one cold January night I waited on the bus stop bench to go to work. My parka hood was pulled up over my head, so I didn't see who hit me from behind and shoved me onto the ground in the street, where I barely managed to roll out of the way of an oncoming car. I jumped to my feet. Three men attacked me, holding my hood down over my face and pelting me with their fists. I fought back. Two fell to the pavement. The third pulled a knife. I ran home. My body was bruised and my front tooth broken. Nothing had been taken from me that night, not my wallet or coat—theft had not been my attackers' intention. I'd been objectified by my appearance as belonging to an unwelcome group. People called it a hate crime. The damage lingered for months. The realization that the same hate that had driven me from my home was here in America hit me like those fists to my gut.

A few months later my cousin Benjamin declared, "I've been observing American culture, and I can see that working in a grocery store is not going to get me success. I need to be a movie star."

He found an audition, and by summer he was in Mexico on the set of *Master and Commander* with Russell Crowe. The casting director, Judy Bouley, told him she needed another Sudanese actor. So the next week I too was in Mexico learning to sword fight, fire a cannon, and climb a tall mast and waiting for hours in a rocking ship's hold in between shots. I learned some Spanish and developed an affinity for carne asada burritos.

Six months later I was back in America. I found a job in the medical records department of Kaiser Hospital, where I worked for five years. Kaiser repaired my left ear, and today I can hear normally.

Benson, Benjamin, and I also spent those five years writing. This book came out in the summer of 2005 and launched me into my new life and career as an author and speaker.

Through all of my setbacks, failures, and successes, I continually struggled against something I couldn't see and didn't understand. It held me prisoner. I kept asking: Who is my enemy?

I'm just now coming to realize that my real enemy is not another human being who insults me, persecutes me, hates me, defames me, gossips about me, judges me, or even attacks me. My enemy is not outside me. My worst enemy is within me.

This epiphany is freeing me. Now I know that when I fear or become angry at a fellow human being, the enemy within me is fighting. When my fellow human beings fear me or judge me, they are objectifying me because of the enemy within them. In this way we wage unstoppable war on one another. I am learning to overcome that enemy and learn a new language called "peace." Perhaps all people can learn to do this. Perhaps all we need is faith in the good of humanity.

A Reading Guide for
They Poured Fire on Us
From the Sky

In this reading group guide you'll find an update from coauthor Judy A. Bernstein, discussion questions, and suggestions for further reading and exploration. For further information and a teacher's and church group guides, please visit the book website at www.theypouredfire.com.

Alephonsion and **Benson Deng** and their cousin **Benjamin Ajak** left the Sudan in 1987 and were relocated in 2001 from the Kakuma refugee camp in Kenya to the United States as part of an international refugee relief program. Since his arrival in the United States, Alephonsion Deng has attended San Diego City College, worked in the Medical Records Department at Kaiser Permanente Hospital, and spoken to many schools, universities, clubs, and organizations about his extraordinary story in Africa and adapting to his life here in America. Benson Deng ran the computer and digital photography system at Waste Management in El Cajon, California, for several years and then went to South Sudan to drill water wells with Water for South Sudan. Benjamin Ajak has worked in factories and spoken to many organizations and schools, sharing his amazing life and insights into surviving as a child of war and a newcomer to the United States.

Judy A. Bernstein is a mother, writer, and volunteer mentor and member of the advisory committee of the San Diego International Rescue Committee. With her coauthors, she speaks at community groups, temples, churches, and schools.

A Note from Judy A. Bernstein

How do we do the right thing?

Three years after I met my coauthors, I received a phone call. One of the Lost Boys resettled in San Diego had been badly injured in a driving lesson gone wrong. I visited him in the hospital, and during the long hours there Ronald Reagan's funeral played over and over on the TV. At one point the injured Lost Boy turned to me and said, "I hate Ronald Reagan."

This surprised me. "Why do you hate Reagan?"

"Because he was president when tanks came into my village with U.S.A. and Reagan stickers on them."

I assumed the painkillers were talking. After all, America had rescued the Lost Boys after years of languishing in a desolate refugee camp. We were their heroes. Absurd to think we might have been involved in what went wrong in Sudan in the first place. Yet I couldn't forget what he'd said.

Few books were available about Sudan in 2004. Google was still in its youth, but I tried to search anyway and typed in "Sudan Reagan" and went from there to "oil" and

"Chevron." I didn't leave the computer for hours. What I uncovered shook me.

For about twenty years, beginning in 1974, Chevron Oil had been exploring and drilling in southern Sudan. Thousands of villages, eventually 7 million people, that were in the way were killed or displaced without compensation or a destination. When the southerners fought back, the United States supplied the northern Sudanese government millions of dollars for arms to protect the oil fields. Yes, we'd been doing business with a government who preferred genocide to sharing oil revenue with its own people.

While I'd been living my comfortable life in the 1980s, with food and water at my fingertips and gas to go where I wanted, little boys had been running for their lives (and dying) to give me that comfort. Some of the same boys I now knew as young men.

When they'd first arrived in the United States, I'd felt good about my country for stepping up and welcoming this group of refugees. I'd been assured they were the victims of religious and racial persecution. I hadn't known that my country had helped to carry out the tragedy in which over 2 million people died and roughly 5 million were made homeless.

This was all before the prevalence of cell phones, their cameras, texting, blogging, and, of course, the Internet. If journalists survived reporting in a war zone like the Sudan in the eighties, they had to make it back out of the country with paper notes and film. Situations like what happened in South Sudan for so many years no longer happen in secret. When a second genocide in Sudan raised its ugly head in

Darfur, pictures and accounts were ubiquitous. Protest groups rose to the occasion.

Awareness of all this injustice and violence can make us feel as though we've been born into the most violent times. However, experts, such as Steven Pinker, have shown that violence has declined in dramatic degrees all over the world.

Technology can now make us aware of injustice in a way never before possible. As Martin Luther King said, "Injustice anywhere threatens justice everywhere." Tools at our fingertips give everyone one of us a voice to protest. Just imagine what might have been different if everyone had stopped buying Chevron gas in the 1980s. We can't do the right thing if we don't know about an injustice in the first place.

I'm hopeful about the future. Since this book came out in 2005, Alepho, Benson, Benjamin, and I have spoken at hundreds of schools. There, I've witnessed unprecedented awareness of global injustices and passionate conviction among young people to do the right thing.

How do we do the right thing? We ask: Where does my gas come from? Are child laborers making my clothing? My cell phone?

Then we act. We speak out. We blog. We join activist groups. We can vote with our wallets and our voices. A small effort by many will have a big impact.

Questions for Thought and Discussion

1. What do Judy A. Bernstein (who introduces the book) and her son find most striking about Benson, Alepho, and Benjamin when they arrive in San Diego? What would be

your own reaction if you were meeting the boys during their first few days in America? Would you find it frustrating? Exciting? What advice would you give the boys to help them adapt to American society?

2. What did you find most troubling about the boys' experiences? Which moments struck you as particularly emotionally moving? Why?

3. How do the voices of Benson, Alepho, and Benjamin differ? How are they similar? Do they have distinguishing characteristics? Was there a writer who you felt most connected to?

4. Benson asserts that hunger "makes you like a wild animal." While enduring years of starvation, how do the boys maintain their humanity? If you were involved in a similarly desperate situation, what would you do to preserve your compassion?

5. Why was education so important to the boys, especially to Benson? How does the boys' desire to learn compare to young people in America who you know?

6. Benson and Alepho have heard some outlandish rumors about America. What were they, and what perhaps inspired their formation? Are there countries or cultures that we make similarly misinformed judgments about today?

7. What are the boys' attitudes toward women? Compare their perceptions of African women to our perceptions of American women.

8. During their journeys Benson, Alepho, and Benjamin each meet many people, some fellow refugees and some not. Which of these secondary characters have the most influence on the writers' stories? Which leave the strongest impressions on you?

9. How do you think the boys' age and lack of guardians affected their travels? Was it always to their detriment? How might their experiences have been different had the boys been older?

10. How do the refugees help each other despite living in the confining environments of absolute poverty? How do they manage to assert some control over their own lives?

11. Why do you think there so few "Lost Girls"?

12. The efforts of aid groups like the UN are sometimes a mixed blessing to the refugees. Why is this? What do you think could be done so that their influence would be wholly helpful?

Suggestions for Further Reading and Exploration

Bixler, Mark. *The Lost Boys of Sudan* (University of Georgia Press, 2005).

Bok, Francis, with Edward Tivnan. *Escape from Slavery* (St. Martin's Press, 2003).

Deng, Francis Mading. *The Dinka of Sudan* (Waveland Press, 1972).

Eggers, Dave. *What Is the What?* (McSweeney's Press, 2007).

Jok, Madut Jok. *War and Slavery in Sudan* (University of Pennsylvania Press, 2001).

Nazer, Mende, and Damien Lewis. *Slave: My True Story* (PublicAffairs, 2003).

Scroggins, Deborah. *Emma's War* (Pantheon Books, 2002).

The Genocide Intervention Fund (www.GenocideInter
 ventionFund.org)

Human Rights Watch (www.hrw.org)

The International Crisis Group (www.CrisisGroup.org)

The International Rescue Committee (www.TheIRC.org)

Save Darfur (www.SaveDarfur.org)

PublicAffairs is a publishing house founded in 1997. It is a tribute to the standards, values, and flair of three persons who have served as mentors to countless reporters, writers, editors, and book people of all kinds, including me.

I. F. STONE, proprietor of *I. F. Stone's Weekly*, combined a commitment to the First Amendment with entrepreneurial zeal and reporting skill and became one of the great independent journalists in American history. At the age of eighty, Izzy published *The Trial of Socrates*, which was a national bestseller. He wrote the book after he taught himself ancient Greek.

BENJAMIN C. BRADLEE was for nearly thirty years the charismatic editorial leader of *The Washington Post*. It was Ben who gave the *Post* the range and courage to pursue such historic issues as Watergate. He supported his reporters with a tenacity that made them fearless and it is no accident that so many became authors of influential, best-selling books.

ROBERT L. BERNSTEIN, the chief executive of Random House for more than a quarter century, guided one of the nation's premier publishing houses. Bob was personally responsible for many books of political dissent and argument that challenged tyranny around the globe. He is also the founder and longtime chair of Human Rights Watch, one of the most respected human rights organizations in the world.

.   .   .

For fifty years, the banner of Public Affairs Press was carried by its owner Morris B. Schnapper, who published Gandhi, Nasser, Toynbee, Truman, and about 1,500 other authors. In 1983, Schnapper was described by *The Washington Post* as "a redoubtable gadfly." His legacy will endure in the books to come.

Peter Osnos, *Founder and Editor-at-Large*